A MEMOIR

Boy On A String

From Cast-Off Kid to Filmmaker
Through the Magic of Dreams

JOSEPH JACOBY

Introduction by Martin Scorsese

CARROLL & GRAF PUBLISHERS • NEW YORK

BOY ON A STRING
From Cast-Off Kid to Filmmaker Through the Magic of Dreams

Carroll & Graf Publishers
An Imprint of Avalon Publishing Group Inc.
245 West 17th Street
11th Floor
New York, NY 10011

AVALON
publishing group incorporated

Library of Congress Cataloging-in-Publication Data is available.

ISBN-10: 0-7867-1711-4
ISBN-13: 978-0-78671-711-8

9 8 7 6 5 4 3 2 1

Interior design by Pauline Neuwirth, Neuwirth & Associates, Inc.

Printed in the United States of America
Distributed by Publishers Group West

For Frances Richman,
my mother.

Contents

Introduction

Martin Scorsese

I MET JOE Jacoby for the first time in the early sixties, when we were students at NYU. Like me, he was born and raised in the city. Like me, he loved movies. And like me, he loved the TV talk shows of the fifties and sixties, especially *The Steve Allen Show* and *The Tonight Show* with Jack Paar. For me, those shows were actually like a gateway to the outside world—they truly opened my horizons. Those shows gave me my first glimpses of people like Jack Kerouac and Bob Dylan, people familiar to those who traveled in hip circles but unknown to neighborhood kids like me, and they exposed me to a kind of sophistication that we couldn't even dream of. Those days are over, of course, because now the talk shows are just part of the massive entertainment machine. It's important for young people to know that they once meant so much to people like us, and why. In fact, the nature of celebrity in America was nurtured by this TV form. Cinema and celebrity became one—in our very living rooms—every night. All this eventually ran its course for me in making *The King of Comedy* in 1983.

I was on the outside looking in. Joe, on the other hand, had actually worked on a show Merv Griffin was hosting and was getting more jobs in television when I met him. He was working part-time on network game shows—at this point in history, TV was still live and a lot of the programming was coming out of New York. He was also doing some work for The Bunin Puppets, the people who did *The Adventures of Lucky Pup* in the late forties and who created Foodini and Pinhead (to many younger readers, I realize that these seem like mysterious names from an ancient era, if not a lost world—they were puppet characters in early television, and they were icons of my childhood). Later, when I needed a straight razor to spurt blood for my short film *The Big Shave,* I brought it up to Bunin's shop. Joe went to work and rigged a small tube and a rubber syringe that my actor, Peter Bernuth, could hide in the palm of his hand.

In 1968, I finished my first feature, *Who's That Knocking at My Door?* I remembered that Joe had made contact with a distributor on Forty-second Street after he'd made his own first feature. I asked him for the lowdown, and he gave it to me: "Marty, this guy's a goniff, but he'll get your picture out." He was right, on both counts.

Joe was the kind of friend you could count on—he knew the score, and you knew that he would always be straight with you. At the time, I didn't know much about his background or his life before I met him. I do remember him as kind of a loner. Maybe I saw something of him in myself.

As I read this frank, touching book, I was astonished to learn that Joe was in and out of foster homes and various institutions from the time he was seven until his eighteenth birthday. That experience—that *range* of experience—must have played a big part in his solitude, and in his worldliness. Of course, it wasn't important that I knew. Sometimes, friends don't need to know absolutely everything about each other—you can just sense what someone needs without spelling it out, and that's enough. That was the way it was between Joe and me. I had lived a sheltered life, at least compared to his, and we gave each other something. I hope you'll find this book by my friend Joe Jacoby as rewarding as I did.

Martin Scorsese
MARRAKECH, MOROCCO
November 16, 2005

In all important transactions of life we have to take a leap in the dark.

—William James, *The Will to Believe*

Part One

This Too Shall Pass

Patient became very agitated and depressed and was

found wandering around the streets with her child . . .

she was picked up wandering with the boy in the streets

by a neighbor and placed in a hotel room for the night. *

* Text in part openers is quoted from family medical records and other sources.

Boy on a String

Brooklyn, April 1948

A HOTEL SUITE. Wall-to-wall beige carpeting. Walls are painted soft white. Room is very clean and orderly. I'm seven years old, running from room to room, luxuriating in both the carpeting, which I have never felt under my bare feet before, and the cleanliness and orderliness of the room—the likes of which I have never experienced before, either. That night I slept alone, in my own big bed, with clean white sheets. And I dreamed: I'm on a roller coaster. But then it suddenly seems to have been burned down where the tracks should be. It reminds me of Coney Island's Thunderbolt—a big dark thing where even the track is thickened with blackness. Suddenly the track seems to come to an abrupt end where the cars can now only fly off. There is nothing but a charred emptiness in front of the onrushing cars. I wake up. It's morning. I look up toward the smooth, fresh, pale white color of the ceiling and am reminded once again that my mother and I are in a clean, posh hotel suite. It does not seem to have been such a horrible dream after all.

The phone rings. My mother answers. "Yes. Okay." She hangs up. Mr. Fisher is downstairs, waiting to take us to breakfast, I think. My mother and I wind our way down the carpeted hotel stairs. At the foot of the landing, just slightly to the right side of the stairs, stands Mr. Fisher—a benevolent, heavy-set, middle-aged, balding man with a well-meaning, kind air about him. I recognize Mr. Fisher as the man who runs the supermarket on Franklin Avenue in Brooklyn, someone my mother obviously knows. With him stand two men in white coats. The ambulance and police car are just in view outside the lobby window. My mother immediately understands what he has done and screams; she backs up the stairs briefly. I watch, recalling now that Mr. Fisher had us put up for the night at the hotel since we had been kicked out onto the street for nonpayment of rent. I remember an old junk truck parked outside the tenement building piled up with our possessions, such as they were, but the only one that I recall is a set of rusty old bedsprings with brown cast-iron bedposts, resting on its back. I was embarrassed by all the junk. I'm standing at a distance, holding my mother's hand. Maybe they'll think it's someone else's.

Gently, the two white-jacketed men come up the stairs. And there, too, off to the side, is Aunt Gussie. That's how I know her, but I think she was really my mother's friend, and no relation. Mr. Fisher must've somehow known her, too. Perhaps she sought his help. I'll never know for certain, but it seems reasonable. Her gray hair is braided like a little girl's, though she's about my mother's age, forty-seven. There's something off-putting, even frightening, about "Aunt Gussie." It has something to do with the gray braids: the old lady as the little girl. Her smile meant to be gentle and consoling, but I find it scary. I think she knew something that I knew, too. Soon my mother is in the ambulance and I am in the back of the police car as we head for Kings County Hospital.

My mother takes off what I believe is her gold wedding band and gives it to Aunt Gussie. I intuit somehow that she doesn't want "them" to have it. They're talking to each other, now, and my mother not only comprehends what is happening, she is also functioning with calm rationality. Somehow I know that she knows it will be easier this way. We're standing outside Kings County Hospital but inside the heavy black wrought iron gates. I'm perhaps fifteen feet or so away; a policeman is holding my hand. My mother now is taken away toward the hospital building, and I am jolted by the reality that she is leaving me behind. I want to go with her. A couple of matrons or nurses try to lead her through the open hospital door, where I see what look like bathtubs. She is resisting. I try to follow her, but the policeman lifts me up near his shoulder, and his chest badge sticks me in the groin. "You're sticking me," I say as I cry after her, "Mommy. Mommy. What did I do?!"

Franklin Avenue and President Street, Brooklyn

My mother is over me, choking me in my bed as I sleep, but I am now awake. My hands are gripping hers, trying to make room in my throat for air. She suddenly stops and turns away. She is in her pink nightgown, I am pleading: "Mommy, Mommy. What did I do?!" She goes back to bed. I fall asleep, too. She tried to kill me.

My mother is now being restrained as she enters the room with the baths. The policeman is carrying me off the grounds in the opposite direction as I cry after her. I'm taken to a children's shelter. One large dormitory room with a thin, mean little old matron in a white nurse's dress, white shoes, white stockings. A cigarette dangles from her lip. She has a silver metal flashlight just like an usher in the movies. The mean old matron is authority. I don't like her.

It's summer. It's very hot. There's no such thing as air conditioning. The large windows with metal gratings are open. The white cast-iron beds are lined up against both walls of the large room, probably a dozen beds against each wall and another two dozen back to back in the center. I hear her shoes hitting the linoleum floor as she makes her way up and down the rows. My bed's the last one, under one of the large open windows. There's no breeze at all, though. Just white sheets on the bed. There's a smell to the place unlike any smell I've smelled before. It's institutional, whatever it is.

Smells were always meaningful to me. I was always looking for a way to find a sense of place, and smell seems to have been one. I remember standing on a nighttime corner with my mother and smelling the exhaust of a bus while waiting for the light to turn green. I like the smell of the gas, and the word "boulevard," which I associate with that smell. I like the sound of that word; the image it conjures; "the bus on the boulevard." I have no idea where we are living but I can't be more than three or four years old. I only know that we have to cross the boulevard to get to our apartment building.

My mother and I were wanderers. Every day was different because we had nowhere we had to be, nowhere we had to go. I had no friends and she was friendless with the exception of Gussie. I had her and she had me. If I wasn't out walking with her, she left me to my own devices.

My best friends on Franklin Avenue and President Street—my only friends—were the cockroaches. They crawled around inside the pantry drawers in the kitchen, except there were no pantry drawers; just empty space where the drawers used to be. I would crawl into this space with my cap gun and shoot at them. My mother had put white powder, boric acid, all over the place, in all the cracks and crevices, too, but that didn't bother me, or them. I still shot cockroaches and they scurried. Nobody ever got hurt, though. And this was the way I played. I had neither fear nor revulsion of getting into small spaces with cockroaches.

Shards of memory. Our apartment on the ground floor. Maggie—a neighbor I think, maybe a teenager, but she could be younger. She teases me by throwing her long, silky brown hair in front of her face and hiding behind it and I grow up believing Maggies do that sort of thing. The wooden walker that I stand up in but can barely get to move along the concrete. Standing in my crib and my mother arguing with a man. Who is this man? My father? My high chair with all the baby food bottles on it. I've learned the foods I like by their colors, and those I don't, disappear. One swipe to the floor. The old man who grows gold coins on a small bush in an empty lot next to our apartment building. Real gold coins. As golden as golden can be. For years afterward, I believe that money grows on trees. The smell of Coca-Cola at the marble soda fountain, as the soda jerk dips his long spoon into the tilted Coke glass under the seltzer spigot and stirs the syrup to a brown fizzy head, putting it in front of me on the black marble counter. Coke hasn't smelled as good since.

I can remember only one meal with my mother, although I can't remember ever being hungry. She cooked chicken soup, and I ate the chicken. She chewed the bones.

Mealtimes at the shelter are at a large group table with the other children. We stand behind our chairs and clasp our hands over our heads as we recite a Hebrew prayer before eating. The shelter must be under Jewish auspices. From all the chaos I have known so far, there is, here, a sense of order, structure—even the metal beds are lined up one after another. I don't know where this will lead. I don't think about it.

One sunny day, only a few months after I've arrived, I am playing with the other children in the backyard fenced-in playground when a young woman approaches to tell me that they have found a home for me. I seem to recall having swapped my yo-yo to a boy for a baseball mitt, a Hershey bar, and the promise that I will be his best friend. I think I got the better part of the deal because he is not too happy, and I am eating the Hershey. The woman explains to me that this is to be a temporary home until a permanent home can be found. Perhaps it's my immediate satisfaction that disturbs the boy so—the instant disappearance of his Hershey bar. The woman is smiling, but I don't know what to make of what she's saying; already I'm on guard. I'm eating a Hershey. Do I want to leave this? Yet I trust her somehow. Yes. I think I want a home, even if it's temporary. I follow her.

The temporary home is in Brooklyn, where I was born. It's a red brick house on the corner of Avenue J, just across from Wingate Field. There are other children here, too, and the foster parents are nice, but now I have no memory of them, not even their names. I don't even remember what I called them, but "Auntie" and "Uncle" would be how I would address my future foster parents. There is an older girl here, probably ten, who wears braces and bathes in the wash sink in the basement, as I believe we all do. I don't remember my own baths but I remember she doesn't like being watched when she wants to get into the sink. I tease her a lot. We eat meals at a nice table in the kitchen that has benches built around it in the corner nook.

The happiest moment I can recall here is Christmas morning (I'm Jewish, but Christmas morning for an eight-year-old is not really about religion). I am coming down the stairs but now the walk is bright with the anticipation of the presents around the Christmas tree. Christmas tree ornaments, especially the colored glass balls and the metal tinsel, have always given me a warm glow inside. When I walked through department stores—Brooklyn's A&S or Manhattan's Macy's—with my mother at Christmastime, I would look up at the clusters of colored balls and fill up with warmth and joy. As an adult I have sometimes tried to recapture this feeling, but it's not the same when you're all grown up.

I have a very clear memory of my Christmas present that morning: a hand puppet with a brown face. My own small hand could barely work its way into the head and puppet arms, which had a pair of white gloves sewn to them—just as Larry Parks did when he played Al Jolson in *The Jolson Story*.

It's a dim, rainy day. The Jolson Story *is playing at the Brooklyn Paramount. Me and my mother are crossing the trolley tacks, now, approaching the theater—a blackish majestic marquee with light-bulbs, flashing sequentially around the marquee, framing all sides. I sit next to my mother and stare enraptured at the big screen in front of me. I want to be part of this world. It is an indelible template for what is possible and how you go about getting what you want. I watched it*

as real life, not something that had been written. I also want to be Al Jol-
son, not knowing, of course, that it is really Larry Parks that I identify
with. Years later, when I find out that Al Jolson looked nothing like
Larry Parks and was certainly nowhere near as good-looking (though
Parks had Jolson's moves down pat, and I'd find out in adult life that
Jolson himself stood right next to the camera to make sure of that), I felt
a certain ambivalence. One could sing, but the other, mouthing the
words, "looked" more the part. To this day, I'd rather watch Parks doing
Jolson than Jolson. My mother had bought the Decca 78 rpm album—
the blue cover with the white gloves spread apart, Mammy-like. In our
apartment, the one at Franklin Avenue and President Street, I would
stand in front of our Victrola for hours on end, mouthing the words, doing
the moves à la Larry Parks.

The "brown" face and the white gloves; from that Christmas morning forward, I would somehow keep communion with puppets, even into adult
life, when puppetry would become my early profession. It would not be
a profession I would consciously seek. It will appear as much through hap-
penstance as anything else. But there are other reasons.

In the late 1940s we had "radio stores," which were, naturally enough,
where you bought a radio. On one cold winter night, standing in front
of a radio store window with my mother, I saw for the very first time a
television set—a bare metal chassis upon which sat a picture tube, surrounded by lit vacuum tubes. On this particular picture tube, there were
two dancing marionettes, bouncing up and down on roller skates. I was
ignited. Something about the strings that went all the way up out of sight.
That could be me. I could be there; I could express myself because I
wouldn't be seen. The strings allowed distance, control, and freedom of
movement. The camera could convey my performance to other people. It
all came together. I had a passion for cameras, all sorts of cameras, but I
would develop a special passion for television and movie cameras.

My very first still camera was a Donald Duck plastic bellows camera (not a real bellows, though) that my mother had bought me and that took regular roll film. I remember I was more excited about developing the results than taking any particular picture. I'd gone down into our backyard, which was nothing more than concrete with weeds sprouting from the crevices, and snapped away at everything in sight, including the crevices. I proceeded then to lock myself into the toilet, take the film out of the camera, fill the sink with water, and wash it with soap—all in broad daylight. I ended up, of course, with a long strip of clear plastic film. Disappointment? Yes. But I have no idea where I got the concept of immersing film into a liquid. This passion for the camera, though—even just the *look* of one—stayed with me.

ON ANOTHER RAINY morning a few months later the taxi pulled up in front of my first permanent foster home, 1565 East Twenty-ninth Street in Flatbush. I noticed the Venetian blinds spread apart as someone peered out the window; they'd been waiting for me. The front door of this private home opened. The social worker opened the door on my side of the car and held my small suitcase, while I looked out hesitantly. A woman in her fifties, though appearing older to me at the time, was standing at the front door in her housecoat with a kind, gentle smile on her face. I can see her now, feel the warm, loving, maternal glow that Sadie Peller exuded, and also feel the shyness I felt. As I got out, slowly, the front door opened even wider and she stepped back with it slightly, her welcoming expression glowing even more brightly now. I walked up the three or four front steps and brushed by her, gently. In a sidelong glance I saw she approved. Okay, me, too. I entered the house that would become my home—both my first experience of a real home, and the last that I would ever feel in my childhood.

We entered the living room, which was the front room with the venetian blind windows that looked out onto the tree-lined street, and the cushiony couch. I sat on it. This felt like a home. I would always call

Sadie Peller "Auntie," and though George M. Peller was "Uncle," the "M."
betrayed his formality and innate detachment. He did not have the
warmth that Auntie had, but he seemed okay. He kept his own shy distance—which was okay with me, too. I was feeling, now, not unlike an
animal must feel, I think, when the cage is suddenly opened and he con-
fronts his new surroundings.

There is something profoundly abrupt and uncertain about being
dropped at the home of two strangers, and knowing that this is to be
your instant home. There's no putting your toe in the water to acclimate
the rest of you; it is a total immersion, all at once, and there is no alternative. One has to come to instant terms with it. Auntie's warmth, the inch-
ing open of the door as I stepped from the cab, even her floral housecoat,
all of this was immeasurably comforting and reassuring. Of all the homes
and neighborhoods I would live in from ages seven to eighteen—there
would be a total of seven homes, one shelter, and a "treatment center"—
the home at 1565 East Twenty-ninth Street in Flatbush would forever be
"my home." I lived here only 2 or 2½ years, but it is here that I would lay
down roots and bare myself emotionally as totally as I ever would.

That sensation of being dropped off, almost a feeling of leaving my body
and reentering, must have had a desensitizing effect on me. In being
plucked from here and replanted there, I learned to distance myself before
acclimating myself. This early forced training must have played some
role in my introspection and self-analysis later, and also my ability to perceive people and situations intuitively, even coldly. I learned, very early on,
to trust this intuition and to be circumspect, and I think here is another
key to my survival. I believe that distance also accounts for the selective-
ness of my memories. My childhood comes to me in bits and pieces, tat-
ters and threads. It comes to me as in flashes of lightning—one moment
illuminated to vividness, the next moment darkened to nonexistence.

Uncle seemed even older than Auntie, and he was a retired engineer.
There were all kinds of small black, soft leather books with cryptic engi-
neering diagrams on the bookshelves, along with a set of small volumes

known as the *Funk & Wagnalls Encyclopedia* (which sounded dirty), and which he pridefully attempted to introduce me to, almost immediately. With the exception of *Babar the Elephant*, a book my mother used to read to me, I couldn't read. And even *Babar* was one I'd recite from memory, turning the pages on visual memory cue (my first acting experience), but not reading in any real sense.

It turned out that Uncle was not only distant, he also could be severely judgmental. One day in front of a friend of mine, he made me distinguish my left hand from my right. I got it wrong. Embarrassed, I insisted my left hand *was* my right, as if insisting on it firmly enough would somehow make it so. Or at least assuage my embarrassment— like when you trip, you look back to blame the pavement. I remember Uncle walked away in disgust. I determined then that I would never again not know my left from my right, and to this day, I visualize standing in Mrs. Silver's classroom, facing the blackboard, knowing that the door to the classroom is on the right. So the other is left.

My room upstairs was comfortable and had a window overlooking an alleyway that looked out onto a house about fifteen feet away. It was the first room I had ever known that was for me alone. Sheldon, a much older foster boy who also lived there, must've been either in the later years of high school or college because he was a whole lot more distant from Auntie and Uncle and because he wasn't there much. I thought of this home as mine alone.

I remember some of my friends on the block, a block that became my world, but mainly I remember the redheaded freckly kid who lived next door—Jimmy Blumstein. At the foot of the upstairs landing, there was a window that overlooked Jimmy's house on the opposite side. He also had a window at the top of his landing and we strung our walkie-talkies between them and I remember how difficult it was trying to figure a way to get the wires strung from window to window (we finally hoisted them with a weighted cord from the alleyway).

His father, David, was an assistant principal at Madison High School nearby. Jimmy was a few years younger than me and his sister, Anita, a few years older. She seemed a lot older. A teenager, probably! Anita was also fair-skinned and redheaded like Jimmy, and she liked to sing songs—Rodgers and Hammerstein's "Oh, What a Beautiful Morning!" or Frank Loesser's "A Bushel and a Peck," that kind of song. I really liked those songs, and they seemed to go with the feeling of my tree-lined world. For those of us who lived in Brooklyn in those years, it was very much a world apart.

I remember, too, Jimmy's mom, who was in her upstairs bedroom, ill with cancer, I think, except that in those days nobody ever spoke the word. Given my inventory, though, I knew.

President Street, Brooklyn

My mother runs into someone she knows. Given my presence, my mother whispers: "Sprecht Yiddish. Fershtate nicht." *(Speak Yiddish. He doesn't understand.) I understand, especially because that language has come to represent terrible things, sickness and death, and most especially because the effort is being made to hide something from me. I must be dying! With a slap to her own face, she whispers again:* "Sehr krank." *(Very sick.) Desperately, fearfully, I stand there, my ear cocked. I make like I don't fershtate. Am I dying of some horrible disease?! What could I have done to deserve this? Maybe that's why my father left; maybe that's why my mother choked me.*

There are times when I am embarrassed, like when my mother picks fights in the street, and I can't stop her, and I go looking in store windows like I'm not there (I probably drove her crazy), or when I don't have enough clothes on, and it's cold, especially in winter, but I don't know that I should not be cold, or even that I'm all that aware of our desperate poverty, so I don't think I take on any responsibility for that, and if I do, I'm not consciously aware of it. And even if I do, how could I resolve such a condition, anyway? (I could always shine shoes, of course.) But whatever they're talking about, it's a bad thing. The sound of spoken Yiddish will provoke fear and anguish in me for years to come.

But in Flatbush for a time, I lived as normal a life as I'd ever known. I remember the names of my childhood friends, the first I'd ever had: Jimmy, Stanley Lerner, Steve Zone and his younger brother Alan, whose home had a red brick porch and metal furniture with a green awning that could be rolled out when it rained, and concrete urns that seemed always to have geraniums in them. I never liked geraniums. Alan Katimsky was one of those studious types I never really got to know. He'd come home from school, enter the short metal gate to his house, and disappear. He wore glasses and played the violin. So you know.

Then there was the girl across the street who I was interested in, but she might just as well have been a million miles away, because I never got to know her. Something got in the way. Something always got in the way. My painful shyness (especially with girls) worked in cahoots with the embarrassment of my second-class citizenry throughout my entire childhood. Straight through high school, I was afraid people would find out I was a foster child and had no family, and that my name was different from the name of my foster parents, who were so much older than most kids' parents.

The fear of being found out would not allow me to get too close to anyone, even though I was likable and made friends easily. I separated my outside life and my "home" life so completely that it became second nature. I could not, for example, ever bring a friend "home" from school. When I was living in Flatbush, my friends were all on the same block and Jimmy lived right next door, so I pushed to the side in my mind what people knew about me, as if doing so somehow kept my secret from them as well. With the exception of Jimmy, with whom I had rigged a hard-wired walkie-talkie connection, and whose father I knew accepted me, I would never cross the line by entering the home of a friend and thus risking reciprocity or being asked questions.

Nor was I welcomed. I was different. The outsider. And I knew that.

I was a foster kid, living with people who were considerably older than my friends' parents and insulated and not sociable with the younger adults on the block. So my intrinsic feelings of unworthiness and differentness were actually buttressed by the facts outside of myself. I needed to have some control over all this. By keeping this distance, I could set the parameters. The girl across the street, of course, was off-bounds because that would have led to conflict in me not only about my foster child status, but also my unrecognized feelings about my mother and what I felt I had done, all of which, in my mind, would have led to her rejection of me as well.

I remember Jimmy's birthday party and a dark-complexioned, pretty girl named Wendy. We were nine or so. I was sitting just across from her eating birthday cake, and I could see her white panties. White panties against dark skin. That was it. I loved Wendy. From that moment on, Wendy was the most beautiful name in the world. I think she liked me, too, but I never did see her again. Something always got in the way. From that day on, for God knows how long, whenever I heard the name "Wendy," I'd light up and inquire. I mean, how many Wendys could there be?

Flatbush was Good Humor trucks in summer, beautiful tree-lined streets, front lawns, fireflies in bottles, and Ebbets Field. Jimmy Blumstein's dad used to take us there in his blue Buick, the one with the "ventaports"—those were the chrome-laced holes on the sides that were there just for show; but who knew? When the Dodgers left Brooklyn, though, I left baseball. Betrayal has a way of closing things down for me.

What I remember was "Happy" Felton's *Knothole Gang*, a sort of pregame interview show along the first base line out in right field. There was a TV camera out there (just one, though) and I liked looking at it, as well as the way "Happy" addressed it. He had a lot of respect for it, and I respected anyone who had respect for the camera. In my eyes, that made them important, too. No matter the mayhem that was going on in the ballpark, he talked to the camera like it was the only person there. He was off in a corner, but on TV he was talking to the whole world. I liked that.

Anyway, the Dodgers left Brooklyn, so the hell with them. But I flipped baseball cards anyway (in those days they came with flattened strips of powdered bubble gum that nobody ever chewed; you bought a box of a hundred individually wrapped cards for a buck and threw away the gum). We played "flippsies" and "against the wall." That and my comic books and stoopball. Stanley Lerner had the perfect brick stoop, and if you slammed your Spaldeen hard enough against the edge of the brick, it would go flying over the other guy's head, which was the whole idea. Yo-yos and peashooters we had—the latter were colored plastic straws, slightly wider than regular straws, that you got for a dime at the candy store around the corner, and you got a box of dried peas, and that was it—and someone's mother was always yelling, "Be careful you don't put somebody's eye out with that!"

Then there was the stuff you sent away for, usually from cereal boxes, but sometimes directly from TV. Captain Video one-way goggles, which let you see whoever you were looking at but they couldn't see you; decoder rings that glowed in the dark (a big thing in those days if you could find a dark, empty closet), where you could hide rolled-up messages (like the teeny-weeny paper inside a mezuzah—every Jewish door had one) that you weren't supposed to open, under punishment of sin (but I did it anyway). There was even the Lone Ranger ring, shaped like a silver bullet, and if you got into your dark closet and pulled off the tip of the bullet you were supposed to see sparks flying. I never saw anything except a lot of darkness, but it was a neat shape, that Lone Ranger ring.

Somehow the anticipation of getting all this stuff in the mail ("Did it come yet? Did it come yet?") held more excitement for me than the stuff itself. It was certainly an introduction to patience—you had to wait sometimes three or four weeks for stuff to come, I don't have to tell you how long that is when you're nine. Except when you were holding in your hands the same item you saw on TV, then you were an "insider." For a child who always felt on the outside looking in wondering what it must be like to belong, this held meaning for me.

I remember standing outside Steve Zone's backyard fence once when they were barbecuing steaks. I don't think I'd ever had steak, and it smelled good, and I stood there watching. I must've looked like a hungry dog because someone gave me a piece of it and I recall chewing it and chewing it; savoring it all, still standing there on the outside of the fence, knowing it was to be the only piece I would get.

I knew, too, that Steve's grandfather didn't like me very much. At the time I understood it was because I was a foster kid not deserving of his grandson's friendship. I was an outsider with no real parents, and was therefore less deserving, and I tried to stay out of his way. Not only did I not question his disapproval of me, I found a way to confirm it. I recall him as a mean-spirited, miserable old man, I think mainly because of a big toe that gave him a lot of pain, which stuck out of his open-toed shoe. I remember him mumbling something about how he wished they'd just cut it off.

Shortly thereafter, I, too, developed a pain in my foot, only in the *back* of it. Unconsciously, I suppose, I couldn't accept having the pain in exactly the same spot—that would've been too obvious, so I had to be creative in accommodating my own guilt. I moved it around to the back. This way, I got what I deserved, and I worried that they might have to do the same to me that they were going to do to him.

This was truly a life-and-death issue for me at the time. I mean, if the old man had a pain in his toe, and I was even less deserving—and I'd had that chew on the steak, remember—it seemed only right that I would develop a bigger pain; this would be my penance, my expiation. There was the time, I remember, when I was lying on the couch in the living room, and my feet were cold. To my mind, this connoted the end of circulation at the bottom. It was just a matter of time, then, before the end of circulation at the top, and I would be dead. So I lay there and waited. This is how this child thought; this was what he worried about.

Uncle wanted me to play the violin, but I felt the violin was for old people, probably because I identified it with him and was more interested in the guitar, anyway, which he succeeded in convincing me was not an "instrument." So I learned to play nothing. I tried the piano, but it was not my idea and I grew bored with practice. Tap dancing, I think, was my idea, though I never got further than heel, toe, heel, toe, with a walk toward the mirror. I liked the idea of black, shiny tap shoes and the "clack" of the large metal taps, and the possibility of meeting girls, but I was much too shy to have done much about that anyway. This shyness, I think, reflected my feelings of not belonging, and my fear of the fore-shortened nature of whatever might transpire (the dream where the roller coaster tracks are burned out). Even earlier, whenever my mother would speak with someone on the street—even when she was lucid—I would often hide behind her, clinging to her dress. I was uneasy that she would try to introduce me. Perhaps I was fearful of unexpected displays.

We had a "furnished basement," as they say in Brooklyn, even though I don't remember much furniture. I think "furnished" meant you could go downstairs, turn on the light, and maybe there'd be a linoleum floor and some whitewashed pipes or something. Maybe a painted metal deck chair that sort of bounced up and down when you sat on it, or a card table. In other words, it was habitable, like what was then called a rum-pus room.

I built puppets down here. They were quite crude, mostly made from papier-mâché or peanuts strung together with sewing thread. I would get cardboard boxes and build puppet stages and scenery, and then string the puppets with sewing thread and I'd have a marionette. I also made hand puppets, but the one thing I didn't like about hand puppets was that they had no feet. Marionettes had feet. They were more lifelike, somehow, and they moved around by themselves. They could even leave the ground. Of course, the "magician" who pulled the strings, and whom you couldn't see, was what really made them move around. He was the one you really wanted to meet, or at least get a look at; he was the guy who was really in control. But with a hand puppet, all you had to do was let your arm show during an actual performance, and I did.

That was showing off, really, pure and simple, but they'd suddenly have to remember you were under there. I got a charge when I did that, letting people in on my controlled "mistakes." I liked that. I had always sought attention, albeit shyly. Cameras and puppets both brought me attention, as well as control, while working undercover.

One day we got a television set. I don't know if we were the first on the block, but we were sure up there. It was *that* new. I recall it exactly: a thirteen-inch RCA Console, mahogany cabinet, with two small doors that opened and closed over the picture tube. The base of the console was covered by a meshlike scrim with a golden braid woven into it that concealed the speakers. A small red light in the center of the console lit up when the set was on. The knobs were all in front, with the large channel knob on the far right. When you changed the channel, you heard the clunk of the mechanism inside, which somehow affirmed that the thing actually worked. The aerial was mounted on top of the roof, as were all aerials in those days, with flat brown wire that ran out the window and up the side of the house—the neighborhood sort of looked like the original WCBS *Late Show* logo, the one whose theme music was "The Syncopated Clock."

The shows I watched were *The Magic Cottage* with Pat Michael (my favorite character was Oogie the Ogre), and *Captain Video* with Al Hodge, Don Hastings as the Video Ranger, and the evil Dr. Paulie, played by an actor whose name I never knew and didn't wanna know. I don't remember much about the plot except that Captain Video operated out of some remote mountain retreat and had an instrument called the *ektaconscalometer* (ek-tah-con-skah-lah-me-ter), which looked like a surveyor's sextant and allowed him to see through walls and stuff. I wondered if he could see through girls' dresses, too.

I also used to watch for flubs, like the time a "frozen" Dr. Paulie got caught talking to someone off-camera, not realizing we could see him, until *he* realized it and froze silly: just a moment, but somehow indelible. That was neat. Or the time someone opened a door and a camera dollied by. That was even neater. This was a time when television was new and everything was just beginning, and they were still trying to figure it out. There was no such thing as videotape, of course, so what went on behind the scenes, and my anticipation of the spontaneous mistakes, were as exciting for me as the things that were meant to happen. More so, even. When the "liveness" of television gave way to videotape, I think something was irretrievably lost.

My favorite show was *Lucky Pup* (CBS), starring the Bunin Puppets— Foodini, Pinhead (hand puppets both), and Doris Brown with Jolo the Clown (another hand puppet)—all brought to you by "One, Two . . . Ipana's for you!" (Do they still make Ipana toothpaste? They had it in bubble gum flavor. I used to eat it.) I watched *Lucky Pup* every weekday after school, except we all used to say we were going home to watch "Foodini" because the pup that inspired the series quickly disappeared. Foodini was an inept but highly self-important magician/inventor and the real star of the show. Pinhead, his assistant, was his foil/scapegoat, because nothing Foodini ever invented ever worked, and Pinhead always got blamed for it. "Dunderhead!" he would yell at poor Pinhead, "Pinbrain! You miserable wretch!" Or if something really stunned him, "Gadzooks!" as his giant eyebrows lifted in amazement. All said with love and affection, mind you. "Gee, boss. . . . what'd I do now?"

I remember Foodini once came up with a cure for baldness. Pinhead, whose age was indeterminate but who sounded like an innocent little boy (he was actually played by Morey Bunin's wife, Hope), had a few tufts of hair but was otherwise totally bald. And so Foodini invented a hairgrowing elixir called "Glitch"—part glue, part itch. And when Pinhead's head started to itch, Foodini yelled "Eureka!" But all poor Pinhead did was itch; he never grew a single new hair (not even with "essence of adolescence," which Foodini sprinkled in, as I recall, for good measure).

Though you knew nothing Foodini did would ever work and even Pinhead knew that, both you and he put up with it, in part, I think, because hope springs eternal (I could invest myself in that, certainly), and knowing, anyway, that Foodini was a paper tiger, a blowhard, bombastic authority, albeit endearing, believing he could make things work, just like we all want to believe we can make things work, and making himself a fool in ways that even adults loved watching. Pinhead would caution in advance: "Gee, boss, I don't know," but Foodini would hear none of it, and that, too, endeared me to him. "Now Pinhead, my boy. Why don't you just step in here." Poor Pinhead, guinea pig that he was. But you always knew it would turn out fine even when you knew it would never work. The show would often end on Foodini, his hands to his face, rocking left to right, lamenting: "Woe is me. . . . Woe is me." (At least he didn't do it in Yiddish.) But he had these outrageous schemes, you see, and nothing ever discouraged him. Or me.

I also remember *Life with Snarky Parker*, starring the Bil Baird Marionettes, and that guy at the piano, Slugger Ryan. Slugger always mumbled something at the opening and close of each show, as he sat there at his upright, bangin' away at the ivories, a cigarette dangling from his lip, his deadbeat eyes suggesting a guy who was tanked. I had no idea what in the hell he was talking about but I liked the way his lower lip moved, and the way he blew smoke. Today we'd say he was "cool," only we didn't say that then. Very Hoagy Carmichael (after whom, it turns out, he was modeled). The rods under his wrists were a dead giveaway (which was okay), and I wondered what else there was that gave him life. I never could follow the show, anyway, so I guess it didn't matter.

Life with Snarky Parker and Burr Tilstrom's *Kukla, Fran, and Ollie* were both too sophisticated for me, but the combination of television and puppetry held me spellbound. As I said, you'd think I consciously planned what followed in my life. I didn't.

Two marionettes dancing on roller skates as I peer through the radio store window, my mother at my side, setting my eyes on the first television set I have ever seen.

ONE DAY, AS I was walking by a building on Avenue M, something must've caught my eye, because I sensed what this place was. I remember a large door was open just wide enough for me to peer in, and a watchman, who must've caught my look of enchantment, was kind enough to let me take a closer look. And there it was, sitting there: an old movie crane that used to have a camera on top of it (and which I severely missed not seeing; it was as if a shrine had been defiled), as well as some other small pieces of equipment, and I knew I was looking at a place where they'd once made magic. I even remember the burst of sunlight beaming through the skylight onto the empty stage area, the dust particles through the beam of light, as if the beam of light itself were being projected. The ghost of magic past. If only walls could talk.

I got the shivers. Goose bumps. I'm not sure where this came from, this extraordinary passion and love for something I'd seen so little of in my very young life. I think I inquired of the watchman if they were going to bring this back, and I suspect his answer was not very encouraging because I got the feeling I'd been born too late; I'd missed it all. I made like none of it really mattered to me anyway, though, just curious. As if the acknowledgment of how much it really *did* matter would somehow have threatened whatever fantasies I held to. So I feigned indifference.

The thing about my dreams and aspirations was that I hid them. This had to do, in part, with my innate expectation that had I not done so, they'd be taken away, just like everything else had been. I could not risk the derision of "Where do you come to have such crazy ideas?" Hearing that would have taken away everything.

A dozen years later, I would be working part-time in live television in New York, writing and holding cue cards for a TV comer named Merv Griffin, who was then also hosting a teenage dance show called *Saturday Prom*, originating live from what was then and still is NBC's color studio on Avenue M in Brooklyn: the very same studio I thought I'd been born too late for.

Let no one tell you ever, *ever*, that dreams don't count.

2

The Home

A FEW TIMES during the year, I would take the subway to what was always called "the Home" in the Boro Hall section of Brooklyn. Upon its arrival at Boro Hall, the subway would make such a sharp turn that it would not only have to slow down, it would also literally tilt and screech its way into the station. With this, you knew you were almost there.

My fate hung on the decisions that emanated from the Home, the central office, the nerve center of the foster care program. Here were the offices of the social workers, the supervising social workers, the supervising supervisors, the administrators. Ida Freedman, who would in some sense change my life forever, was a supervising social worker. I went there regularly, for my annual physical and dental examinations, to pick up clothing twice a year, to see my social worker. That my foster parents themselves referred to it as "the Home" acknowledged a fundamental truth: this was the seat of authority and control; of power, pure and simple. My foster parents, whether they were "permanent" or temporary, were nothing more than designated hitters; theirs was a franchise subject to revocation at any time, as well as abuse. I was the ball in play, on loan to the people whose home I shared, as they were to me. This reality would, in time, breed both fear and loathing in me.

My few blocks' walk from the subway station to the Home was an obligatory undertaking tinged with the embarrassment I would feel as I saw lettering emblazoned in brass on the building's brick facade: THE BROOKLYN HEBREW ORPHAN ASYLUM. Assaulted by these words, I would speedily and jauntily hasten up to the glass outer door that was the entrance to the building, turn right, and step up to the next glass door, which led directly into the linoleum reception area. My walk, my bearing, would disown the fact that I was the one referenced on the sign above. If I got in quickly enough, perhaps no one would notice I'd even entered. An orphan was alone and unwanted; I had myself, and I really did have a mother—it's just that she was sick. "Asylum" was even worse; it said to me "crazy house." That was my mother, not me. What was wrong with these people?! These words said to me and to the world that I was not as good as other children. No doubt there was a touch of my own guilt—as well as a gilded affirmation of it—in my embarrassment, but I needed to retain *some* vestige of "goodness" for my dreams to happen. My dreams were very important to me, and they needed me, too, so I needed myself.

These words said, too, that I was second-best; a reject; a hand-me-down; a child requiring pity, as one might feel a certain pity for the handicapped, the abandoned, the needy, one of the less fortunate, a charity case. Somehow I would transcend this definition as well. And while I was Jewish, "Hebrew" was just taking this too far (especially given the fear I connected with spoken Yiddish); it belonged to an ancient time, before I was even born!

"Brooklyn," on the other hand, meant the whole wide world—including Ebbets Field, the Dodgers, and Coney Island—and there wasn't a thing wrong with that. But the unfortunate grouping of words in the Home's name was a potent negative force field, from which I could find no affirmation and with which I wanted no identification. (Besides, there was no such thing as the Brooklyn Hebrew Orphan Asylum. Over the years it was reorganized and absorbed by the bureaucracy. For most of the years it dealt with me, it was the Children's Service Bureau. Then it was the Jewish Child Care Association of New York. Nobody bothered changing the advertising.)

Rejecting these words involved an *affirmation* of who I was and *who I was to become,* the latter being my salvation. My mother had bought me paint and a paintbrush; she bought me a shoeshine kit and a bellows camera and even a projector she could not afford. And I could set up my own "store" in our apartment even if I didn't sell anything. I could play the Victrola over and over again and *be* Al Jolson. There, at the earliest moments, was support and confirmation.

For me, self-invention was ongoing and without alternative. If necessity is the mother of invention, then invention was, for me, the mother of life itself. I would find both solace and salvation in my dreams for the future. They were more than escape; they were a rescue net, so to speak, woven with thread from an indefinable source. They were doors to worlds that seemed far happier, more expansive and more liberating, than my own. Besides, I could *make reality*; through the viewfinder I could *select it*, even *invent* it. I could take the pieces and put them together in new ways, ways that were mine. All these years later, I have not changed that view, and wonder, sometimes, how I got it so right so early. The empirical truth of this is the fact of my ample survival. There was a dignity, after all, in my being. But there was no dignity at all in the emblazoned bronze advertisement above the brick facade.

∞

FLATBUSH WAS A fair-weather friend all weather long. It had just stopped raining one early spring day, and I remember walking along the curb, exhilarating in the clear rainwater streaming by me; watching an occasional tree leaf swim by, when suddenly a free-floating single dollar bill rushed past (one box of a hundred baseball cards!). Whose dollar bill could this have been? And as I bent down I wondered, "Is this allowed?" Surely I'd have to let it dry. Ambivalence? Of course. But heaven, still.

Auntie was a mother in the old-fashioned sense. She cooked, she cleaned. I don't recall her ever going to a movie or anything else. I don't even recall her having friends—I don't remember any coming over to the house. She was more a presence, a benign one that left me free.

In winter, Jimmy and I built snow huts that we could actually crawl into. Maybe it still snows in Flatbush, but when you're nine, everything is so much more, and even the street where you play stickball is ten miles wide. Jimmy had Lionel trains. I liked American Flyers best, though, because they had tracks with two rails that looked just like the real trains, while Lionel's had three rails and they didn't look real. I don't know why, but there was a prejudice for Lionel and against American Flyers. It's like Goya beans. Somehow, Goya beans weren't Jewish or something. Maybe it was that "goy" (but the goyish girls were awfully pretty). I don't know.

A block of kids needed organizing, and organizing was something I liked doing. It gave order to things and everybody belonged, including me—especially me if I did the organizing. I was founder/president of "The 29ers." There were five of us, maybe six if you include Alan Katimsky down the block, but I don't remember if he ever showed because he was always busy practicing his violin. We met in the low-slung toolshed in back of Jimmy's house, where you really couldn't stand up but there was nothing to stand up for anyway, and bending down to get in kind of made it forbidden. We had our own dyed blue T-shirts with the words "The 29ers" stenciled on them. I took attendance at our meetings in the same kind of long narrow manila attendance book that the teachers used in public school (I think Jimmy's father had brought one home), enjoying its fine-ruled order. I have no recollection at all, though, of what we did or talked about at our meetings, except that I liked taking attendance and collecting dues. Dues were twenty-five cents, which was how we financed our T-shirts. Order. Order, and control of that order—I think those are what sparked me. I had the need—indeed, the passion—very early on, to pull things together, people or otherwise, whatever was within my grasp, in a world that was, for me, continually coming apart and one, too, from which I felt excluded.

One day I was with a friend on East Twenty-ninth Street and we came to an empty lot. In those days, there were plenty of empty lots all over the place. You could see clear across Flatbush Avenue to where the Nostrand movie theater was. (The double feature on Saturday was twenty-five cents, and for an extra fifteen cents, I think, you could sit in the loge—which was like a first balcony, but lower, with fat seats that were plushy—but that was for people with money, and I never got to sit there. Even the special tickets to get up there were fat.) Anyway, you could also see the back of a grocery store, its back door open. In the lot, up against the fence, were wooden crates of brown empty beer bottles—*refundable* beer bottles. So me and my friend reached in, pulled out a bunch of bottles, and brought them around the front for our "refund." I recall that after four or five trips, the grocer caught on and chased us the hell out of there. We were selling him his own bottles!

I also sold Power House candy bars from my homemade "sales wagon" at a price that was above fair market value. This was quite an achievement when you consider that the candy store was just around the corner. That did not seem to faze me. In fact, I doubt the *reality* of it ever crossed my mind. As I recall, business wasn't all that bad, either, maybe because I sold Kool-Aid with them. Maybe that was the key to my success, the package deal. And I delivered the *Brooklyn Eagle*—my own paper route. I had my own bike, a Schwinn, made collections once a week, and wrote them down in my brown cardboard subscription booklet, until the book got soaking wet in the rain. I think that was the end of the paper route. Nobody ever forced me to go out and make money, though. I had this entrepreneurial spirit at the outset, even dating back to the days with my mother and my first shoeshine kit.

Eastern Parkway, Brooklyn

A brief walk from our apartment on Franklin Avenue. My mother has bought me the shoeshine kit that I have wanted, with the brushes and orange gook in the bottle. (It smells good, too. Good enough to taste, really, and I'm tempted, but I'm not that dumb.) This is the same kind of kit I have seen professional shoeshine men use, and I proceed to solicit takers. I think I charge three cents a shine and have a taker or two—mainly, I suspect, out of their bemusement at the thought of a six-year-old "professional." My intent, though, is quite serious. I am out to do a job and make money. I like the idea; it's fun.

I remember painting a slatted wooden door that, for whatever reason, was lying on the living room floor. My mother had bought me a 25-cent can of Red Devil paint and a brush. I painted the entire door green, and before it even dried, I took a piece of white chalk and marked a price all over it: $1.98. Then there was the time I set up my first store, right next to the living room window that overlooked a narrow alleyway three or four stories down; the same window I'd thrown lit paper napkins out of, making believe they were Nazi planes, and watching them drop to their kamikaze deaths. I decided to sell 78 rpm records. I moved together a couple of large black trunks, the ones with the brass corners (I guess they were furniture). Putting together a "store" filled me with expectation, as if the "putting together" would lead to a result. I must have been an optimist at a very early age: taking an event into my own hands, perhaps sensing a dilemma, and hoping that I could lead us out of it. It never occurred to me that nobody'd ever come (in spite of the large sign I'd placed in front of me). But I had a record store. I was in business. (I doubt the Jolson album would've been for sale, though. I don't think I could ever have sold that.)

Then there was the time I decided to open my own movie theater, replete with projection booth. My mother had bought me one of those opaque projectors that had a slanted mirror and a lightbulb inside; I would cut the funnies out of the newspapers, slide them under the glass, and project them onto the wall. I moved our largest trunk to the back of the living room and tore two squarish holes in a sheet. I'd noticed the tiny windows up in the projection booth in the movie theaters where the beam of light came out of. When you looked up you saw all that dancing dust and realized that way back up in that booth is where the "magic" came from (someday I'd have to get up there).

So I was all set to go except that the projector's cord wasn't long enough to reach the outlet. I tried using my mother's cone of string to lengthen it—running it from one corner of the room to the next until I'd pretty much run out of string—hoping somehow I'd extend the cord and get this thing to work, but all I got, finally, was a shock when I stuck my finger in the wall socket.

Whether or not, on some unconscious level, I was trying to ease our financial plight, I cannot say. Surely I knew and felt the struggle. It had something to do with me; I was in some way responsible. Therefore, I expected to be punished: if not disowned or disposed of in some way, then the even greater punishment of physical sickness and death. The fact that my mother would speak Yiddish *(Sehr krank)* clearly meant to me then that she was shielding me, out of love, from this terrible news, and that this, apparently, was something beyond even *her* control. I was going to be punished by a higher power. The fact that she had choked me one night, but had stopped as well, just proved how much she really did love me, but also how unbearable a burden I was in spite of it. And though I had no idea what I had done to deserve this, there was never any question, for me, that this was all my fault. I had sought ways to alleviate our suffering; my mother's mainly, and my own painful responsibility for her plight. I once found change on top of the medicine cabinet in the bathroom. Lots of coins—maybe a dollar's worth. For some reason I reached up and felt them. It was like magic that they were there at all. Eureka! I'd struck gold! I gave them to her, thinking this would solve our problems. Whether it was through a "record store," shining shoes, or painting a door, if I could prove my worth, I would be forgiven.

The defining moment of my childhood, and the confirmation of all I'd suspected, would be my mother's abandonment of me. My screams to her that day at the hospital were my cry for forgiveness, and not from my sorrow that my mother was ill and required institutionalizing. That would have been the adult's view, never the child's. I knew she was being taken from me and that I could not go with her, and I even understood, I believe, the reason (she was crazy), but I could not divorce myself from it as the principal cause.

My recollection of her pain, as well as my own feelings of responsibility, would only serve to compound, for me, the enormity of my crime. "No wonder you drove your mother crazy!" is something I would later hear in a foster home, and may even have heard more than once. It rang true. Atonement by whatever means—sickness, death, rejection—was now inevitable, as was my expectation of abandonment for all time. In spite of my own quest for survival, I would not let myself get away with this. A child knows fair from unfair; just from unjust. I had driven my mother crazy, and I expected that I would be punished, and through my punishment, perhaps, she would forgive me. If she didn't, then I would try even harder still, and expect rejection all the more. Besides, I knew now: love leaves.

Confronting dreamless blind alleys where the face of hope for a future shows itself not, children will sometimes resort to violent lashing out. Without a future, there is no downside to any aimless risk taken in the present. Indeed, taking a risk is propelled by the perception of potential reward. The dreamer embraces risk because of goals believed attainable. The lost soul does so because there is nothing left to lose. The enlightened dreamer will risk because, for him, the unrealized life is not worth living. It is the man in the middle, the mediocrity, who will ask for nothing, exact nothing, and risk nothing, for lack of desire to achieve anything. Like a potted plant, he digs in and awaits periodic watering. Notwithstanding the sheer waste of misguided passions, of misspent, flailing energies, there is more in a child who risks everything, often tragically, in the hope of attaining something, than in a whole world of potted plants.

I lived a childhood of perpetual loss, and I survived to the extent that the very concept of risk became foreign to me; my very life had been defined by it. What terrible thing could I imagine happening now that had not already happened? What could be taken that they had not already taken? What could make me not survive? My mother could slap her face and pronounce: *"Sehr krank!" That* I had lived in fear of, and of *that* I was totally deserving.

No doubt the residual trauma of the loss of my mother and my expectation of future loss helped set in motion a process of conflicting and conflicted means and ends: I *tested* for fidelity. This testing had its roots in my expectations of eventual rejection, and would bring about the very result I'd sought to avoid. I was not only a conjurer of dreams, you see, but, in this, my own fate as well. I was a kid throwing jabs in anticipation of being knocked out. "C'mon, c'mon, hit me. I dare ya. Let's see what you can do to me. Huh?" and then . . . BAM! "I'm calling the Home to take you away!" Oh. Now she's gonna threaten me: "Go ahead. Go ahead. Call the Home. I dare ya." BAM! BAM!! Now she's lifting the goddamn phone: "Mrs. Freedman, I can't handle him anymore. Take him out of here." "I *knew* you were gonna do this!" This pattern was taken to its unbearable extreme.

I think most kids test and need to know there are boundaries. Nothing I ever did was violent, but I would act in a threatening way, to see where the limits were. These older foster parents were simply not able to establish those kinds of boundaries. Ironically, by the time the breaking point was reached, *their* breaking point, and they called the Home to have me taken away, the reality of that would set in and then none of us wanted it to happen. In the face of the rejection I'd brought on, I pleaded for acceptance and a chance to prove my worth.

The continuous battle for survival was the only life pattern I'd ever known. The pain of the "knockout" was real, of course, but so was the sustained pain of anticipation; suspended animation in expectation of that which, while I set it up, I considered inevitable anyway. My subsequent remorse, and that of my foster parents, were equally real. Without exception, they tried to reverse the decision to have me removed. But the institutional wheels had been set in irreversible motion. I was out for the count. And refundable to boot.

I had developed, early on, an instinctive ability to psychically distance myself from demoralizing, threatening, or otherwise undermining circumstances. This distance allowed me to sustain whatever thread of continuity and promise to my world that I could conjure in an otherwise precariously uncertain existence. I was perpetually monitored by authorities whose very measurements destroyed any semblance of normalcy in my life and were, in and of themselves, threateningly judgmental. Mine was a continuous process of internal reinforcement. Children often retreat to themselves when unable to cope with threatening forces around them, and yet my own dreams were not so much escape as a foraging for resources. I reached for, and created, alternatives in the midst of uncertainty in an ongoing process of self-reliance and self-reflection that created resilience. The inner life is sanctuary taken when external paths are blocked. That one should meet up with the transcendent is not surprising.

In all of this, though, I remember feeling a sense of control, as well as of *self-control*. The "acting up" was precisely that: convincingly staged behavior, pseudo-emotions that paraded themselves as the real thing for real effect. It was never beyond my ability to stop, instantly, if I so chose. In fact, at my stunned moment of "success," I *would* stop. I was not a child "out of control," though the net effect was largely indistinguishable from the real thing, and the toll it took was as real as the real thing. But once my need to bring about the needed effect disappeared, so, too, did this behavior.

While still in my late thirties, I would meet a child psychologist

whose children shared a class with a child I helped raise. At a school func-
tion one evening, I revealed that I had been a foster child. He seemed fascinated by this. His suddenly widened eyes were quite telling—I looked
and acted nothing like a foster child. We became friends, and not long
afterward he commented, with a mixture of mused perplexity and admi-
ration, "I don't get it. You should either be dead, on drugs, or in jail."

Self-control was my best defense always, my weapon of choice. By holding myself in check, even while acting impetuous, impulsive, and angry
(feigned or real), there was always a point beyond which I would not go.
This discipline of "protective detachment," in a sense a form of passive
resistance, was there at the outset, as remarkable as that seems even to me
in retrospect. In the absence of other defenses, it is effective, and when it
is effective, it reinforces a capacity for observation that, after all, helps you
see things clearly.

"Seeing things clearly," for a child, can mean trusting intuitive perceptions, revelations, glimmerings—the resonances of things past as
points of reference. The clarity with which a child perceives, be it the truth
or deceit and denial, is unfettered by the emotional bias of concealment
or adjustment. The accumulative jaundice we call experience is only a
knowledge with which we cover over our perceptions and inner truths,
concealing them even from ourselves. A child's perception is of the purest,
a lucidity that is both crystalline and unadulterated by life's protec-
tive/defensive mechanisms. This is the primary asset, I believe, of the artist
in society, and is particularly potent in a child sensitized to loss and
abandonment.

"I'm calling the Home to take you away!" Just as I have no recollection
of the names of my temporary foster parents, I have no recollection either
of the moments of separation from my "permanent" homes. In fact, the only
moments of separation for which I have a vivid and detailed memory were
those with my mother. Perhaps, in having lived such trauma once, and at
so young an age, I was simply incapable of fully facing it again, and I effectively closed down. And I accepted the separation as inevitable. The pain

of separation, though, was no less felt. In leaving Flatbush, I understood at once the irreversibility of the "program" that had been set in motion, and my own inability to affect my ensuing destiny. And yet, in another psychic conundrum, it showed me that I might.

My awareness of the will's power to bring about an outcome, even a painful one, produced, at some level, a confirmation of my own ability to survive—particularly since I was in a position of weakness, my destiny perpetually threatened by others, ravaged by punishment at the earliest stages of life. It was as reaffirming of my inner strengths and resources as it was empowering. The practice of will, then, would become the one tool, or weapon, I could achieve early "success" with. I could, for example, get even—with them as well as with me. The paradox of this success being, of course, its self-defeating aspect. I believe, however, that it forged in me a lifelong capacity to accomplish goals that seemed impossible to others. An observant yet baffled film editor with whom I worked years later, watching me put together a film with no visible financial support, described my ability as "self-levitation."

I cannot describe in words the profound sense of loss at the sudden disappearance of all I had truly come to feel a part of and to love. Being taken away from my home on East Twenty-ninth Street in Flatbush would mark the second time I was taken against my will, but a first, really, in terms of losing a daily life that was genuinely not torn by the exigencies of basic survival. This had given me my first room, my first friends, even my first tree-lined street. I had invested myself in Auntie, I think, as much as I had my own mother. Auntie even changed her mind, wanted to have me stay and try again, but the bureaucracy would not allow it. These had been 2½ vital years, ones with an emerging consciousness for me, as well as the first real sense of community and continuity of life that I'd ever known. So when all that I'd believed would be "permanent" was lost to me, the expectation of loss was all I would ever come to know, and would remain the only certainty I could ever count on. I was ten or eleven years old now. In a moment, it would all be gone. Even Chubby.

3

Shutting Down

IN THE THREE-BEDROOM, ground-floor apartment of Rose and Ben Kessler at 1365 East Third Street in Brooklyn, I would share a room with an older foster boy named Morton Levine. Uncle Benny's and Aunt Rose's bedroom was just off the living room and had two glass-paned curtained doors that closed it off. Who knows what went on behind these doors? (These were people in their mid- to late fifties, but when you're eleven or so, that's ancient.) Uncle Benny was always kvetching, coughing, spewing up phlegm, and complaining that he had congestion in his chest. He smoked, too (I knew even then, somehow, that this wasn't good), and I would've imagined that he was going to die, as I believe he himself imagined it, except that Aunt Rose wore a nonchalant "what a pain in the ass," tight-lipped grin and a knowing twinkle behind her horn-rimmed glasses that somehow signaled he'd survive. I liked Aunt Rose a lot, and found the calming effect of her "What, me worry?" attitude reassuring, as I'm sure Uncle Benny did, too. There was just nothing Uncle Benny could come up with that she couldn't handle. By proxy, then, if Uncle Benny was okay, I was okay. Aunt Rose's nonintrusive, nondemonstrative nature somehow created a sense of security for me almost as soon as I got there.

A congenital kvetch such as Uncle Benny, though, was a whole different kettle of fish from, let's say, Milton Sperling, who really *was* dying, and to whom Aunt Rose and Uncle Benny took me on a visit once. He, too, coughed a lot, but I recall this as being the real thing: Milton Sperling undoubtedly had TB, and thus became my prototype death model. Even though he had stayed way on the other side of the room, it was from him that I must've caught the disease, which included back pains but excluded the coughing part, which I apparently saw no need for. This must've been a dead giveaway to the pediatrician, though, who would later examine me, pronounce me fully healthy, and refuse to give me a chest X-ray in spite of my insistence that he do so. I was certain he'd missed something. I would have to live, now, with the uncertainty of his certainty.

The third bedroom, incidentally, was empty, and would remain so enshrined, in memory of Aunt Rose's mother, whose room it had been and who had already died. Fortunately for me, this event transpired some time prior to my arrival and, with the exception of the folded wheelchair against the bedroom wall and some other antiseptic-looking accoutrements—eerie remnants of a person's passing—there was nothing here that was overly worrisome, except that the room was suspiciously still. I was not permitted to enter this room, which was just as well, actually, because a spirit might still reside there, and God knows I had enough to worry about without having to encounter one of them. Besides, who knows what you could catch from an empty room that someone might've died in?

This room also expressed for me, if ever so subtly, Aunt Rose's capacity for sentiment. That was reassuring, somehow, for it made everything else she did all the more believable, and spoke to the truthfulness of the sense of security she promoted through her reassuring unconcern for what was genuinely not worth worrying about.

Aunt Rose would set my breakfast out for me each morning, usually a choice between Mallomars and a glass of milk or something else. I'd pick Mallomars, of course. On Sunday mornings Uncle Benny would put on his mackinaw and drive his green Chrysler Town and Country—sort of a cross between a car and a station wagon, with wooden-styled doors, over to Avenue U to pick up the Sunday *Daily News* (which had the funnies), lox, bagels, cream cheese, and jelly rolls. I have no idea how jelly rolls got into this Jewish feast, but they were my breakfast of choice for Sunday. The other stuff, which I might have nibbled at, was serious food, and the lox was just too salty for my taste. I didn't know from nova back then, which is not as salty as lox, and might've been too expensive for our neighborhood.

Once again I was free to do what I wanted, within reason. Already television provided me with friends who traveled from home to home with me. Now I was old enough to visit them, and I would get on the subway and go to television studios whenever I could, whatever the weather. Game shows were usually five days a week. I don't think I played hooky—I've checked my reference books and there was a time when *Beat the Clock* broadcast on Saturday, and that's what I recall as well. I almost always went on my own, riding the subway to Manhattan. I'd probably sent for tickets at least once, so I knew the address of the theater. All shows were live in those days, so if you knew when they were on the air you knew that if you showed up you had a chance to get in. I don't remember ever not getting in.

Getting a white oblong envelope in the mail with the NBC or CBS logo on it was as good a moment as Christmas morning because you knew there were tickets inside. You opened the envelope and there was a sort of pocket folio that you flipped up and there in a slit were the tickets. Just looking at those tickets was a thrill. It was a continuing passion even into high school, when the biggest thrill was the *Jackie Gleason Show with Ray Bloch & His Orchestra*. You waited months for those, and even when they came, they were dated at least a month in advance. *Caesar's Hour*, with the incomparable Sid, was another passion. The first incarnation of the *Tonight* show, starring Steve Allen, broadcast live from the Hudson Theater beginning at 11:30 P.M. I was there once. But there were other times, other shows.

While I was at the Kessler home, I would walk a small child, no more than six, perhaps, to school every day for a dollar a week. He lived just across the street, and his mother trusted me with his charge. I felt quite proud of her trust in me, although I cannot recall how she came to know or sense my worth. The dollar offered both confirmation of the value of my service and its utter seriousness. I would take that little boy's hand, he would reach for mine, and that made me feel proud and responsible. I remember that feeling vividly.

I remembered Chubby vividly, too: he was my dog, and he was still back home on East Twenty-ninth Street, and I missed him and Auntie very, very much. So on my way to public school each morning, about a block from the school I would pass a candy store where there was a telephone booth inside. I knew I was doing something wrong, but I couldn't help it, and I was very careful to make sure that no one ever saw me go into the store and I'm pretty sure no one ever did, and I made sure I had a dime. Sometimes I would make believe I was actually going to buy something (and maybe I did, just to even it up, as penance), but the phone booth was in the back, so I would sort of work my way up to it, very unsuspiciously, of course; make-believe unconsciously, just in case someone thought I was actually going to make a call. If someone did see me, he or she would have wondered who I was calling, since I didn't have anywhere else to call except home anyway and everyone would've known that if they caught me.

In those days the phone was in a private wooden booth that had a brownish quilted metal lining inside it, and a seat, and when you closed the door, the light went on, and no one could hear you. And I would call home. I knew Auntie was waiting for my call and I pictured her sitting in her floral house dress at the phone table, which was down at the foot of the stairs. I would tell her how much I loved her and missed her and Chubby and we would make arrangements to meet on Ocean Parkway after school (which was somewhere between East Third and East Twenty-ninth streets) and she would bring Chubby, too, on his lanyard.

Just as we had had peashooter and yo-yo seasons, and other seasons, too, I remember a lanyard-making fad. Lanyards were made of different-colored plastic strips that you'd sort of weave together, with a metal clip at the end, which you could always use for keys and stuff. I made Chubby a long lanyard leash, and I can remember him pulling at it when he saw me coming toward the bench where he and Auntie were waiting for me on Ocean Parkway. He just pulled and pulled, his tail wagging, and Auntie stood up and we all met in the middle. Auntie looked sort of awkward holding Chubby's leash like that, but the sight of my leash and Auntie holding on to it said to me that part of me was still with them. Chubby was an ordinary dog—a brown, wavy-haired mutt, really—but it was a wonderful feeling when he came into my life. I don't remember quite how and why that happened, but he was the only live anything I'd ever had, and I knew and he knew that he belonged to me, and that *I* was responsible for *him*, and I knew he would never reject me.

Two long, narrow, tree-lined, cobblestoned islands ran parallel to each other on Ocean Parkway. Each was flanked on either side by rows of stone and wooden benches, lined up, seemingly forever, one after the other; the foot traffic flowing between them. Here little gray-haired old ladies sat on a summer's day, kibitzing. Little gray-haired old ladies are still sitting, still kibitzing, only now it's their daughters holding court. It is a timeless scene of impermanence.

This stony way station was a physical expression, really a metaphor for my feelings of estrangement and of being stranded. I could not go home. I had no more home. But I had Auntie and Chubby on the parkway. The pain of knowing that I could not have what I'd had, that this would only last a few moments or so before I would have to go back to East Third Street, that this clandestine rendezvous in broad daylight on this homeless island with nowhere to go with its imposed limits on intimacy amid the cacophonous breeze of passing cars, would not only remind me of the limits placed upon my deepest heartfelt feelings but also reinforce the momentariness of my reprieve from separation. The foreordained parting was, in a very real sense, a replay of all I had come to know about the nature of relationships in life, and I would feel such sadness and despair, such aloneness and isolation that the moment itself was fraught with a yearning for a sense of belonging. I could affect nothing, no matter how much I loved, no matter even how much I was loved in return (and I was), and no matter how much I yearned to go home. I could not. It was not permitted. Where was home?

One night when I was in my early forties, I had a dream of being a young man, or boy, at night in the city (probably Brooklyn). In it, I am on my way home, and as I walk down the street I see the lights on in the windows of the apartment buildings across the street. The cars, their headlights beaming, are passing me. I am eerily disconnected from it all. Who are these people behind the lights, inside their cars, inside these buildings? Everyone has each other. Everyone belongs. I am isolated, removed. Suddenly, as I am walking, I realize I do not know where I live. I have no idea where my home is. I am groping, trying to recall a street, a location, a familiar landmark. Try as I might, though, I cannot find my way home.

It is one of the most vivid and disturbing dreams I can ever recall, all the more terrible because it is set at night and all the windows are lit, which means, presumably, that there are families inside who belong together. I have an overwhelming sense of aloneness.

∞

ONE DAY, CHUBBY was gone. Auntie came to the parkway without him. She told me he'd run away but I don't think I believed that. Maybe she *gave* him away because she knew I would never be coming home again. I don't remember if I saw Auntie ever again after that. I just don't remember.

∾

MORTON LEVINE, WITH whom I shared my latest room, had been living there by the time I arrived and must've been all of eighteen or so. He would stand at the foot of his bed each morning davening (rocking back and forth in prayer), wearing tefillin, two little black leather boxes that contain religious parchments written in Hebrew, which he wrapped around his left arm and forehead. I watched him strap these things on, wondering how he got it inside himself to do this stuff. I found it, somehow, old-mannish and somber, with no happiness attached to it, probably because its clear association with Judaism could only mean trouble, given my experience. I had seen old men davening in shul (synagogue), and so to my mind, it was all tied up with illness or impending death. Why else would old men pray unless they thought they were going to die and wanted terms? Or, better yet, were attempting to negotiate a deal, offering penance, not to die. I wasn't about to offer anything; I didn't even want to be reminded. Besides, I was already dying—pains in my back and incurable TB, a very big item in the fifties, and for which I'd already identified a human prototype.

Since I *am* Jewish, I was always placed in a Jewish home, but "Jewishness" was not something I felt any great joy about. What I'd seen of Judaism, so far, was not very encouraging—a downtrodden perspective, truly, and one I could not identify with, in spite of, or more appropriately, *because* of my own situation. Things like my own survival (ironically, the most primary concern of Jews for millennia), my adjustment to dense confusion and disorientation, my lack of any compass except the one I could find within myself, took precedence. The only god I could grasp was the god within me, and that had more to do with my protected fantasies for the future than anything else.

Even though I'd gone to cheder (Hebrew school) in Flatbush and been taught to read the siddur (prayer book), all I could really do was recite the Hebrew words by rote. I had learned to read them, but I had absolutely no understanding of what I was reading. Nor, frankly, did it ever occur to me to wonder. I suppose reading out loud was just a performance. Not exactly Al Jolson, maybe, but something was better than nothing. I did what was expected; nobody ever said I had to understand it, too, and I doubt *anybody* ever did, anyway.

Besides, talking up was something I was good at, and enjoyed it even more when I was told to "shut up *zen pisk*!" (shut your mouth!). I never did shut up, however, which was just another reason why I was thought so difficult to handle. I still haven't, of course, but in the adult world, speaking up for what you want and holding beliefs that are original or even antithetical to social norms are often admired. Children are neither empowered nor licensed in these ways; rather to the contrary. So much more so for the child with a different last name.

Cheder was an obligatory undertaking in preparation for bar mitzvah, a rite of passage for all Jewish boys at age thirteen (still some years away for me). But I could never feel any affection for, or identity with, the process, so I could never invest myself in it. Besides, by the time you got to be thirteen and bar mitzvahed and a "man," you *immediately* stop going to Hebrew school and forget everything you've learned, even the stuff you haven't learned, including the reading of the siddur. That's the end of it; everybody feels *naches* (pride) because you/they did the right thing, and life goes on. This is tradition. What did I care about this? I was trying to get used to the bed I was sleeping in. But for a kid who disavowed his Judaism. . . . Jesus, how it stuck!

∞

I CAN REMEMBER almost nothing about school. I hated it. It bored me. I have only a few scattered recollections about public school during these years, and no sense at all of continuity (which, in my case, I suppose, is not all that surprising). In the summer, all I could think of was how hot it was in that damn classroom and how long it would take for that big black bell to ring. But one incident stands out.

A gray-haired teacher named Mrs. Silver used to have us stand at the start of each school day, face the blackboard, and pledge allegiance to the flag. One day, for whatever reason, I decided not to stand. Even after several stern warnings, I was still rooted in my seat. Before I knew it, Mrs. Silver had grabbed the flag from on top of the blackboard and rushed up to me with the clear intent of hitting me if I didn't stand up.

So I stood up, turned the other way, and ran. In those days, desks and seats were lined up one behind the other and nailed to the floor, just like the public education system itself. I wove my way up and down the aisles, with her in pursuit and the whole class cheering me on, enjoying it, and with me enjoying them enjoying me. This, of course, pissed her off even more.

Finally I realized that this up-and-down-the-aisle business wasn't going to get me anywhere and that she might catch up with me anyway, and buoyed by the cheering, I stopped, turned toward her, and as she approached with that flag, I kicked her in the stomach. Now, I didn't really kick her in a way that connected, mind you; it was more of a "get outta here, leave me alone" kind of kick.

I probably gleaned more from this episode than I'd learned in school until then. I'd stood up to her, and away went her patience and authority. I'd humiliated her, the kids had seen it, and she'd seen that they had. I reveled in the encouragement of those who, if only by proxy, liked to see authority challenged. Realizing, I suppose, that she could not "handle" me, Mrs. Silver went to the front of the room and called the principal's office on the intercom. I was undoubtedly punished in some way, like being sent home, which would've been no punishment at all. I wish to hell they'd kicked me out altogether.

❧

A VESTED PINSTRIPED suit. A fob watch. And a Germanic accent. Sigmund Freud? Close, but no cigar. A psychiatrist, who I found out later was Wilfred Hulse (pronounced HUL-see). It would be a single session. A

projective/subjective summary judgment, a general evaluation, administered to me at the Home by this one man. From this my fate was sealed.

I don't know why the Home felt I needed to be examined by its Great
Man just then. Of course, I had no idea what the point of it was. Whatever the point was, though, I knew I'd probably failed it. I still felt I
could make up for whatever it was I had done. In one form or another,
I was selling; always selling (could I interest you in a slatted door,
unhinged and freshly painted, a dollar ninety-eight?).

Somewhere in Brooklyn

*My mother sells blouses in a shop that I believe is her own. I cannot be
more than five years old. The store feels threadbare, including splin-
tered floorboards, but has glass fixtures in which there are blouses, most
with colorful sequins and rhinestones. Many of the sequins are heart-
shaped. My sense is that few blouses are sold and this venture ends in
failure. What remains atop the closet in the apartment on Franklin
Avenue are big jars of sequins and rhinestones. There is a certain smell
to the rhinestones, too, and a sort of dry, muted squeak to their texture
when I hold them in my hand and rub them together. I don't understand
why there are problems when there are rhinestones.*

Years later, I will see a copy of my birth certificate. It identifies my
mother as having been born in the United States. Occupation: house-
wife. It says that my father, whom I am never to know, was born in Russia. Occupation: salesman.

I bet I could've sold the blouses.

∞

MY GREAT ESCAPE was fourteen inches square. It was the top of a small
white metal cabinet that sat snugly to the left of the doorway to my

room. There I would execute my ultimate fantasy: my own miniature "television studio."

I would pull up a chair and get very close to the cabinet, virtually hovering over it, protectively, secretively. Carefully, I would knead my gray modeling clay into sets (slabs), actors (sticks), "mike booms" (inverted L-shaped sticks), and at least three fully equipped television cameras (rectangular boxes) operated by cameramen (more sticks) "hugging" the camera, of course (wraparound sticks for arms).

The cameras were your standard studio type: black-and-white-image orthicons (the nomenclature for the early black-and-white camera tubes) with hydraulic pedestals, except for camera two, which was on a dolly, replete with dolly pusher. At the front of each camera protruded four tiny clay sticks, each slightly longer than the other. These, of course, were the primary lenses on the camera's turret. This predates the advent of the Zoomar lens, which made the turret obsolete, and was as dreadful a day for me as when the Dodgers left Brooklyn. Worse, even. It meant there'd be almost no reason at all to move the cameras. All the cameraman had to do was pull a plunger-like stick under his viewfinder to zoom in for a close-up. But I needed to see the cameras move, like Jolson turning up the house lights just "to see faces."

Half the drama of "live" production (from my point of view *behind* the scenes) was the choreographed movement nobody saw. Maybe I couldn't dance, but I could sure as hell choreograph a clay production like nobody's business. Left alone, I would sit there for hours on end; moving cameras, getting shots, and creating the illusion for the "home audience" that there was a lot more here than met the eye, that there was order. Actually, there was a whole lot less than met the eye. When looked at from behind the cameras, there was the semblance of total chaos. Chaos, you see, was the thrill of it all. But at the same time, the apparent randomness of the behind-the-scenes machinations was illusory. It was controlled chaos, where every move had meaning, where it had all been fashioned and rehearsed in advance. Reality was what you made.

Order came from the illusion of chaos, while the "reality" in front of the camera was, paradoxically, the real illusion. I could even run the credits in the toilet—the toilet paper roll made an excellent credit scroll, providing you were close enough to the paper that you didn't see the tiles.

That was important. Whatever existed outside the frame, outside the camera's field of vision, did not exist, and what appeared within the frame—I could control that. What a stunning metaphor, what counterpoint, unconscious to me at the time, for an everyday life in which I controlled nothing. If the world was a stage, for me the stage was a world, a world I could control, and in so doing, control both. What a comeuppance! I could deliver my own destiny, my own salvation. All I needed was a box of clay. A dime.

On occasion, Aunt Rose would pass my room on her way to the bathroom, which was, more often than not, I suspect, a pretext to see what I was up to, especially when I'd been quiet, and *most* especially on a sunny day, when I would be ordered to get some fresh air.

Upon my awareness of Aunt Rose's encroachment, I hammered my clay structures flatter than pancakes; subtly, nonchalantly (lest I raise undue suspicion), eliminating all the incriminating evidence. This was especially frustrating when I hadn't even completed the components of my studio. I was convinced the clarity and detail of my creation would instantly give me away, and somehow equally instantly result in it being taken away. Like the cat that swallowed the canary, my embarrassed, undoubtedly guilt-ridden expression must've read something like: "Studio? What studio?" Aunt Rose would invariably say, "How could you be inside on a day like this! (BEAT) C'mon. Go out and get some fresh air!" The next thing I knew, the shades were flying open, and the windows, too. "C'mon. Look! Look how beautiful it is out!" How could you argue? "It's not healthy being inside like this." Nobody was ever going to tell *me* what was healthy or not healthy. My antennae knew about such things, and fresh air had nothing to do with it. If Milton Sperling had come over, I would've run like a bat outta hell. But he never did come over. I undoubtedly protested about leaving my room, as any child might, but sunny days were here again, and that was that.

I never quite understood what it was with sunny days, except for the guilt they instilled when you tried to ignore them. Apparently, though, fresh air came out more often on sunny days than on all other days. Nobody ever mentioned fresh air, for instance, after a good rain, which was ironic, really, because nothing smelled fresher than the air after it rained. But this really wasn't about fresh air, anyway. It was about solitude. *My* solitude. The roaches had transmuted to clay. And whatever friends I'd had in between were, somehow, more dependable tabletop ones.

But I'll tell you a secret: Not a shred of what was on that tabletop, *not a shred*, mind you, would have actually looked like anything to anyone except me. Just globs of gray modeling clay, ten cents a box. But *I* didn't know that, and I was profoundly embarrassed that I'd actually taken control of something within me, allowed myself the joy of dreaming and, by extension, control of my destiny. What right did I have to do such things? I could not expose this passion, this evidence of my identity, this inner voice, to ridicule and even possible extinction. The risk of this exposure was unbearable. What if they took it away? Then what?

4

A Life on Loan

AND THEN TO think, after weeks and months of waiting, I'd almost overslept! Of all the dumb things that could've gone wrong, that would've been the worst! The *worst*! And had Morton not woken me up that Saturday morning, tapping at my feet like he did and smiling in a big-brotherly sort of way, I'm sure I would have. I'd twisted and turned all night, just from sheer excitement, and to think that I'd almost missed it! *Geez!* I think I even dreamed that I'd gotten up and gone!

When I saw that he was already dressed, I suddenly realized. "What time is it?!" "Well," he said, in a teasingly urgent sort of way, looking at his watch as if to make the obvious more obvious, "if you don't hurry up and get dressed, you're gonna miss it." I bolted out of bed, my dreams that morning as visible as I'd imagined my clay cameras to be. There are three mornings of my childhood that I will never forget, the first being that morning in the hotel. The second was the joy of Christmas morning when I discovered the gift of my hand puppet under the tree. This would be the third.

I quickly donned my clean, pressed Boy Scout uniform, knowing, of course, that this would be an occasion when "costume" could make all the difference in the world between standing out and being overlooked. We took the subway to one of NBC's television studios, the New Amsterdam Theater on Forty-second Street, just off Times Square, which, like so many television studios of the fifties, was a converted legitimate theatrical house.

NBC's *Rootie Kazootie* was one of the few Saturday morning children's shows that had what the *Howdy Doody Show* used to call a peanut gallery. But while Howdy's gallery seemed to have dozens of kids, Rootie's had only twelve, onstage, selected from the studio audience itself. And while Howdy's kids were not really active participants, except as a sort of cheering section, Rootie's kids were contestants in the show's quiz format—"Quiz-a-Rooties," to be exact. Of the twelve selected, three would be chosen and asked a question by the show's host, Big Todd Russell. Rootie's dog, Gala Poochie Pup, would bark to indicate whether the question had been answered correctly or not (nobody ever answered *incorrectly*), and then the contestant would punch one of four balloons to see what prize he'd won. And so, while I never really had a yen to attend a *Howdy Doody Show* (I watched it, as you did, of course—assuming *you're* old enough to remember), *Rootie Kazootie* was another matter entirely.

Howdy and company were string puppets (marionettes), while the Rootie characters were all hand puppets, which have always lent themselves, I think, to a more intimate exchange with children. They are lithe, accessible, and less physically protected—less vulnerable to being yanked at, for example. As an extension of the puppeteer's hand, their movements are immediate and exact, and therefore more suited to physical contact and engagement, and they respond easily and immediately to children touching them. And while some people consider marionettes more "magical," hand puppets are grounded and easy to get close to. My real interest in Rootie was that if you got lucky, you could stand right next to him as a contestant and actually play-act with him. As much as I wanted to push the cameras, I wanted to be in front of them, too. And that is precisely what I'd dreamed of the night before.

When I arrived, I squeezed myself up close to the doors, they opened, there I was, she saw me, and she picked me. I was in and that was that. That fast. She saw the uniform. I *knew* she'd see the uniform. Now I had a chance to become a Quiz-a-Rootie contestant, answer a question, and win a prize. I'd even get a feather in my cap. Only three winners; hence, three feathers. Once again, the uniform cinched it.

Now the shocker: *Rootie* was rigged. I don't mean Kazootie himself (all puppets are rigged, in one way or another), I mean the *show*! (Mind you, this predates even the fifties quiz-show scandals.) Here's how it worked: right before "air," the lady who picked me at the door took me backstage (where I got my first glimpse of Rootie hanging upside down on a hook and looking absolutely wooden), and asked me the magic question that Big Todd Russell was going to ask me on the air. While Rootie himself may have been in on the scam (I'll never know), Gala Poochie Pup provided plausible denial—it was *his* quiz. Big Todd would ask the question, I'd answer it (correctly, of course), and Gala Poochie would growl "R-r-r-r-*right*!" It was a slow growl, strictly for the home crowd, and while it made you squirm a bit, it had dramatic bite and always came up heads. Rootie was delighted (but never implicated), and Big Todd was approving (though I'd never spoken to the man before, *or after*). The kids loved it, too, and frankly speaking, I had no problem with it myself. And here, kids, was the question the woman asked me.

"There was a king in fairy tale land who had a magic touch, and whatever he touched turned to gold. What was his name?"

I answered: "King Arthur."

Now, don't laugh. First of all, I was not the guy to ask this particular kind of question; I had no point of reference. Second, you have to remember that I was about eleven, and I still really hadn't ever read anything. At least I had something to open with. She was very nice and, lowering her voice to a whisper, she told me, "King Midas." Just between her and me, when Big Todd Russell asked me that very same question, I should answer. . . . and I filled in, whispering "King Midas." That was good. Very good. I got it. So I spent the entire half hour repeating to myself "*King Midas, King Midas . . .* ," while at the same time trying to explain to the kid sitting next to me what the cameras (there were three of them) were doing moving back and forth, and what went where, and when to worry about smiling and having a good time, when it didn't matter because nobody was actually watching you anyway, and how it all got from here to people's houses.

My turn came. I stood next to Big Todd Russell and Rootie and looked directly at camera two (whose red tally lights were on), while Big Todd told me I had a "Quiz-a-Rootie partner" at home who'd sent in a postcard with his name on it, and who would win whatever prize I'd win if I answered the question right. Then I'd get a chance to bust the balloon and he'd read the prize on the paper that fell out with the confetti. I *knew* all this stuff already, but he just kept spieling on and on, hogging it all for himself, not even taking a breath even, not even a period or a comma, and then, finally, trying to tell *me* which camera to wave at! Can you imagine?! I practically did this for a living and he was going to tell *me* where to look?!

Still, if ever there was to be one glorious, memorable moment of my entire childhood, this was it—no clay cameras or doorknob-in-the-bathroom cameras here, but real live image orthicons all. So when I waved to my Quiz-a-Rootie partner at home, tally lights aglow, I was waving, really, to my bestest, loyalest, and most familiar friend ever: *the camera;* a friend I'd known ever since my Donald Duck bellows camera on Franklin Avenue. Maybe, even, come to think of it, I was waving to my mother, too. This wave, though, this wave of the moment, had a buoyancy and a joyousness to it that, as I look back and see myself, I do not think I exhibited anywhere else. Perhaps I was reaching for an acceptance without fear of rejection: distant and silent, the camera posed no threat and imposed no judgment (none, at least, that I would worry about). It was a wave that I would savor, as I had savored nothing else before it; not even that chew on the steak.

I was forever seeking out the camera, if only just to look at it. When NBC did live remotes during the Christmas holiday at Rockefeller Center, I would stand there for hours, looking at the camera, communing through sidelong glances, not quite knowing how best to inveigle its interest in me, nor, for that matter, what I might be seeking from it. But I never tired of the search, either. In a few years I would spend entire days walking around New York City looking for a camera. When I found it, something welled up inside me. My dependable friend, who made no judgment except the judgment that was mine by extension, it threatened no consequence except the consequence I imposed on it, and allowed for choice that was my choice as well.

I cannot recall giving any thought to being a "director." The physical components of a production were what consumed me. The visible choreographed machinations were, for me, the soul of the machine. Assuming the position of overseer in my clay fantasies never occurred to me. Nor did it occur to me that the camera's handler was less than the master of its fate. The physical connection to the camera drew me viscerally.

"There was a king in fairy tale land . . ."

"KING *MIDAS*!" "R-r-r-*right*!" And that was that. I busted the balloon, won the prize (couldn't take it home, though; they'd ship it), and the rest was all downhill.

On the subway back to Brooklyn, nobody recognized me. *Nobody.* Not even when I stood up and made myself present. In school, when Mrs. Silver called attendance, I would yell "President!" Here, though, "present" was too important to leave open to argument. This was as present as I got: "driving" the train out the front window adjacent to the motorman's cab and wearing my bright yellow distinctive Quiz-a-Rootie baseball cap, sideways, with feather. *Still*, nobody noticed. And you got that feather only if you'd won. *Nothing.* How could this be? All these people on the subway and *nobody* watched?! I wondered, maybe, if Norma watched. Wait'll I get home. She *had* to be impressed.

Norma Aarons was her full name. She was about eleven years old and as pretty as Mitzi Gaynor, whom I also had a crush on. Not bad, huh? I think the Kesslers knew her parents and I was over there one day with them. There was this talk about her piano lessons, and then someone suggested that I might take them, too, but then someone else said I was too old to start (oh, oh—missed it again), and there she was. *Boing-g-g!* The best part, though, was that Norma liked me, too. But even though I rode my bike past her house, I was much too shy to approach her. Sometimes I'd ride my bike by more than once; sometimes six or ten times. Or even fourteen or nineteen. *More* even. And if she'd see me through the window, sometimes she'd come out. Ringing her doorbell would have been unthinkable. I had, *at best*, an only uncertain sense of my own worth (I harbored terrible secrets that might get out and ruin everything, especially if I got too close), and no real foundation on which to expose any joyous feelings, and I understood the futility of having these feelings, anyway. They'd be taken.

So even though I knew she liked me, I could not extend myself beyond the moment or I would just be leaving myself open for rejection. I could like her as long as I didn't tell her and scare her away, and something in me too, of course, was scared of what I felt. The closest I ever got to showing her how much I really liked her was when she let me give her a ride on my bike. She sat on the bar between the handlebars and the seat and I rode her around the block, and it was really wonderfully scary being this close to her and all, which was as close as I'd ever gotten to a girl. When we came back, her mother was standing outside her home, sort of smiling, and I saw she saw that I liked Norma, and she knew, and I knew she knew, but I made like it didn't matter. As far as I was concerned, I was just taking a ride, counting birds or something, and she just happened to be there. I wondered what her mother knew about me.

I remember feeling deep sadness in knowing that mine was a temporary life, with no real grounding, that I really didn't belong to anybody except the Home, and that sooner or later everything was going to be taken away again anyway. I was a foster child, and even when the Home said that someplace was going to be my permanent home, like the one before it, nothing permanent stayed that way because I was really alone, with no legitimate standing, and when you came right down to it, my life was really somebody else's decision. I knew I could never keep these feelings for Norma permanently, like kids with real homes, and so I could no longer risk the emotional torment of loss and the knowledge of its inevitability. The exceptions, of course, were my dreams. They traveled with me; they *belonged* to me. I could trust me.

She didn't watch. I rode my bike by her window. I must have worn my cap and feather that day. I *had* to. Nothing.

Eventually, my A. C. Gilbert Atomic Energy Set came. I'd waited months for the green Railway Express truck to deliver it, and every day after school, I'd anxiously inquire, "Did it come yet?! Did it come yet?!" When it finally did come, the "Wilson Cloud Chamber" was busted. I used the two small aluminum lights that came with it as spotlights for my puppet theater, so it wasn't a total waste, and besides . . . I still had that moment. Nobody took it away. Nobody could.

∞

WHILE I CANNOT remember what led up to my leaving East Third Street, my behavior, including my dysfunctional behavior at school, was undoubtedly part of it. I must have known, somehow, the consequences of "acting up" and constantly pushing the envelope, as we now say, to its limits. My foster parents were old, unsophisticated and malleable. I could conjure their complicity in any playlet I'd devise, take control of the moment, and effect a predictable outcome. I felt license to both express and elicit the behavior that would fulfill my expectation of punishment and rejection. I would actually dare them to lift the phone and call the Home to take me away. Success came at each and every turn. It was a complete lose-lose. All children act out. And while I acted out in the extreme, in two of these homes (it was only two), the environments were permissive. I felt license to both express and elicit the behavior that would fulfill my expectation of punishment and rejection.

I knew I was bad—I had my mother's attempt to choke me when I was six as proof, as well as her own outcome to confirm it. Given the absence of my father, and my mother's refusal to tell me where he'd gone, I could imagine what I'd had to do with that. (She said California, but Al Jolson sang "California. . . ." and she probably got that from him. I could smell evasion.) Later, they would never let me see her, even when I asked and when I was told how sick she was, because they were secretly protecting me, perhaps from a terrible fate—my fate, which could never be spoken of, only imagined. The terror of not knowing was the ultimate terror, and I would live with this throughout my childhood. Like all the stuff that was said in Yiddish, it was best I never knew.

I had assumed the guilt for my mother's outcome, so by emulating her behavior, wearing it as one would a cloak, I could provoke a response that might put me away, too. I would also be dealt the punishment for what I had done to her. I really didn't know what I had done, but I knew I must have done something, because I knew she loved me. One way or another, I might find my way to penance and forgiveness. I doubt that my mother gave me a model for behavior, given my overwhelming fear of and embarrassment about hers. But the echo of a child's observation transcends thought and reason, so the influence remains.

Whatever the specific cause, leaving would never again have had the tug or underpinning of leaving Flatbush. I never again made the emotional commitment. The passive refusal of the Kessler home to be inveigled into participatory behavior precluded whatever emotional pyrotechnics I might have otherwise played out.

Aside from Norma, I cannot recall a single friend during this eighteen-month period. The fewer roots laid down, the fewer that got torn up. I never did have the chance to say good-bye to Norma, though. I would never have had the emotional wherewithal to do so. How would I have explained to her that I was being given back, which would have betrayed me as an impostor in the first place? Besides, she would undoubtedly find out what happened after I left. What would she have wanted with me then, anyway?

For many years afterward, whenever anyone with the name "Aarons" would appear in my life, I'd inquire if they knew a Norma. I mean, how many "Aarons" could there be? And you know something? I'm still doing it. So Norma, just in case you're listening, give me a call. I promise I'll remember.

∞

I DIDN'T WANT to go. Ida Freedman promised I wouldn't have to if I didn't want to. All that I was being asked to do was look at the place before making up my mind. And if I didn't like it, I didn't have to go. *That was the deal.*

Ida Freedman, like almost everybody I ever met in her profession, was full of shit. The fact is, a decision had been made long before I'd ever seen the place, and, even more significantly, as it turned out, before being sent to my next home, which, I was informed, would be temporary, pending the availability of space at the "treatment center." So I guess I thought that if I didn't like the center, they would just find me a new "permanent" home.

Perhaps she thought that if I saw the place—the kids, the cottages, the blossoming trees, and the expansive grounds—that somehow I might feel different. I knew even before looking, though, that there would be nothing I would see that would make me want to relinquish my freedom. Would anyone in his right mind want to do such a thing? So I went along with it (I had no choice), wanting to believe, against my own instinctive doubts, that somehow I had control of the final decision. She knew, of course, that I did not. This act of deceit was her way of getting me up there with a minimum of fuss.

Besides, if I were willing to conspire against my own freedom, that would have ameliorated any guilt or discomfort she might have felt, so it was worth the shot. What's a little lie between a supervising social worker and a child, anyway? And if I remained closed-minded, she could always argue, as she did, that I was being "stubborn," and use this as further evidence that I needed "treatment." It was cynical and Kafkaesque at the same time. I've seen three-card monte games that give better odds. The fact is I was scheduled to be sent up to Hawthorne Cedar Knolls School, as it was called, and the decision was irreversible. *"You're going whether you like it or not."* Those were the most honest words Ida Freedman ever spoke to me.

The lie, whatever its motive, taught me one of the most important lessons of my life: you must never lie to a child. In the first place, they will probably see through you, and while they will perhaps not always be able to articulate it, they will "hear" the lie as well. In all of this, you stand a very good chance of never being forgiven. You will, most certainly, never again be trusted. And by almost equal measure, if you bother to take notice, they are as incapable of lying about a fundamental truth to you as you might be in covering a falsehood from them. And finally, as you may have noticed, they do not forget.

On my visit to Hawthorne Cedar Knolls, I was invited to have lunch in the dining hall, which occupied a long, squat building off to the left side of the main administrative building, which appeared front and center as you drove onto the grounds of the institution. There were perhaps seven cottages with about twenty-four children to each, and each child was assigned his own cubicle area downstairs for shoes and belongings. The atmosphere could best be described as "raucous summer camp." And I mean that in a positive sense; the kids seemed to own the place.

The food was served cafeteria-style from a steam table. You took a tray, lined up against the wall, and waited your turn. There was a sense of community and purposeful order here. On the surface, you would find little here to distinguish these kids from any other bunch of kids. Off to the right as you left the steam table were the staff tables, and this is where I had my first meal when I visited the place with Ida Freedman. It was almost inviting, seductively so, particularly for a child who'd seen so little security or structure, so much uprooting, and not a whole lot of country. Besides, it didn't seem like it would be very difficult to make friends here, either. I could understand, perhaps, Ida Freedman's gamble. But this was not summer camp. This was a place for emotionally disturbed children, some of them very disturbed.

There were girls here, too. They lived on the opposite end of the "campus," but they never ate with the boys, for reasons I never understood (but didn't spend a whole lot of time thinking about, either), so we never got to see much of them.

But the illusion of normality and openness was omnipresent. There were no physical bars or fences here, and a social worker would often cite this fact with disingenuous satisfaction—just in case you were thinking of leaving. So not only would the premise of my residency turn on a myth compounded by a lie, in addition the place itself was tempered by illusion, sustaining itself in large measure on the sustenance of its own smug mythology.

One of the school administrators, who also may have been a social worker, joined us at the table. The main course was chicken; the dessert, Jell-O. I never cared much for Jell-O, but I love chicken. My mother used to make it. I remember the chicken tasted good. I never did get a whole lot of chicken, anyway. I remember beginning to think that maybe if they served chicken often enough, maybe I would be willing to let them take me away. That I even considered this makes me realize now just how willing I was, in spite of everything, to allow myself to be convinced, and that I was more open-minded than even I thought. I couldn't have gotten even that far just from chicken, though. It must've been the Jell-O.

∽

AFTER ALL THIS, they had no room for me, so I was sent to a temporary home until Hawthorne had room. But the Kesslers suddenly didn't want me to leave any more than I did. Redemption redux. All over again, just like with Auntie! Ida Freedman, though, would have none of this. Returning to the Kesslers would only postpone the inevitable and perhaps lead to the false hope that the Children's Service Bureau would cancel their decision to send me to Hawthorne, and I would once again feel safe to act out my old patterns. They were not about to be duped. For the sake (mine) of scorekeeping, I entered my fourth foster home by age twelve.

What is most interesting about my three- or four-month tenure at the next home is not only the things I remember, but those I do not. I cannot now tell you the street I lived on, the address, or even the section of Brooklyn (all my foster homes were in Brooklyn), and yet I can remember all four of the "permanent" homes without difficulty. I think, in knowing that this would only be a way station between here and Hawthorne, I simply closed down. I could no longer make any emotional or psychic investment at all. Nor did I have any hope that I could affect my destiny, as I had at my very first "temporary" foster home, where I envisioned a future as open and limitless as that joyous Christmas morning. I could not get on with life, and I could not go back to anything I'd known. I felt utterly isolated. I no longer dreamed about the future. Even my clay models stopped.

And yet, something different happened here. I'd never known anything like it. It was a house of rules. The structure, the discipline, the defined boundaries were unlike anything I'd ever experienced. You could not mistake right from wrong because both were overt and straightforward. You could not walk into the house with your shoes on. Shoes were removed and left at the front door (I vaguely recall beige wall-to-wall carpeting). We—there were three boys—were not allowed to sit on the clear plastic-covered sofa or the chairs in the living room. When watching television, we sat in front of the sofa, on the floor. The bathroom upstairs had a large white card pasted directly behind and above the toilet: "Lift the seat." There were other numbered rules, too, but I forget them. What was important was that I knew the rules, I knew the limits, and I knew they applied to everyone. I was affirmed in my behavior because expectations were spelled out.

Dinners were served with place settings and napkins. We took turns setting the table. Though I can't remember my foster father's name, I remember his gentle, respectful instruction to me the first time I had the chore of laying down the place settings. Today I cannot get the knife and the fork right, but I had it down there once it had been shown to me. Ditto the dishes. They gave us responsibilities we were expected to fulfill, and in so doing, they gave us trust and respect.

A sense of respect, of worth, and defined boundaries were precisely the things I had never before experienced in my life except through subjugation and punishment. Show a child simple respect for his intelligence and self-command, trust that he will deal with them accordingly, and let him see that you both encourage and acknowledge his competence and individual worth—my God, he will not let you down.

Though I got along there, I could not make ties, knowing I'd soon be moving again. These foster parents were as emotionally reserved and noninvasive as I was needful of my barriers, all of which contributed to the relative harmony that I experienced. Still, when I walked the streets of this neighborhood, everything felt barren and nothing familiar. I'd been told once again to get out, get fresh air, and make friends. It was truly torture for me having to go out when I didn't want to go out. I had no idea of how or where, or even why, to make friends, no idea of what to do with myself. Usually I would just circle the block, straddling the curb, one foot in front of the other, trying to make up games in my head and hoping that the time would pass so I could go back in. I was, quite literally, marking time, living the limbo existence that had been imposed on me.

While this foster mother had the very best intentions, this was her life, her home, her neighborhood. She had her past here and her future, as did,

I believe, the other boys. I did not. Perhaps, though, she was signaling an expectation, however unconscious or unintentional, of my extended stay here, but if that was her expectation, I exhibited only a life of stasis. A holding action. Waiting for whatever came next, unable to lay down roots.

While I do not recall what I did when I was in the house, it was the less painful way to spend my time. I did not read during this period of my life, not at all, but I watched a lot of television. Television was a protective and protected environment that I could reach for without risk of having to take part, except, of course, through fantasy. It was a "neighborhood" I could invest in because it would presumably follow me wherever I went. It was a reliable reality, unlike my constantly changing everyday one. Even the inhabitants of this electronic genie hung around much longer than people in real life. To my young mind, this was not only a predictably loyal alternative to family, but also instantly accessible and, unlike the movies (which I loved, but for which I lacked both money and access), it was free. I was a "couch (or floor) potato" long before we knew what such things were, and would shortly become a TV studio groupie, again, before that word had even been coined, perhaps the youngest in history (age twelve).

This was the television of the fifties, the "golden age" of black-and-white, and it was a live medium (most of it originating out of New York). Programs stayed put in one place long enough to create continuity (Uncle Miltie, Tuesday at eight, Channel 4), which enabled this infant medium to establish a dependable identity. Millions of Americans extended their loyalty to it, quite literally scheduling their lives around it (Ed Sullivan, Sunday at eight, Channel 2).

My passion for what I called "instant movies" emerged when both television and I were very young. In the not-too-distant future I would enter a television studio and see there, up on the stage, the familiar settings I'd watched at home in drab shades of gray. My excitement at seeing gray in the flesh was palpable; confirmation, I suppose, that life in the color gray could hold excitement and be real, both.

The cameras, technicians, lights, booms—all were there as I'd imagined. Even the musicians were real. Within this small space, a world came alive. One did not need a lot of space to create the illusion of reality. That, somehow, captivated me, and matched my own life. The peripheral was incidental as long as you focused on the subject. In later life I would abandon or ignore the chaos around me but sustain a focus on the subject. That the semblance of sublime order, meaning, and continuity could flow from such surrounding disorder captivated me and still does. Order. I have always been in need of it. I have always "manufactured" it when it was not there.

Seeing all this live tangibly confirmed the future I'd dreamed of. My endless hours of imaginings at my small metal cabinet became not evidence of some crazy kid's fantasy, but rather a secret agenda far more real and uplifting to the spirit than fresh air could ever have been. Even if I'd had a neighborhood familiar enough to call home, *this* was my neighborhood; *this* was my home. This was one reality I would build.

I do not know where this passion comes from, although I suspect it comes in part from a soulfully rooted search to conjure worlds that are the escape hatches to salvation. Its circumstantial roots lay with my mother—Jolson on bended knee; a radio store in Brooklyn, a television set in the window; dancing marionettes on roller skates. Maybe that's still not enough. Maybe there's divine intervention. I don't know.

∞

IDA FREEDMAN SAID to get ready: Hawthorne had room. I'd almost forgotten. So had everyone else.

I didn't wanna go. Nobody wanted me to go. Nothing had even happened here: no tantrums, no enactments, no reenactments of past enactments. Nothing. Nobody'd even called the Home screaming, "Get 'im outta here!" So it came as somewhat of a bolt to me and my foster parents both that I would suddenly have to pack up and leave, even though this moment had been foreordained. What had *not* been foreordained, not even

by the prognosticators at the Children's Service Bureau, was the remarkable turn of events that had occurred here. I had been conscripted to this
home on a temporary basis only; I recall with certainty that these foster parents would not have taken me in otherwise. Now, after three
months, they were asking that I be permitted to stay. My foster father
even took a day off from work to go down to the Home on Court Street
and implore them to reverse their decision. I knew, though, that his
effort would be in vain, just as I'd known Ida Freedman's earlier assurances could not be trusted. Having been sensitized to control and co-
option of my destiny at so early an age, I understood that they were not
about to cede control to a child's or a foster parent's wishes, regardless
of the evidence at hand.

And I understood them. A decision that I was incapable of functioning in a foster care setting had been made (a notion, heretofore, not
unfounded). The system would not reexamine their prior decision in
light of current circumstances. That would have acknowledged limits
to their crystal-balling. Such an admission would call into question the
omniscience of their original judgment. This authority did not like its
voice questioned. I'd intuited then, and now know, that the ministrants
of foster care can be an arrogant, self-serving, manipulative, and power-
driven lot, whose charge over hapless, powerless souls for whom there
is no practical arbitrating body goes largely unchecked.

Ida Freedman's ready answer was simple enough: knowing that I was
going to Hawthorne, I had been on my "best behavior." My foster parents' experience of me, therefore, was rendered bogus and irrelevant.
While it was true that I'd lived a life of emotional stasis—not knowing, literally, if I was coming or going—I had no idea whatever that I
had been on my best behavior. Nor had I any idea of the penalty one paid
for that.

Part Two

Lockup

Patient's thoughts are preoccupied with her sickness

and her relationship to her dead mother. She is greatly

concerned about the fate of her son and will cry bitterly

whenever he is mentioned.

5

Hawthorne

I REMEMBER THE music. The theme from *Moulin Rouge* was playing on the car radio; I remember the haunting melancholy of the lyrics: "Whenever we kiss, *I worry and wonder.*" It was early morning on the Sawmill River Parkway on the way up to Hawthorne, and the rain was pelting hard against the windshield of Ida Freedman's small foreign car, the wipers squeegeeing back and forth with the cold beat of a metronome. The song, its nuances and foreign tone, eerily captured the moment. I was sitting in the front seat next to her. She smoked with a straight-ahead focus. I don't think we said much. There was something military and detached about her as she drove in that beige cloth raincoat, the cigarette dangling. Was she, perhaps, avoiding the implications of a decision made that she herself felt guilty or uncertain about and just wanted to get this over with? Or was she thinking about something else entirely? I'd always felt her authoritarian coldness somehow fit her Germanic accent, but stolid detachment was something even more chilling. It spoke of irrevocability.

I doubt it had fully hit me yet that I was on a one-way trip, any more than it hit my mother until the actual moment when she was forced toward Kings County's entrance and away from life's freedoms, no matter how hellish. While the word "school" appeared in its name, Cedar Knolls was and is an institution for "emotionally disturbed children," a term that had particular resonance in the fifties. Maybe the darkness and the rain would slow things down a bit and forestall the inevitable. Maybe the place was farther away still, so I might steal some extra time. I stole empty beer bottles. Why not time? I worried and wondered.

In leaving Brooklyn for Hawthorne in Westchester County, I might as well have been leaving one country for another. That they were relatively close to each other geographically never entered my mind; Hawthorne felt a million miles away. I'd never left Brooklyn except to see a live television show in "New York," and since there was no real place that I could call home anyway, once I left a home, it no longer existed. What had been tenuous was now evaporative. It had finally come down to my marking time walking the streets. Someday I'd grow up and this would all be over. And I would. And it would. And I'd still have me.

I was literally deposited with my suitcase in the linoleum-floored waiting area of a small brick building and left alone. It was surrounded by offices that I would soon learn composed the clinic where you went to see your social worker. I remember feeling hopelessly trapped, like a boxed-in animal, abandoned, with no exit. I yelled, screamed, kicked— anguishing in a way that, when I think about it now, mirrors how my mother must have felt when she suddenly found herself led away with no escape. This was another instant reality, one discontinuous with anything that had come before, except, of course, the inherent discontinuity of all that had come before. But this time, no streets to walk; no "outside." I recall her screams.

The difference here, of course, was a child's sudden loss of freedom, which had only twelve years of life behind it. My mother was forty-seven when she lost her freedom, although hers was a loss coupled with relief of release from life's unbearable daily burdens. Hers was to be a foreclosure of a future. Mine was but a preamble to one not yet lived. I screamed and tantrumed in that linoleum-floored vestibule. If I had not been responsible for my mother's illness, then why were they putting me away?

Consciously and rationally, she'd taken off her wedding ring, her last worldly possession, and given it to Gussie. They were not going to get it. Or maybe it was just for safekeeping. Perhaps she gave Gussie something to hold of hers with some thought, some expectation, that she'd get it back someday. On the one hand, perhaps hers was a moment of absolute awareness of what was to come. In one sense, a preparation for surrender. In another, an expectation of a future time. I saw this, too. I do not remember her saying good-bye to me. But it was all so sudden.

She was leaving a life of unbearable burdens. I was part of those burdens. But all I knew was that she was abandoning me.

Someone came to take me to the dining hall just around the bend. It was the expansive hall I'd seen on my earlier visit, alive now with the dinnertime fervor of hungry boys. I had been away to camp before, when I lived with the Kesslers, a sleepaway called Camp Ramapo, and this had some of the same energy to it. Suddenly there was something here that was undeniably inviting and adventuresome. No doubt this was precisely the response Ida Freedman had gambled on the first time. But given the choice between freedom and confinement, as opposed to my acceptance now of a fait accompli, I could find the good. My perceptions, as well as actions, were often dictated by lack of choice, but when choice was present, I would invariably opt for the least painful alternative. There was something here, too, about not being the focal point; I could get lost in this drone. And I could belong. The steam table was straight ahead. Kids lined up along the left wall, grabbed a tray, and waited their turn to be served.

There were seven cottages, and each had its own dining alcove in the long dining hall adjacent to the main building. I was assigned to Cottage 7. There were three junior cottages and three intermediate, each on opposing sides of the long campus lawn. At age twelve, I was a junior. Way, way up at the head of the lawn, sitting front and center on an inclined slope and looking majestically down at the other cottages, was Cottage 23, the senior cottage. That, for me, was the prize to win. Not because of its balance between the cottages on either side, although the metaphor is there, but because living there meant not only that you were more grown up but also somehow more "normal" than the rest. The distinctions among junior, intermediate, and senior, as I remember it, had as much to do with "emotional classification" as with age, although the juniors were the youngest. Tim O'Neal and his wife (whose name I don't remember), a nice Irish couple well liked by the kids, were the cottage parents at Cottage 7. "Mom" and "Pop," we called them.

Hawthorne, like any institution, had rules. And rules, especially when they are fair, understandable, and noninvasive, promote order and define boundaries, which provide comfort and security for a child; they are like guardrails. As in my foster home before this, if I followed the rules, I had less pretext for, or expectation of, rejection. If it was so easy for me to be on my best behavior, and that was really all there was to it, then why hadn't I thought of that in the homes I'd been in prior to the last? But, of course, it was not about good behavior, or bad behavior, but about my guilt.

Except for the boundaries I'd conjured through the lens of a Brownie camera or a piece of clay, and except for my home prior to Hawthorne, this external structure was something I'd hardly ever known. My adherence to the rules, which I adapted to, lessened the uncertainty of my daily existence and also provided a society in which I could actively and purposefully participate. In time, I even let go of my penchant for hypochondria. I was just too busy now to think about it and, besides, if anything happened to me here, it would be on their watch, not mine, the operative words being "their watch." I was off-duty. And while I maintain it was an overly controlling environment, administered by an obdurate authority intoxicated with its own power, I could let go. I was absolved.

Hawthorne was a closed loop and entirely self-sustaining: cottages, dining hall, school, trade shops, social workers, and even a synagogue. The classroom, with its fixed number of hours in a day, was organic to this highly structured residential treatment center. There was no clear delineation where one part ended and the other began in terms of how they dealt with you, what they expected of you, how they thought of you, and what you experienced. The daily life I lived here was total immersion in a protective, seamless continuum, an enclosed faux environment. This child never went home after school.

As I entered my cottage, the community living room was just to the right and the cottage parents' residence was to the left, with Mom and Pop's small kitchen in the middle. Their kitchen door was often open in the morning when you could see them, usually just having coffee, but I don't remember ever going in. We had our meals over at the dining hall after morning assembly, and Pop accompanied us and had breakfast with us, too. Two paneled glass doors led into the living room, where we had a TV set and even a piano. The bedrooms were upstairs, four beds to a room with a small wooden dresser and lamp next to each, with a drawer on top and a small door below for clothes and stuff. There were probably twenty to twenty-four boys in each cottage. The bathroom and community showers were downstairs, below the main floor as you entered the cottage, as were the toilet stalls. The recreation room with our cubicles for shoes and coats was opposite the bathroom facilities. We had a Ping-Pong table down there. There was even a small door that led into the space just beneath the stairs, bigger than a crawl space but you couldn't stand up, and where I set up what I thought of as my darkroom.

I was given an allowance, which I recall was then at twenty-five cents a week, just enough for Canteen on Friday nights (i.e., five candy bars, or four and a soda, or any combination thereof—a nickel a shot). There was a farm (with cows), an outdoor swimming pool, a gymnasium with a projection booth on its ceiling for movies (more later), an infirmary, all kinds of walking trails with huckleberry vines, and even chickens. At Cottage 7 I helped build a chicken coop, and I had my own pet chicken—name of Buck-Buck—and a garden with so many tomatoes that we'd have rotten-tomato fights. I remember when we built the chicken coop. We poured the cement foundation and buried our "cottage list," a sheet of paper with all our names on it, as a sort of time capsule, and I reminded myself to remember to come back when I grew up to see if it was still there, but there are things I remember that I'd just as soon forget.

We played baseball and football on the rolling fields behind the cottages, and in winter we'd ride our sleds right down those hills and into the adjoining woods, where you could get off your sled and run away if you went in far enough. As a matter of fact, you could run away any time you wanted. There were gateposts at the entrance, but no gates. And if that didn't convince you freedom was everywhere, there were no bars anywhere. What was I complaining about?! Who would trade this for real life, anyway? Why was I always asking when they were going to let me out?

Some kids ran, though. Usually the officer of the day would go after them, or maybe he'd call the cops. A kid hopped the train once and got as far as New York City. When I heard that someone had gone AWOL (I learned a new term), I'd root for him, but it was really anticlimactic because I already knew the finish. They always got their kid. I had no desire to run. I was afraid that when they caught me, they'd keep me here longer, or worse, they'd send me to Warwick, a reformatory they whispered about all the time.

And besides, where would I run?

That doesn't mean I wanted to stay. I made up my mind to get out the day I got in. I'd known freedom, and despite the artifice of a gateless, no-bars-anywhere setting, this was incarceration, including emotional incarceration. My having been sent to Hawthorne confirmed the worst about me. Clearly, I was not fit for the world. For me, Hawthorne was punishment, which, in fact, was how it was intended for those who'd been remanded here by the courts. There was hardly a session with a social worker when I didn't start with "When am I getting out of here?" Part of the question was really "What has to happen before you let me go? What am I expected to do or become?"

I needed some kind of goal line. I needed to understand what they were after. I wanted to be normal just like every other kid living outside. If I knew what they wanted, I'd deliver, and that would be the end of it. And there was something else I needed: I needed to take back some control. I could trust myself. It was the external that could not be trusted. I was understandably not trusting of authority generally, and even less so of this opaque authority that played it close to the vest, revealing nothing of itself except a palpable authoritarian and controlling need. From my earliest childhood all I'd known was the usurpation of my will by strangers, people I didn't belong to any more than they belonged to me but whose property I'd become anyway. Hawthorne was the very pinnacle, the condensed version, of this experience. Somehow I had to reclaim myself, take back ownership, wrest control.

"Look, Ma—no bars!" Hawthorne was not what it appeared to be. They got information, they didn't give information. This was the very bedrock of their treatment, with which they could validate almost any prejudgment of you, frustrate and piss you off in the process, and then in having pissed you off, use that as confirmation of their original judgment. Catch-22. On a hot day you might remark "It's hot." "How do you feel about that?" "Hot." "Do you want to talk about it?" "No!" "Why're you so angry?" "I'm not angry, I'm hot." "You sound angry." "You're making me angry." "I see. We can talk about that if you'd like." The social workers and staff at Hawthorne methodically insinuated that anything you did was aberrant whenever it did not conform to a pervasive, parochial worldview, insulated from real-world exigencies, just as Hawthorne itself was. They were particularly insinuating when you called their arbitrary judgments into question.

The layers of control here, built upon an endemic allusion to openness, were themselves as fragile as the "treatment" premise itself, and virtually immune from open challenge because, as a child, you have no power, and while you can feel it, you cannot pull back the curtain to show this for what it is: control and manipulation. If it is a myth built upon a fabrication and you are forced to play on this faux field long enough, you will fear reality when the time comes for you to face it again. Confinement, at an early age, leaves an imprint. Notwithstanding acknowledged benefits that may be gotten, there are dangerous trade-offs. An inevitable consequence of this "treatment" environment was that I'd not only left the outside world behind me, I'd left a certain amount of me there, too. Whatever had put me here to begin with, I knew, would have to be kept out. In other words, I would *now*, to use Ida Freedman's words, be on my "best behavior." If I'd be "good," and do whatever was expected of me, they'd let me out. Not that I knew when.

Depending on the child, his inner strengths and resources, he may gradually reemerge, as I did. But it can take years. And when the time came that I could once again be who I was to begin with, I was a young adult and no longer a ward of the state. I made the adjustment, though. And in spite of myself, even, the place grew on me. There was plenty of immersion here. There were lots of kids. And yet, in spite of everything, in spite of it all, I wanted to go home. Wherever that was.

I have always felt that the people who made these rules were themselves victims of limited vistas, whose overlordship was to some extent created by their own fear of the world, and that many, though by no means all, found refuge in this protected, monasterylike setting for precisely this reason. The Wizard of Oz was alive and well at Hawthorne. In this tyranny of treatment, the only ones who shot from the hip were the kids.

My social worker, Mr. MacWharter, had a calendar on his wall. I pointed to it: "There. Give me a date. Pick the date. Go ahead. *You* pick it. I *want* you to pick it." (Let *him* be in charge.) If I had to, *I'd* pick the date for him: "What's a good day for you? How 'bout this one?" I wasn't letting go. I challenged him to make a commitment and give me an answer. He'd get nothing from me until I had a date from him. I wouldn't get off it; I insisted on a date. He finally did it. He actually gave me a date. Even as a kid I was always being told I should become a lawyer. My argumentativeness and prowess at persuasion had manifested themselves early. I don't remember if I believed him—probably not, but maybe. There's always hope. I certainly wanted to believe him. I knew he was of sufficient authority to influence them—whoever "them" was—to let me go. But he'd been a little casual, a little arbitrary in the date he agreed to. Still, my being here was arbitrary.

I went back and forth, circumspectly stunned. I'd actually forced a direct answer (even if he didn't mean it) in a place where no one was direct (except the kids), and where nothing was what it appeared to be, and where your questions were usually deflected by their questions, which were calculated to imply that yours were somehow symptomatic of some emotional disorder.

MacWharter had agreed to that date, so I had something now to hold him to, just in case he'd lied to me. When the date came and went, I confronted him with a broken promise, and it was over. I'd been seeing him twice a week then, and for the next several weeks, at my appointed time, he'd come looking for me over at the wood shop, where I might be turning a lamp on the wood lathe. I'd sort of sneak sidelong glances out the window, and when I'd see him coming, I'd feign preoccupation until I felt a gentle tap on my shoulder.

Clearly, I was anticipating his pursuit. I recall actually liking him, even though he'd lied. But I'd been the provocateur in the lie and complicit to the extent that my persuasion had boxed him into a corner, and I suspect I knew it. The pattern, while subtle and perhaps not immediately recognizable, was as familiar as an old shoe, only this time I had inveigled my social worker as coconspirator, and this time it was being played out with quiet persistence in a controlled environment.

This "rejection" cycle extended over weeks and was more complex than my earlier foster home experiences, not just because it was free of "acting out" but also because his biweekly entreaties ceded me a certain legitimacy, as well as something else—control of the field. While part of me was still willing to go back to our regular appointments, the better part of me could not give it up. If he'd just keep coaxing, I felt, I'd relent. I sat there with him on the front steps outside the building as he tried to convince me. The simple fact that I had walked out with him was telling. From his vantage point, the situation would not have seemed intractable. But I suspect I would have raised the bar indefinitely. There was a "prove it to me" component in all of this, and that was the familiar part. Prove to me you like me; prove to me I'm worthy, because down deep, I don't believe it. And ironically, my very presence here confirmed it. I'll keep rejecting you to see how much it takes for you to finally give up (i.e., reject *me*). And after quite a few weeks of noble tries, he stopped. While I may have felt a tinge of remorse, I did not feel the angst of rejection. And I never went back.

I did not truly feel his giving up as rejection, although I felt the loss of power. I had set up a pretext by which I could reject him if he had lied to me. And when he did and I walked out I'd see if he'd come after me. If he didn't, there'd be no downside, no rejection, because the second stage of this pattern, removal from a home, could not be played out. I was punishment proof. And I was pretty sure they didn't send you to Warwick just for rejecting your social worker.

But he'd lied to me. And if he could lie to me once, he could lie to me again, so what was the point of talking? I still didn't have a release date, though, and that was really what I wanted. Soon afterward, another social worker was assigned to me. Everyone had a social worker. Whoever the others were in the three years I was here were cumulatively forgettable. All except one, yet to come.

MacWharter was Sherman's social worker, too. Sherman was my best friend. We'd coined a rhyme together: "MacPenny, MacNickle, MacDime, MacQuarter." (His name was Royce, but we never called him that.) It said we liked the guy. I must have told Sherman that I was finished with MacWharter and that he'd lied to me, and Sherman must have shown me his compassionate hangdog look that always came out when something we'd shared went bad, conveying disappointment with a note of understanding and confirmation that I'd probably gotten it right, notwithstanding any reservations or regret he may have felt to the contrary, which I could usually sense through his pensively extended lower lip. If I could get him worked up over some injustice, that lower lip might extend still further, accompanied by spittle that would require frequent wiping with the back of his hand. That meant I'd gotten him fighting mad on my side. Or maybe just damn enthusiastic about whatever scheme I'd dreamed up, and I was always dreaming up something. I knew that Sherman valued our friendship and would have done nothing to threaten it, even if it meant agreeing with me when he really didn't—which is always a good thing in a friend, especially when you're twelve.

He was a gentle, tall, gangly fellow, flat-footed, and always in Keds ankle-high black sneakers with the white rims. His passion was model railroading. Maps on graph paper of pencil-lined track layouts including complex switch-track formations were his stock in trade. He was at it constantly, one could say compulsively, sitting at the edge of the Ping-Pong table downstairs, his genuine engineer's cap on, penciling on his graph paper. You could usually tell he was worked up about something when the spittle seeped out the side of his extended lower lip, which the back of his hand quickly took care of. I could tell from a distance when Sherman was on to something big. His absorption was total, his discipline ironclad. Sherman's intricate track formations on graph paper were as real for him as the building of clay cameras and settings had been for me. For both of us, reality could be a construction in the mind. Passion was in short supply around here; I'd found a kindred spirit.

I teased him mercilessly, though. A gentle giant, he'd put up with it until I'd pull the graph paper from right under his nose and he'd yelp and howl, "Hey, goddamn it, Joe" (realizing it's me), "gimme that! Jesus fucking Christ." No real anger, mind you. A wipe of the mouth as he stood up. "I'll make you another one. Don't take that one, goddamn it." For Sherman, the one that he was working on was always the most important one. He just loved to spew those cuss words, in a tone that was more imploring than threatening, and I gave him plenty of pretext. Boy, the spittle would really fly as he flat-footedly chased me around the table, the heel of his palm wiping his mouth. After about twice around, Sherman would show that telltale grin, layered by protest that cued his pride in and appreciation of the value I imputed to his work, the attention I'd paid, and the affirmation I'd given just by absconding with it.

I would always relent, of course, knowing how much this meant to him, and I was well aware that he trusted in that. His earnest exuberance was something I understood all too well. This was his "work," after all, and his dream of becoming a train engineer was not something I doubted, assuming there was nothing really wrong with him in the first place. And aside from his flat feet and penchant for cussing, I never could figure out what was. It was in large measure a shared understanding of our passions that was the fundamental basis of our friendship.

I suspect, though, that model trains held a special meaning for me, even beyond the fact that every kid in the fifties loved trains, especially at Christmastime, when those metal cars came out of their individual red Lionel boxes and when the plywood layouts went up. I think that in sharing this world with Sherman, I was also recapturing my life of just five years past, which, when you're twelve, is a very long time ago.

I must have seen a picture of a Lionel train set in a magazine during the Christmas season, and had decided right then and there I wanted this more than anything in the world. My mother bought me colored construction paper so I could make my own trains. I tried, but no matter how

I bent the paper or glued it, it did not look like the picture I'd seen. And it didn't run on a track and make smoke. She knew how much I wanted those trains and she took me to Macy's or Gimbel's and bought me a complete train set that came in a large brown carton with individual cars packed in their own red cardboard boxes, along with the track and transformer. The trains she could not afford she had bought for me anyway.

There was a wonderful song I heard playing in the record department—"Johnnie Fedora and Alice Blue Bonnet," sung by the Andrews Sisters. My mother had taken me to see the Walt Disney animated movie Make Mine Music, *which features the song, among others, but I only remember this one. It is about two hats that love each other. One day, a customer buys Alice, the girl hat. Johnny is left alone in the window of the department store, but he has hope that Alice will always be looking for him, and he is told to not give up hoping and not give up dreaming. It is a song that will haunt me for years to come. In the sixties I will look for and find an old 78 rpm record of the song. It haunts me still.*

They might never tell me anything here, and I never knew when they'd let me go, but they couldn't stop me from going home in my head.

Sherman may have been a bit eccentric, but because of his passion he seemed perfectly normal to me, especially relative to some other kids around the place. For example, take Edelman. He was always banging his forehead against the wall at all hours of the night, causing a persistent boil. His banging somehow escaped notice of the night watchman, who, while making his nightly rounds cranking his clock, had a knack for shining his flashlight in my face. If Edelman hadn't have woken me up I wouldn't have known this, and if I'd opened my eyes the night watchman would have suspected me of God knows what.

Then there was Stadtmore, whose face showed perpetual bemusement about something known only to him, and who was constantly singing some dumb song about his Li'l Inky Pup.

And then there was Bovar, the quintessential juvenile delinquent.

Rumor had it he'd actually knifed somebody on the outside (nobody ever shot anyone then, we hadn't advanced that far), so nobody could figure out what he was doing in our cottage, and everybody was scared shit-less that he might strike again, but I got along with him. I remember thinking they put him in the wrong cottage—he belonged with the older boys in Cottage 9 or 13, across the way.

Greenfield jerked off a lot, but so what.

Finkelstein was gay before gay was fashionable, and when the word itself connoted happiness. He'd taken a liking to me, and I remember once locking myself in a toilet stall in the morning to get rid of him, although you never knew when this guy was going to strike. It never went beyond the nuisance stage, though. There was always a sort of safety with the other kids being around, and besides, we had to hurry to get dressed in the morning for our walk to assembly and the main building for breakfast.

Meister was as happily excitable as his flaming red hair, and he said everything—*everything*—with emphatic punctuation and repetition, usually with his head bent downward in concentration and his finger jabbing toward the ground, jackhammerlike, which in turn propelled his body forward like a human chicken. Rube Goldberg hadn't even dreamed of this one.

I got along with all of them. Since the cottages were segregated age-wise, and I suspect in other ways, and given the control mechanisms in place here, I recall that my exposure was pretty much limited to boys of my own age group, and even if there were worse behavior problems in other cottages, these kids, with maybe one or two exceptions, didn't seem to need to be separated from the rest of the world. They came from all over the country. Sherman, for example, was from Baltimore (how Sherman wound up in Hawthorne I'll never know), and quite a few came from Brooklyn. I haven't a clue where the girls came from because I never saw them. Their cottages were way on the other side of the campus, and that's where they ate as well. In my three years at Hawthorne, I never ran into a girl. Think about that. (Today, girls and boys at Hawthorne take classes together but are otherwise still segregated.)

A *New York Daily News* headline, which I recall having seen at the time, referred to Cedar Knolls as "a school for wayward boys." I don't know if anyone had to define the word "wayward" for me (nor do I recall any mention of those mysterious girls on the other side of the grounds), but I could not connect myself to that headline. A puzzlement. What was I doing here? I'm not sure this disturbed me so much as it heightened my sense of importance. After all, they were writing about us. I was part of something big. The adage "any publicity is good publicity" is one I would have undoubtedly subscribed to. If my name had been there, I would've made sure they'd spelled it right. I liked the attention, as I believe most kids do.

Today, some people walk the streets of New York talking to themselves all the time, some even *without* cell phones (I know I do. *Now*, not then.) There was a lot of eccentricity back then, too. Even if all Stadtmore could do was smile and sing, he wasn't a whole lot different from the kids I'd known on the outside. If these kids were as bad as it got, then I think, in retrospect, our threshold for emotional disturbance has been heightened through the decades. Or perhaps I fit here just right, and then everything, of course, was filtered through my sense of what normal was.

Nah.

But I still think the social workers had the bigger problems. And they were beyond redemption.

Just to be absolutely clear, though, except for one incident, my years at Hawthorne were free of physical abuse. After the O'Neals retired, a new couple, the Bedfords, took over. They were a British couple who had a grown son, probably then in his midtwenties, who played soccer. He sometimes took charge of us when his parents weren't available, and one day, while I was alone up in my room, he ordered me to do something and I refused. At that moment he grabbed hold of my head, as if I were the soccer ball, and began banging it against the floor. While this was an isolated episode, what was pervasive was the feeling of having no recourse. Had I complained, I feared, I would in some way be punished still further. And if I ever expected to get out of here, it would go against my record. I never spoke of it to anyone. The distinction between physical abuse and emotional suppression was moot, as was the distinction between incarceration with no bars vs. with bars. Hawthorne had its genesis as a reformatory. In the fifties, vestiges of that mind-set lingered.

∾

SUNDAY WAS VISITORS' day at Hawthorne, and Sherman's parents came up often from Baltimore. He was the spitting image of his father, who actually built model trains himself. Trolley cars, too. I remember falling in love with a red trolley he had made for Sherman, which except for its color looked just like the trolleys that ran on Coney Island Avenue in Brooklyn. I loved everything about them. I liked the colorful trolley-car transfers that came in narrow coupon books with a perforated coupon at the very bottom that read A.M. and P.M. Trolley motormen used to give me their unused transfer books, which I collected. I also liked the coin changers on their waists, and the way they gave the change without looking down, and the clicking sounds as the coins dropped into their hand.

The detail work on Sherman's trolley was exquisite, and I especially relished the realism of the poles at the top of either end of the car, which were tied down by a pulley-and-spring mechanism. The motorman would tug up and down on the pole until he got the groove of the small wheel at the tip of the pole in contact with the overhead power cable. It was sort of a hit-or-miss thing, but when he finally made contact—bingo! This was clean-air technology before we ever used the word "technology." For me, watching the motorman yank up and down on that pole was a sort of spectator sport, not unlike the game at Coney Island where you had to get the dangling ring at the end of the fishing pole over the neck of the bottle. Tricky stuff.

Prospect Park, Brooklyn

I'm sitting with my mother on a bench—I can't be more than six—when the trolley makes its slow turn and jumps over the stone I'd placed on the track when my mother wasn't looking, causing the trolley to tilt slightly, and the pole to jump the wire. Suddenly the trolley stops and the motorman exits the car to examine what has happened. I watch in awe from the distant bench. In my utter powerlessness, I have exercised an awesome power—stopping a trolley car. That I have the power to effect an outcome through my action— destructive on the surface, but to me simply mischievous in the extreme—is a lesson I would not forget.

Sherman asked his father to make a trolley for me, too, and since I would be paying for it, cash on the barrel, I asked if I could have mine in green—just like the ones in Brooklyn. The trolley kit cost ten dollars. I'm not altogether sure where I got the money to pay for it, but it was probably from Aunt Miriam.

6

Instant Family

ONE DAY, OUT of the blue, my social worker told me that an Aunt Miriam, *my* Aunt Miriam, whom I never knew existed, had somehow magically found me, or had herself been found, and that she had offered to both spend time with me and even contribute to my allowance. I remember that her monthly contribution would be six dollars, and I even recall a check in that amount. Don't laugh—a lot of money in the fifties, especially for a kid with zero expenses.

One of the goodies that came with this stipend was spending time with Aunt Miriam at her home in Nyack, New York. Everyone thought that would be a wonderful idea, including me. I remember it was during the summer months because she bought me a pair of open-work leather sandals. Aunt Miriam was about sixty, but unlike the foster parents I'd known, she was a savvy, educated woman, clearly independent and apparently of some means. She lived with a boxer—not a prizefighter, a dog. As I recall, her husband, who had passed away, had taught mathematics at a Brooklyn high school, and I remember that just the word "mathematician" left me with an indelible impression of probable genius, and she talked about him that way, too.

What made Aunt Miriam's dog very special, though, was that it was a trained Seeing Eye companion. Aunt Miriam was blind. This may sound like a scene out of a Neil Simon comedy, but I accepted the situation as unquestioningly as everyone else. Having never known a single relative in my entire life, aside from my grandmother—and even her I recall meeting only once—Aunt Miriam's sudden appearance was, quite literally, a bolt out of the blue. It never occurred to me to wonder where she'd come from or even why. But the feeling I had when she did appear was that this was a strange sort of gift. It gave me a feeling of belonging somehow, something I'd never imagined possible. I never did figure out who she was to me, though, and whatever explanation Aunt Miriam may have given me, if she gave me any at all, was somehow overridden by the fact that I sensed she was withholding information that I actively sought. Withholding it for my own good, just like my mother did when she spoke Yiddish. One late afternoon while sitting alone with her in a dark-ish room at her home in Nyack (being blind, she tended not to turn on the lights), and having just read her some of the stock quotes from the paper, I asked her what happened to my father. She fell silent, gazing outward with a sudden detachment from the fact of my sitting there. My sense was that Aunt Miriam knew stuff she just wasn't giving up. It was the fear now that I felt of my not really wanting to know what happened to him, because I knew she knew that I shouldn't. Whatever had befallen my father would probably happen to me. I must say I didn't have a whole lot of fun when I was with her, though I was amply equipped to deal with feelings of isolation.*

* I found out later that she was Miriam Morgenstern, born Miriam Finkelman in Russia in 1894. Her father was David Finkelman. My mother's mother, Minnie Finkelman, was born in Russia, and her father was Joseph Finkelman, also born in Russia. I am probably named after Joseph, my mother's grandfather. Miriam and my mother were about six years apart. I don't know this for fact but I assume David, Miriam's father, and Minnie, my mother's mother, were Joseph Finkelman's children. So Miriam was related through her father to my mother's mother and therefore my mother's first cousin. Miriam Morgenstern died in Duluth, Minnesota, in 1972. She was seventy-eight.

In retrospect, spending time with a blind aunt is not really a child's idea of having a good time, anyway, especially when you're reading stock quotes from the newspaper. Aunt Miriam left my life as mysteriously as she'd entered it, and the monthly "allowances" stopped, too. But I think that's how I got the ten bucks for the trolley, and even some more for a camera, an Argus 75 twin-lens reflex. And I think I read enough quotes to have earned them.

For months after, whenever I asked Sherman where the hell my trolley was, he worried that I might not be his friend anymore (I never said it, but I knew he thought it), and he would write his father imploring him to send Joe his trolley. And finally, one day, just in the nick of time for Christmas, my trolley came in a tissue-packed shoebox. Truly a work of art. Green, as ordered. Poles and all.

But I would have been Sherman's friend no matter. He probably reminded me of me when I was at the Kessler home making my clay cameras. For reasons I don't know, I'd stopped making them. But puppetry continued, as did my love for the camera in all its forms, especially my passion for live television, which would manifest through my arrangement for group "field trips" to New York.

Once I wrote away to *Caesar's Hour* (starring Sid Caesar, Carl Reiner, Howard Morris, and Nanette Fabray; telecast from the Century Theater on Seventh Avenue in Manhattan) for twenty or thirty tickets—and got them. Hawthorne had a regular yellow school bus with the words "Hawthorne Cedar Knolls School" printed on its side (like many schools), and I somehow convinced them to take the whole cottage one evening to see the show.

When Sid Caesar stepped out of the wing off to the corner at stage left, just seconds before air, the theater audience went wild with applause, and I leaned so far forward I might've fallen off the balcony. I would have liked to have gotten closer still, maybe next to the camera, but I was close enough. It was live television, and I was alive.

∞

MY NOT HAVING visitors on Sunday was no big deal. Not every kid had them anyway, and usually the kids who did ended up divvying their care packages of cookies and other munchies with the kids who hadn't gotten any, and Pop O'Neal made sure of that.

I met other kids' parents fairly often, but I don't recall ever wondering why they had parents and I didn't. This hand was probably so familiar to me that I just took it as normal, although I had an instinctive shyness, and felt a certain awkwardness, about being too visible when other kids' parents were around. Besides being an only child, and a fatherless one at that, I had never really known what "family" was. So I'm not sure I could truly have felt a loss of something. Except, of course, of my mother.

Occasionally some of us took field trips with volunteer Big Brothers, who were quite generous in giving their time. One, I recall, was an attorney with NBC, Howard Monderer. These were very decent, professional men who were simply interested in showing some of us kids a good time, when we might otherwise not have gotten off the grounds. It was actually on certain Sundays, while other kids had visitors, that those of us who didn't were treated to these excursions. One Sunday, we took a trip to Coney Island's Steeplechase, which, historically, was one of Coney's great amusement parks, with hot dogs and corn on the cob at Nathan's and cotton candy on the boardwalk.

In time I was offered a "permanent" Big Brother, Fred, and was introduced to him and his lovely wife, Ethel. This was an effort, I believe, to assimilate me into some kind of family structure, and I was even allowed to take the train into the city on Sundays to meet them. Not long after, I met the rest of their family, and began a relationship that would last beyond my tenure at Hawthorne until eventually it, too, ran its course. I could never really assimilate into a family that was foundationally not mine. Closeness was not something that came easily. Even before the loss of my mother, aside from the occasional passing cockroach, I had not a single friend for the first seven years of my life with my mother. No friends at all. And later, as I moved from home to home, relationships simply stopped, friends vanished, and so except through my fantasy with television, I never really had any permanent or long-term anything up through Hawthorne.

What I knew about family life I knew essentially through observation in my foster homes, never as an organic member but rather as a lodger of sorts. Even in my home in Flatbush, where I'd clearly bonded with my foster mother, there was really no family life. I was always the perennial outsider, a sort of hand-me-down (like much of the clothing I would wear at Hawthorne), the foster child with the different last name, marching in the shadow of the shingle of the former Brooklyn Hebrew Orphan Asylum, a transient, a citizen of sorts but with no real claim or rights, and yet fortunate enough to have ended up here. I had enough to deal with just reconciling this, distancing myself from the pain of loss and at times distancing myself from others when I couldn't reconcile the discrepancies.

It is no wonder, then, that I wouldn't risk it with Fred and Ethel. Always the outsider no matter how genuine the effort at inclusion. Or perhaps it was just another handout. Either way, while I made the effort, in time I grew away. I would bypass all entreaties at inclusion, and this must have hurt some of the people who tried with me, though certainly I did not intend that. Nor did this rejection come from my fear of rejection. Being alone was somehow in my nature. It was, after all, the die I'd been cast from. It would be a trait I would carry with me throughout life, and I suspect the roots of it lay in self-protection.

One day, a social worker seemingly casually wondered aloud whether I would ever be able to experience a loving relationship. At age twelve or so, I cannot be sure how I took this concern, if in fact I gave it much thought at all. In hindsight, what was being posited, I believe, was whether I had the capacity to love *and* accept love, given the burden of guilt I had unduly assigned myself, and not whether I was worthy of being loved. I recall the proposition as having been declarative rather than inquiring, but that's a thin line.

It strikes me as an odd subject to put to a child; risky, to say the least. If I took this as an expression of doubt as to my capacity to express or experience love, I would not, I *could* not, have lingered with it. I knew how much I loved my mother, and how much I had loved Auntie and Chubby, and what I'd felt for Norma when I felt she liked me. I knew what a wonderful feeling that was, and so if that's what the social worker was talking about, I already knew these things.

But if the social worker was telling me something that I may secretly have already known, that I was not *worth* loving, then maybe this was someone I should listen to because I was hearing confirmation now of what I had suspected all along. I could not assign its root cause. If you're not worth loving, then whose fault is that? And while they didn't speak Yiddish here, if this is what I was hearing, then the news was not good. I knew how much I loved my mother, but I wonder if I knew for sure that she still loved me. I asked my social worker when I could see her, and I may have asked her where she was, but I was given an evasive answer. They were probably protecting me by not telling the truth, just as my mother never told me what happened to my father. I could only imagine.

While I can understand where their doubts and assumptions about me must have come from, my sense was that the social workers sometimes used me for practice. Many of their prognoses and observations had more to do with their acquired dogma than with any real need to understand my problems.

This need would reach absurd and unnatural heights. By age twelve or so, most boys begin to show an interest in girls, whom the wisdom of this authority kept sequestered on the opposite end of the grounds. I do not recall thinking about them, because they weren't there. Girls had never been a consistent part of my daily life anyway. In a sense what you didn't have you didn't miss, not consciously, and I cannot help but conclude that sexual awareness was calculatedly sublimated. Honest boy/girl relationships in this setting would also have proven anathema to its carefully monitored therapeutic environment. They would have created real and spontaneous issues, which would have required real and spontaneous responses and, perhaps, counseling. The unpredictability of open heterosexual relationships would have threatened their control.

What would prove even more threatening, long-term, was the consequence of this enforced isolation of the sexes. Just when my interest in the opposite sex should have been emerging, the exclusion of girls only compounded my own inclination toward isolation and my uncertainty about my worth. While Hawthorne made every effort to *appear* open and free, its highly structured, rigidly controlled environment was in important ways antithetical to the natural development of certain emotional growth patterns. With its hodgepodge community of children, some remanded here by the courts, and others, such as myself, by social agencies, its fundamental mission as a treatment center was incoherent. It could not make up its mind what it was or who it was meant to help. And to this day, I can't either.

In addition to not offering me things I needed, I was offered things I didn't need—for instance, that I was not destined to suffer my mother's kind of illness. It had never occurred to me that I would. Then a social worker expressed doubt as to my ability to finish high school. At age twelve, I doubt I'd thought much about it. Another said that I had an ability to lead others. I knew that kids had always followed me, but taking charge was a way to avoid being taken charge of. More than that, my enthusiasms were contagious. I was also told that I would make an excellent file clerk—I was good at organizing file cards in typing class. My adeptness at organizing file cards, while perceived in limited terms, no doubt, had larger meaning. I'd been making order of stuff from the very beginning. Devising order and context, if only illusionary, kept me swimming, regardless of the tide, in a world that had shown me nothing but chaos.

"Have you ever thought of becoming a writer?" Mrs. Williams asked. I don't know why she asked that but she was looking over my shoulder in class one day at something I'd written. She told me her husband was a writer and clearly she was being encouraging, although this wasn't what I wanted to hear. I thought she was telling me what I *couldn't* do. I suppose it beat being a file clerk, but I had much bigger things in mind. Being a writer was never a thought in my head. Even thinking about it felt claustrophobic. Writers didn't get seen. They got holed up in a hot room all by themselves, probably in a suit, and nobody ever knew they were there. It was very important that somebody knew I was there.

If Mrs. Williams didn't think I should be seen, I had already taken care of that because I did things where you didn't have to be seen to still be recognized. I wanted to make stuff happen and I wanted to entertain and everybody had to show up, including me. I wanted an audience. Even though I came up with the idea for our newspaper, the *Jr. Round-Up* (and even drew a cowboy with a lasso as its masthead), I didn't see writing as making stuff happen—it wasn't performance, and there was no audience in front of you. I don't recall what I wrote about, but it wouldn't have mattered as long as I was editor in chief.

I liked the idea of being able to think things up and then put them down and print them up, though. Making reality was something I was used to. Still, I do not recall having read a single book up to that time, except the *Babar* book that I "recited" from memory to my mother.

I always liked the look of books, though, especially the bindings and book jackets, and the edges of the pages that often had muted colors when the book was closed, but lost their color identity as individual pages. I liked those colorful trolley car coupon books. But reading wasn't doing. Dreaming up my own stuff was. Writing was perhaps a useful tool for selling, persuading, and making up stories, an indispensable adjunct to putting on shows. I wrote the puppet shows I did at Hawthorne, in part, because there were other players, too. So the fact that I could write and still not have developed a reading habit may not be so mysterious.

I remember an evening on the porch with my mother in Seagate, Brooklyn, when I had a fountain pen in my hand and scribbled something out that looked impressively like cursive script. It just poured out; I don't know from where, and I vaguely recall that it even caught my mother's attention, which was probably what I was after. There was no admonishment, but she saw it was nothing at all. I couldn't even write my name, let alone anything else, but I remember liking the impressive look of that meaningless scribble. I even thought I might have said something. That would be wonderful if you could say stuff so easily. It would have been nice if it had been something. It looked like it could have been. Even she thought that.

The balloon wouldn't bust. I'd written this show where the marionette jumped into the basket of a hot-air balloon, and the balloon was supposed to rise and then it would bust and the audience would gasp, and it would fall back to the ground. And the marionette? Well—is he okay or is he not okay? I forget the rest of the plot, but that was the shocker. Deus ex machina. God at work. As the balloon began to rise, I lowered a sewing needle on the end of a piece of thread, which was supposed to bust the balloon but instead it just sort of slid around like a feather. So I lifted it again and dropped the needle like it was deadweight. Slip-sliding around. Nothing. And meanwhile I'm raising this balloon with the marionette attached, and it just won't bust, and I've only got two hands, for crissake, and I can't keep lowering and raising this balloon or it's going to look phony and it won't bust and I had a fit.

That was it. End of the world. I dropped the controls. Show over. I didn't even lower the curtain. I quit. Pandemonium. Everybody's running around crazy. Mrs. Williams wasn't too happy with me, either, because I was always sort of the leader, and if I went nuts all the rest of them went nuts with me. I recall reaching for the fire extinguisher in the hallway but Mrs. Williams got there first. If I was looking to put something out, I had the right idea, wrong solution. But after a while we all got our heads back and everything got back to normal again, such as normal was. Nobody had taught me anything, though, but maybe I learned a few things anyway. Three things, actually: the laws of gravity; rehearse; control your frustration. The fire extinguisher probably wouldn't have worked anyway.

I have not even a vague recollection of an academic agenda, except that whatever agenda there must have been was flexible, seamless, not force-fed, and complemented by activities such as woodworking, printing and even typing, in the trade school building across the way. Whatever subjects we had academically, be it reading, arithmetic, or anything else, seemed to flow one into the other. Somewhere along the way I learned stuff, almost in a lazy Susan self-selection style, but I can't for the life of me recall rigid boundaries for subjects, in part, perhaps, because we had one teacher for everything and a general classroom atmosphere without the rigidity of the public schools I'd known, an atmosphere conducive, no doubt, to learning stuff. If I wanted to put on puppet shows, for example, I'd better know how to read and write because without a play there was no show and so the connection between need and motivation was established.

Much of what happened in the classroom at Hawthorne was within a framework—a consciously conceived and structured framework—that allowed for this kind of creative expression and initiative, within fair and acceptable bounds. The approach toward teaching was radically different from anything I'd ever known before and was certainly a lot less authoritarian, with a tolerance for noncompliance, though clearly not for madcap mayhem. Meaningless curricula that did not reflect or address my real interests, offered up in a rigid environment, was all that school had ever meant to me. This was a treatment facility, after all, and the rules that applied on the outside would certainly not have worked here in any event. And you really didn't have to learn anything anyway, if you didn't want to. Somebody had apparently grasped the notion that learning did not come through force-feeding.

I came to this place, however, with certain assets—my passions. And when my passions were given room for expression, I was motivated. Whatever method of teaching this was, my noncompliant predisposition toward school and learning would be forever altered.

My first day in class I was sitting in back of the room near an open window, with the sun shining through onto the green blackboard in front, a soft breeze at my back. The desk seat was movable and not riveted to the floor, and I luxuriated in the sense of freedom I felt just from being able to move around in it. My desk in public school, you'll recall, was nailed to the floor, and except when Mrs. Silver chased me up and down the aisles with the American flag, I'd always felt nailed to the floor with it. I'd never seen a green blackboard before. Even the chalk and eraser looked fresh. In public school the chalk, if you could find it, was usually broken white stuff and the erasers looked like dead rats. And here there were trees outside the window, too, not to mention the country air, less noise, and only ten or fifteen kids in the class, not the thirty or forty I was used to.

Within the overall confinement of this institution, I felt comfortably unconfined in the classroom. If I had brought a predilection for resistance with me, it quickly vanished under an absence of tension and regimentation, leaving me a feeling of both relief and disbelief. There was nothing here to rebel against or do battle with. There were no windmills to tilt at. The windows were open. No one was going to chase me down the aisles for not pledging allegiance. If I was doing something I wanted to be doing, I'd look forward to going from morning assembly to the main building. I had quite a few teachers at Hawthorne, but the only teacher I can remember, and I'm not really sure why, is Mrs. Williams. And even though she thought I could someday become a writer, I liked her anyway.

I am sure why I remember the projection booth that hung high up on the ceiling against the wall opposite the gymnasium stage. I remember it because my passion was up there, though for the life of me I can't recall a single movie. How I finagled my way up the vertical metal ladder leading up to the booth right out there in the open, without being stopped, I don't know. It was as if an energy field surrounding my purpose allowed me to turn invisible. I did not have to admit to passion openly to the man in the projection booth; maybe he just saw it in my eyes. After all, he was a projectionist himself. Once in the booth, though, I was in a temple. God's disciple ran it, and I yearned to be a disciple. I felt as I did when, guided by some invisible force, I wandered into that abandoned movie studio on Avenue M in Brooklyn. This was not my mother's trunk in our apartment on Franklin Avenue where I'd cut slits in the sheet, this was a professional projection booth with two 35mm carbon arc projectors (just like the ones in movie theaters), with pedals that you hit with your foot when one projector was about to run out of film, so that the reel of film on the second projector could take over.

I think the projectionist may have let me make one changeover. Changeovers were a big deal. They're what kept the movie flowing seamlessly. Taking control of a changeover was a profound responsibility. The whole show rested on your shoulders, or to be more exact, your foot. You, your foot, and your timing were in charge. I took responsibility very seriously. If entrusted, I could be counted on 100 percent. When you did it perfectly nobody was any the wiser. Just like being a puppeteer: nobody saw you, but they knew you were there, and you were running the show. I knew I was there. After the changeover, you shut down the projector as the film's tail leader noisily ran its way through the projector's transport mechanism for the changing of reels. The clanging and commotion contrasted with the stillness and continuity down there. I liked that; I knew that; I understood it. It was my clay world come to life, with a real audience. In truth, I was probably up there only once, but my imagination sometimes made up what I wanted to have happen. It was almost as if making it up *made* things happen. But I know I was up there.

As luck would have it, I got the measles. I was bedded down in the infirmary, which was when I fell in love with Annette on the *Mickey Mouse Club*, just like millions of other boys of my generation, except I thought it was personal. Who knew?

Movie night was coming up, though, and I had to get out somehow and help run the show and I remember assuring and reassuring the nurse that nothing bad would happen to me if she'd only let me out but she wouldn't, and here I was convincing *her* I wasn't dying, hypochondria be damned. And even if I had been, I'd have waived it. Visceral necessity transcended sickness and death. It was no different from my passionately needing to get to that TV studio in New York for *Rootie Kazootie*. I had literally dreamed my way onto that show, but this time the show went on without me, and I cannot imagine anything that could have disappointed me more.

Nor can I recall ever going back up again. And I don't know why. Maybe I was embarrassed at having let someone down. Did I let my God down (but I wasn't religious)? If I'd been turned away when I went back, it would have been an unbearable rejection.

7

Seminal

THE PROSPECT OF my own bar mitzvah appealed to me in a secular sense, not that I could have said that then. For a kid who had been a loner, an outsider passing under the shadow of the shingle at 150 Court Street in Brooklyn, bar mitzvah meant something about being included. And it came ready-made. You didn't even need parents for it. I was as entitled here as anyone because—and I do not mean for this to sound religious—it was not up to anyone but God. It was what we would today call a level playing field. Equal membership had resonance and my implicit, unquestioning acceptance.

Although I didn't have any parents, I would have an audience. And as if that weren't enough, you got gifts. A suit, a tie, a yarmulke (skullcap), and a tallis (a prayer shawl), and I was in show business. "Today I am a man," or, as tradition only half jokingly puts it, "Today I am a fountain pen," because a fountain pen is the traditional bar mitzvah gift. (It might be ballpoints today, I don't know, but back in the fifties, ballpoints were just coming in. I remember my first Paper Mate, with piggyback refills.)

I always wondered what bar mitzvah had to do with pens, anyway, but I suspect now it's preparation for paying bills. A lot of kids might have known this then, but I was something of a purist. My chance to perform would have far outweighed any consideration for material compensation.

More than that, I felt I'd achieved something. Here I had a marker, a goalpost, a finish line. In a land where nobody told me anything about anything, and where what I was doing was everybody's business but my own, I had something solid to hold on to: a white leatherette, gold-trimmed Bible in a deep blue textured box, with my last name printed across the box's label, in ink. Just my last name. Not even my birth certificate (something I would not see until my thirties) has my first name. I don't know why she never gave me a first name. From as far back as I can remember she always called me Joseph, and even sang it to me. I still have my Bible, though. I just looked at it. I never liked my first name anyway. Too goyish.

I put my bar mitzvah Bible in the drawer of the narrow wooden side cabinet next to my bed. I remember that something in the drawer smelled awful, and after a while the Bible began to smell bad, too. I can't remember what I'd put in there, but it was an odor I just couldn't get rid of. I had no other place to put the Bible, though.

One day I asked the social worker when I could see my mother again. It must have been about the time I'd been bar mitzvahed. I was thirteen now and it had been six years since I'd last seen her. The social worker told me that my mother was too sick to see me, but I had a hard time grasping the idea that someone could be that sick for so long. It had to be something else, then, something they weren't telling me. Maybe my mother didn't want to see me anymore. They just couldn't tell me that because they didn't want to hurt me. "Would you like me to see if I can get you a picture of your mother?" the social worker asked. I couldn't see my mother in person, so they were trying to give me the next best thing. While I can understand now any number of reasons why I might not have been able to see my mother, they weren't saying anything, so by not explaining and sharing those reasons with me with candor and openness, by maintaining what was by then the familiar, though thinly veiled, shroud of secrecy that I could clearly sense, I could imagine only the worst. What is left unsaid is fertile breeding ground for misunderstanding, and confirmation of a child's worst fears, particularly when that child is already burdened with responsibility and guilt. A child's resilience and capacity for understanding transcend the limitations of the belief that a child must be saved from himself. Concealing information is an aspect of control, by which authority puts its own interests—maintaining its authority—ahead of the child's. This is antithetical to a child's innate sense of fairness, and it breeds contempt.

I don't remember wondering when the picture was coming, though, and I'm not even sure I believed it would come, because that would have been just another disappointment if it didn't. When the picture came it was a five-by-seven black-and-white photograph, quite clearly posed. I was told that my mother knew she was taking it for me. Maybe it was true. And if she did know it, then my mother was somehow closer than she felt. While contact for me was impossible—a million zillion miles away—it wasn't for them. If she was taking this picture for me, though, then she wasn't angry at me anymore. The social worker commented that my mother was pretty. I didn't think so. I think I was embarrassed about my mother—ashamed, really—so how could she be pretty? Her eyes were the kindest eyes and she was smiling kindly with them. At me? She looked calm. There was a serenity I'd never seen before. I'd never seen her so much at peace. She wasn't angry anymore. There was nothing wrong, really. Then why didn't she want to see me anymore? If everything was okay now, why did I have only her picture to look at? Was it something to do with me? There was something they weren't telling me. What was the secret here? Why wouldn't they tell me?

I put her picture in my bar mitzvah Bible for safekeeping and for concealment. The things I wanted most in life I tended to conceal. Besides, where else would I have put it? The thought of displaying it would never occur to me. I doubt I thought anyone would steal it, but perhaps I was ashamed. If I had a mother, then why wouldn't she visit me? How could I explain this? The other kids called me "foster." Maybe that was better than knowing that my mother was crazy or that she didn't love me anymore. I was bothered that the drawer still had that smell in it, though. I would open it and look at her picture from time to time. I'm not sure why. Maybe I was searching for some hidden meaning, some understanding. Or maybe just taking in the memory of it so I didn't have to keep it in that smelly drawer. But my Bible was all I had to share.

I was increasingly detached from her, just as her picture itself was a moment frozen. It was as if the option of seeing my mother again was somehow foreclosed because I now had her picture. I think I let go. Each time I looked at the picture, she grew somehow more distant. It all felt past tense somehow. I seemed to understand a finality, for reasons I knew not, and yet I must have hoped for something or I wouldn't have kept opening and closing the drawer. What could I have been looking for?

One day I opened the drawer and tore up the picture. I don't know why. I wasn't angry. I hadn't given it any forethought. But I could not have a relationship with a picture, so tearing it up would be a resolution. The drawer smelled bad, anyway. I didn't want her picture in a smelly drawer. It was like trying to turn that construction paper train into one made by Lionel—I tried but I couldn't do it. My imagination wasn't strong enough to bring her back. If she didn't want to see me anymore, then what could I do? From that day forward, my mother had died.

∞

GEORGE WAS A social worker not without guile. Let's face it: in this job everybody's got an act. But George's guile stunk. It just wasn't real. The fact that George just couldn't put on a good act, however, only heightened the genuineness and warmth of the man who was standing at his desk before me, trying his heart out for me to like him. His was not a soliloquy. If I didn't join him in his act, I'd have felt I'd let him down, and I couldn't let him down. I just couldn't hurt his feelings.

He was a small man, in his mid- to late thirties, a gentle man. His humility right there on the surface. He was open, somewhat vulnerable, and yet confident of who *he* was and therefore he could afford to be equally respectful of who I was. Unlike the rest of them, I couldn't smell an agenda or predisposition. As I sat down he opened his center desk drawer and threw five candy bars onto the desktop. He offered me any three. I just couldn't have all five. He was no dummy and neither was I. "You're trying to bribe me. You just want me to talk."

He nodded: "Sure."

Oh! "Well, what if I don't wanna talk? Do I still get the candy bars?"

He looked nonplussed, perhaps, that I could doubt his sincerity. "Of course."

I must've had a moment there for reflection (he was good) and hesitation (I had my own act to muster), but those five candy bars were staring me in the face, and so I reached out and took one. Making first like I really couldn't make up my mind which one to pick next, I finally took another. Checked again, and took another. No hitches. Invitational theft. Beer bottles were never this easy. I picked my favorites, of course, and I didn't have to talk or do anything. I could just sit there for an hour and stuff my face with candy bars. I doubt I had much to say that day anyway, because when you're eating candy bars you're just too preoccupied enjoying them to pay attention to what's being said *or what you're saying* (the radar, though, is still surveying). Candy bars are a great gimmick. They kind of loosen you up, and it's a great way to make a friend. Ask any horse. By now, I'll bet everybody's using candy bars.

His act was simplicity itself: if you want to make a kid your friend, nothing works better than a bribe. And nothing's more suspect, either— and he knew that. And I think he knew I knew that and that I knew he knew that and I just liked him all the more for it. Look at the extent to which I was willing to go even before the proposition was broached. In truth, I had no idea what was coming. I just knew I liked the guy. He wasn't actually bribing me, anyway, as much as making me an offer to please trust him. And an offer, you could say, I couldn't refuse. From the moment I stepped into his office, his ease of body language, his tone, his natural willingness to engage me on his level, as if I were a person, all spoke to a genuineness that kids just have a way of knowing. Why was something so simple so impossible for the rest of them?

Discovery through sharing and openness is, by definition, a two-way street. If one side is a front, like the ones they prop up on Hollywood back lots, then you might as well be talking to the wall. Walls don't talk, and fake ones can't even hold themselves up. George was the real McCoy, and I believed he liked me. He must have liked some of the other kids, too, but when you were with George he made you feel like you were his only friend. And that made me feel special. There was a sort of conspiracy here, me and George against "them." Or maybe it was me and George and let's ignore "them." That might have been part of the act, too, of course, but who cared if the candy bars were free, the answers straight, and you never felt lied to or bullshitted.

Me and George could make sense of just about anything that made sense, and he wasn't afraid to tell me what he thought, either. And he didn't have to hide or keep control by asking you questions about why you were asking questions, or check in somewhere to find out what he thought about something because he already knew. Sometimes he'd answer questions I hadn't even asked because he'd sense I might have something on my mind I'd want to talk about. Whatever psychology books he'd read, he and I were on the same page, which was really quite a feat when you consider that I hadn't read anything. By then, of course, I was able to read.

I recall meeting George at about the time I had begun my freshman year at Pleasantville High School in Pleasantville, New York—the next town over. George may have been instrumental in this, but I was about fifteen by now, had made it to Cottage 23, hadn't run away yet, and they must have realized I probably never would, so they trusted me to walk down that hill every morning, take the public bus, and head to school. They also must have realized I wouldn't be here forever, something I hadn't thought of. Going off-grounds to high school was a very big deal for me. High school, in my mind, sounded terribly grown up and perhaps an inch closer to self-determination and freedom. One of the social workers had earlier expressed doubt as to my capacity to finish high school, and I always used such doubts to set mental goalposts, in which in my mind I would move still farther away as I approached them, just to be able to top myself. One way I could get even with them was to defy their predictions and expectations, which is not to say that I wouldn't have done what I did anyway, but the challenge of it just gave it that extra kick, you might say. A kick in their ass.

I'd been here for about 2½ years now, a long time when you're a kid. Unwittingly, I'd gotten used to the place, to being enwombed at Hawthorne. Too much so. I was now quite good. My freshman year at Pleasantville High School was more a way station between real life and institutional life, a sort of daily parole, one foot in, one foot out. Of course, I viewed this as an achievement, and clearly I had something to prove. But I could forge no relationships, and I spoke to no one except my teachers in the classroom. No one. At lunchtime I ate alone from a bag lunch I'd been given.

The simple truth is that I was painfully shy and unable to connect with anyone. My deep, dark secret was that I lived in an institution for emotionally disturbed children, which I returned to after school every day. I had no home. As always, friendship threatened unthinkable revelation and consequent shame. Who would want to be friends with someone like me anyway? My clothes, especially my shirts, which were issued to all of us at Hawthorne in previously worn condition (though that never really bothered me and I was never concerned with clothing in the confines of Hawthorne and similarly dressed kids) were usually two inches shorter than my arms and I was painfully self-conscious of this among kids not dressed in Hawthorne style, constantly tugging at my cuffs in embarrassment. I would not complain, though. That might have been interpreted as failure, and in my mind, that was not an option. Since I knew, with certainty, that I had the self-control to be good, there was no fear, but having been away from any real freedom for so long, I felt insecure. What Hawthorne had apparently instilled in me, more than anything, were the reins to hold myself back with. A reinforcement of my inherent badness, and a bridle now to contain it. Straitjacketed, and now my own jailer.

I had always been an open, talkative child, and this undoubtedly helped me insofar as getting people to like and trust me. But I didn't like myself. I could control and compartmentalize the guilt and feelings of unworthiness and inadequacy, but they truly never left me. Ambitious? Yes. Deserving? No. I didn't feel an ounce of self-pity here, just self-patrolled isolation, embarrassment, and estrangement, familiar territory for me.

I did everything absolutely right, and the few teachers I can remember seemed to have liked me. For algebra I had Mr. Koechlin, a kind teacher who had an animated way of smiling and talking at the same time, with an extraordinary conservation of lip movement that left half his mouth open for talking and the other half shut for smiling, up and down, as he punctuated his mathematical nimbleness with pointed chalk in hand and the sort of "gotcha" self-satisfaction that signaled a sort of slap on his own back. Mr. Koechlin liked teaching algebra and I liked Mr. Koechlin, and I was good in algebra, too.

The only thing I didn't do well in was an IQ test. I had never taken a test before that I hadn't at least prepared for, and in the pressure and formality of the testing environment I was self-conscious, nervous, uncomfortable and unsure of what they wanted. But with a little encouragement, I'm sure I could have done better. I can still vividly see my track coach, whose name I can't remember, yelling "Jake!" especially when I was winning the race. "C'mon, Jake!" Very encouraging stuff. I'd literally never heard this kind of vocal encouragement ever before in my life. I'd never known what it felt like to be cheered on in front of everyone else. It signaled belief. Magic. Pure magic. Encouragement for a kid is everything.

∽

ONE DAY I was walking with George up the hill that led to the entrance to Hawthorne's grounds (me, no doubt, with candy bar in hand). There was something he wanted to tell me, but he wanted me to get in front of it, so he put it as a question. "Let me ask you something." He stopped for a moment, as if to consider his own incredulous question. "What're you doing here?"

I just stopped dead. "Huh?"

Seeing my difficulty, he matter-of-factly repeated himself, looking nonchalantly toward the ground as we continued walking uphill. "I mean," and here he paused and looked at me with incredulity, "what're you doing here?" implying somehow the inherent rightness of his own conclusion and prompting me, almost imploring me, to see it his way.

The question's tone had the surreal implication that *I* had somehow made the wrong decision. But it might have been George's way of telling me that someone else had, and that he couldn't understand it any more than me. Or that maybe there had been a problem, but it's not there now. But that incredulous look, with no sense of hidden agenda, no shadows on his face, spoke of such bewildered sincerity that I knew where he was going. It was like we were a team, and he was asking for my concurrence.

I had long ago stopped asking. I had honestly stopped wondering what was going to happen to me. The thought had never occurred to me whether I would be here forever. For me, Hawthorne had become a monastery. I have no other way to explain it.

"I don't know," I finally said. "Why?"

"I mean, you don't belong here."

"I know. I know I don't. Can you get me out?"

"Sure." That's all he said. "Sure." And we just kept walking.

I'll never know for sure what George truly believed when he asked me that. But I have come to believe that had I met George two years sooner, I would have been out of there within six months of my arrival. Maybe less. And I might not have been so "good." And that might not have been so bad.

∞

ONCE A YEAR there was a Saturday ceremonial event known as Citizenship Day, when all the boys were dressed in jackets and ties and brought to a sit-down assembly at the center of the campus near the flagpole. At this ceremony, one boy would be named Hawthorne's citizen of the year and given a special citation. I distinctly recall wanting to get a picture of this, for what purpose I do not know because even though I'd started the *Jr. Round-Up* publication, it was a one- or two-page Rexographed newspaper without photographic capability. (A Rexograph was a machine that printed differently colored pages using alcohol instead of mimeograph ink—and it smelled good.) So maybe I just wanted to take the picture because I liked showing off and I liked taking pictures. An important event such as this was a natural. Or maybe I just wanted to use the pretext of the camera for another reason.

As I sat among the other kids that sunny day, Hawthorne's director, Jerome M. Goldsmith, gave his little speech, and as he drew close to announcing the name, I stood up slowly in my seat to make sure I had a clear shot over the heads of the other kids. And on this bright, sunny day, I lowered my head close to the ground glass of my Argus 75. I put my hand up to my face to block out the sun. And that's when I had the surreal sensation of hearing Goldsmith call my name. How could he have done that? How was I going to take a picture of me? What was I getting an award for? I couldn't imagine what I had done differently from anything I had done before. But the award symbolized something for me that was unmistakable. I had become "good."

I was as stunned as could be. I put my camera on my seat and went up to receive my citation. Proudly, I'm certain. Whatever they had wanted me to become, I had succeeded. Perhaps they had succeeded. It really didn't matter to me who got the credit, though, as long as I had the citation affirming that I'd become whatever it was I was supposed to become. I was absolved. As I think about this now, though, to be perfectly honest, something else creeps in: I knew something. There was something in the air that morning in Cottage 23 when the cottage mother made certain my tie was on straight. Something was cooking. And so the stunned modesty I displayed was an act. But I had it covered: if I prepared myself to take a picture, and didn't get the award, I could cover my disappointment behind the lens. The camera was my shield. I never did get the picture, though.

∽

IN THE END, when the time came, I didn't want to leave Hawthorne. I was simply too afraid to give up a life in which I had grown all too secure. My fear of leaving Hawthorne, after years of demanding that I be let go, shows the extent to which I had been successfully programmed into this "community." The downside of Hawthorne for me was that it would take me years to unshackle, run free, and return to me. The combined pressures of emerging adolescence, an underlying fear that now that I had been officially pronounced "good" and that disappointing them might bring me right back, coupled with my old feelings of displacement and uncertainty, caused me to further retreat into myself and return to my fantasies and their passionate belief in my future.

Hawthorne provided structure for a prepubescent kid who had never had any, but without the structure, I'd owned me: I created and internalized a structure of my own. Now I was in the formative years of what would evolve into a lifelong independence from, and distrust of, authority, and in fact my evolving disdain for authority may have been the best thing I took away from Hawthorne. But no child, in my judgment, could successfully adapt to Hawthorne without relinquishing, or at very least sublimating, whole chunks of himself in the process (a faux indicator of "wellness"), and run the risk of losing something of himself that might otherwise be in good working order. In my case that was a loss of connection to the outside world, which was later compounded by my continuing second-class citizenship as a foster child. I was a resident at Hawthorne for nearly three years, a long time in childhood development. I adapted to it well. If the paper evidence is any indication, as well as they would have liked. I turned out good. Too good. Shut my mouth.

You can emotionally straitjacket, shackle, and bridle, and you can reinforce guilt through incarceration. You can change behavior through intimidation while masking it as benevolent authority. Children, particularly, will seek approval and try to please, especially when pleasing equals freedom. Working backward, you can manipulate a result to confirm your expectation and then reward that result and yourself, both. I got the Citizenship Award for Outstanding Achievement in Our Community at Hawthorne and even had my camera at the ready to take a picture of the winner. I knew I'd won, but wouldn't have wanted this authority thinking they'd won. Either that, or I knew I didn't deserve it, and wanted them to believe that I believed I didn't deserve it. The paradox being that my knowing I didn't deserve it was proof positive of my goodness, and vice versa. And if I could demonstrate that I knew I didn't deserve it, then they'd be confirmed in their judgment of me, and in my having confirmed them, I could accept my award without guilt. As if winning, deserving, were a *Shandeh* (a shame or disgrace). "Good" meant not having.

Was a treatment center for emotionally disturbed children the best place to deal with what had brought me there? Could it address the underlying guilt that had made my life in two foster homes intolerable? The daily structure, routine, and surveillance simply straitjacketed the underlying causes and directed them inward. My behavior was better now, by their lights. But at what price? And for whose benefit?

Fear and resentment would follow me for years after. But I understood the pattern of staying clean and keeping low. Somehow I was still waiting to grow up and get out—both get out the "me" of me, *and* get out of the system. The one thing about getting older was that it happened without you. And in my case, the older I got, the better it got. In time, I reemerged, fundamentally the same me, I am convinced. Like a piece of Silly Putty that's been deeply thumbprinted, in time I rose back to my original form. And with the joyous acceptance that came with gaining responsibility for myself, there also came an acceptance both by myself and by others of who I was. Nor did I, for a second, question my capacity for survival.

Sending me to Hawthorne was a mistake. In writing this chapter I have found it hard to express outrage for the ways they damage people because that's not the person I am, and have tried diligently to paint a picture with fairness. After I had left the system, I was told by my last social worker, Jean Bernstein, who had become a friend, that Ida Freedman had never believed in the decision to send me to Hawthorne, particularly in light of the evidence of the last home I'd been placed in. Though she might not have known the psychiatrist who decided to send me to Hawthorne by name, Wilfred Hulse, M.D., was a renowned figure in the psychiatric community. To this day, psychiatric awards are given under his name. Freedman did not have the authority to override Hulse's judgment. Another psychiatrist would tell me of Mr. Hulse, "He was boss." There was a telling smile on his face when he said it. That arbitrary. That simple.

Part Three

Good Boy

When asked whether she would like her son to visit with

her, she was hesitating and then said she didn't mind,

but she wouldn't talk to him. "Why?"

"Because I wouldn't tell him the truth."

8

Brooklyn Redux

THE DAY I left Hawthorne, a new social worker delivered me to my new foster home, in Boro Park, Brooklyn. I hadn't come home, really. I had no home. I had simply come back to Brooklyn, and to a part I had never known before. The expectations of others were high in my mind; I didn't want to slip up. There were worse places they could send you to than Hawthorne, so whatever I'd gotten wrong before I'd better get right this time.

That I had returned to freedom was never a thought in my head. In some ways I felt even more isolated, less secure, and certainly greater trepidation than ever before. What Hawthorne may have added, it had more than taken away. I was no longer free to be me. The identity of "me" was now uncertain to me, defined to a large extent by what I understood of other people's expectations of me: foster parents and teachers and anyone else in this new world I might come across in a position of authority.

I had returned from a freeze-frame life only to find that real life felt like a still life because I had literally no idea how to live. Living was an art I had yet to learn. What I could do was follow the rules, and I did so now with even greater caution than I had at Hawthorne. Having just spent nearly three years in limbo, it would take a while to get used to the new me, whoever that was.

Not that I ever felt nostalgia for Hawthorne. Never. I had never looked back at anything, really, except my home in Flatbush, which by now was forever gone as well. It would never have occurred to me—*only* five years later, but also a lifetime ago—to walk back to Twenty-ninth Street and ring the bell. I was simply no longer the same person. I also looked different; I was no longer that cute little boy. Had I gone back, Auntie might not have recognized me, or worse, might have found me unattractive and no longer lovable. I was simply not able to run the risk of this rejection; to face the reality that, even there, I was unworthy. This would be reliving my abandonment by my mother. And so I never consciously thought of going back. Not here. Not again. Childhood was something to get past, and I ran from it just as fast as I could.

This foster home was essentially a place for me to eat and sleep. It was a two-family brick house with an apartment on the second floor. My small, narrow room was just off to the right of the stairway, down the hall a bit, away from the rest of the apartment. While it was not quite a bedroom, it was large enough for a bed, dresser, table, lamp, chair, and a metal clothes cabinet. There was even a window facing the street below. The bed was not very long, so my feet kicked up against the metal cabinet at night, but I was able to adjust. I was not complaining. In fact, complaining would have been the last thing I did, lest I run the risk being sent someplace worse. Besides, what if I complained about something that was actually my fault? If I could avoid kicking the metal cabinet, and I kicked the metal cabinet, then whose fault was that? And if I could be faulted, then again I'd be at risk. They did good at Hawthorne.

I was the only foster boy here, but there was a sweet younger boy of about ten, whom I recall was their biological son, although it struck me as odd that this older couple in their late fifties or early sixties would have such a young son. Besides, they seemed too improbably old to me to have had sex. They also had an older son, who had just been inducted into the air force and was soon to fly out. One morning I commented to my foster mother about the risks of flying, and my own ambivalence about it. Unbeknownst to me at the time, my comment had so disturbed her that she reported it to my social worker, who admonished me for it. Why had I said such an insensitive thing? she asked, finding it hard to believe that I could not have been aware that it was.

I was startled that my comment had left any imprint at all. I'd meant no harm, though I understood now that I had been unwittingly tactless. As strange as it may sound, I was probably trying to commiserate, to show my concern. From that day forward, though, I was exceedingly careful about anything I said or did. Going from my room to the dinner table or the bathroom, I would make myself as scarce as possible. I spoke very little. Small as my room was, I kept to myself inside it. And while the apartment itself was not all that big, I would never see all of its rooms.

The dinner table turned out to be the one place, though, where I didn't have to worry because nobody was allowed to say anything anyway. This foster father was a parochial, authoritative, and constricted man. A dispatcher for the subway system, he was adept at dispatching the dinner traffic as well. As he sat, he would loosen his buckle a few notches and shore up his leather pen and pencil pouch to the rear of his belt in a way that conveyed that he could just easily remove the belt entirely if he so chose. He always seemed displeased about something, underlining it by a sigh that implied the weight of the world was on him and that his anger was on a hair trigger. I was implicitly forewarned. His family and I were guests at his table, and the ritual belt loosening and holstering was a sort of tribal reminder of who reigned. Then he'd pick his nose while reading the newspaper and literally gulping down his food, all of which he somehow did in tandem, behind a cupped palm—just so you wouldn't notice.

If his younger son inadvertently slipped and said something, there'd be a hushed silence while his newspaper slowly lowered and my eating pace hastened, as if to distance myself from responsibility. I remember now how grateful I felt that I'd never slipped, and had there been a book for Brownie points I would have filled mine many times over. So bad it was that I get it right. I also would have done anything to gain weight, so eating-no-talking was fine. His dutiful wife alternately sat and rose, rose and sat, and sometimes rose only to realize—"Where're you going?!"—that she should've been sitting. When he was ready for whatever dish came next, she rose again. I was long past any kind of emotional belonging anyway, and this was just another stop en route to my destination. I was a passenger waiting to get off.

Nonetheless, George had been right: the older you got, the better it got, because childhood was no fun and because after, you had more freedom to live your life the way you wanted. That gave me a lot to look forward to and implied a universal truth that somehow lessened the pain I felt about my childhood. Whether he was really right about the first part or not is debatable; he might have tailored his opinion for my consumption. But time would show he had gotten the second part right.

At sixteen, for example, I could get working papers and make my own money. Just the idea of being able to buy my own clothes, or a clock radio, was extraordinarily liberating. I suspect, too, that George may have implied the confirmation of my dreams, based on my own expectations and my deeply rooted belief in their ultimate fulfillment. George was such a positive person that if I'd said anything his response would have sounded encouraging, such as "Why not?" Just like that chew on the steak, I could make a little bit of encouragement go a long, long way.

A woman I met many years later said to me, "You turn over every stone. Every stone. And then, when you've turned over *every* stone . . . you find more stones." That survival mechanism had been in me from the beginning. In that sense, at least, given my absurd dreams, I had the will to believe and an inherent fearlessness of risk, born from having nothing to lose.

The week I turned sixteen, I not only got my working papers but also an after-school job at Bernstein's Department Store on Thirteenth Avenue as a stock boy and cashier in the candy department. (I liked work, but given my acne, I stayed away from the candy.) Making money meant independence and an acknowledgment of my worth. In spite of the abject poverty of my childhood, though, I never once dreamed about making money or getting rich. Even when I sold stuff, somehow it wasn't about the money. Perhaps I saw the inconsistency between making money and fulfilling my passion, and if I had had to choose between the two, there would have been no choice. Why do kids sell lemonade? I don't think it's primarily the money. I think it's the sense of budding independence and the transient entry to and effect on the grown-ups' world.

Not having money, of course, was all I'd known. The Andrews Sisters were singing "Money Is the Root of All Evil" and vowing (as I recall it) not to "contaminate myself with it." And worse, "Take it away, take it away, take it away" (at least three times they said that!). Maybe I took comfort in knowing that not having it was a blessing! A child who cannot effect change will subscribe to the next available, albeit wishful, option.

But I also knew that not having money is what made my mother unhappy and created all of our problems. I was never able to pay my way, either, so since I had let her down when she needed money (so I thought), having money for myself was unthinkable. Throughout my adult life I have been ambivalent about it. It controlled lives; it had controlled ours; and later, when I saw how adults used it to control others, I determined it would not control me. In spite of some very rough times, I found greater freedom through fearless risk-taking, because it gave me unfettered freedom to pursue whatever I believed in, including myself. Ultimately, the real value of accepting the risk must be embraced if one's goals are ever to be realized. Luck and fate and persistence play a part, but in the end, passion so strongly felt transcends everything. I never had a choice.

My independence, however limited it might be, was very important to me. In Boro Park I saw my first rock-and-roll movie, *Rock around the Clock*, starring Bill Haley and the Comets. In fact, it was *the* first rock-and-roll movie. A famous disc jockey of the fifties, Alan Freed, came to Boro Park for the show, bounding onto the stage before the movie started with the same incredibly high energy he had on the radio, assuring everybody (and I had a feeling himself, too) that rock and roll was here to stay and it would never die, and of course we all whooped it up. I'm not sure I believed him, because I never believed anything was here to stay, but I was there by myself and I wasn't going to say anything anyway, and in those days there were plenty of people who were trying to steal the music, so it was us against them, and that's probably part of why I was there in the first place. Being by myself, though, didn't mean I felt alone. The fact that I was sitting there at all, that *I had showed up*, said the music was part of *me*, and me was part of *us*. I never gave it a thought.

I remember earning enough to buy that clock radio, and a suit at Robert Hall for $29.95 (the high-end suits on the back racks went for as much as $79.95). I aspired to an Arrow shirt, while a Hathaway might have to wait until I grew up, although I never could get a fix on that guy with the patch. Bostonian and Florsheim shoes were a notch up, of course, but Thom McAns were trendy and affordable. If it didn't have a recognizable tag I didn't know how to measure it.

In my own way, I was trying to join up and get noticed. And I wouldn't have minded if the girls noticed, too, but clothes can go only so far. Had they noticed, and one did, I could go only so far. Given my fundamental insecurity, inherent shyness, discomfort with my appearance, and uncertain sense of worth, I never had a girlfriend in high school. I simply could never accept that a girl would find me attractive, and my fear of rejection, once she discovered the rest of me, precluded any show of interest on my part.

Fortieth Street in Boro Park wasn't so much a part of a neighborhood as it was a colorless concrete street. But I was also no longer a kid growing up on the block, anyway, and there was nothing here to take me home. I had become a lodger, spending more and more of my time at school and in extra-curricular activities after school.

> *Ten thousand girls, ten thousand boys*
> *United in these high school halls.*

Those were, and are, the opening lines to New Utrecht High School's school song, which I can sing to this day, and if I knew how to write music, I'd write it out for you just so you could get a feel for why it held a certain inspiration for a sixteen-year-old. Inclusion was something I embraced, and our alma mater was not only about inclusion but also about a glorious future.

> *To share in studies and in joys*
> *Await the day when service calls*

It was clear sailing ahead, very up and optimistic, which, for reasons of willful wish fulfillment, I had always been anyway. There was a certain hallowed quality to the piece, and I felt reverential pride whenever I sang it, which I suppose is what such anthems are supposed to make you feel. It felt almost Talmudic, not in the sense that it sounded Jewish, mind you, but in the sense of its traditionalist values.

I started my sophomore year at New Utrecht High School, which provided me with a social structure within which my sense of self would gradually reemerge. My biggest obstacle was my painful shyness, exacerbated now by acute acne and the fact that I had developed into a five-nine, rail-thin ectomorph (learned that one in high school). I often wore several layers of clothes just so as not to disappear entirely, particularly in profile.

As in my freshman year at Pleasantville High School, I did reasonably well as a student, but now I was not umbilically tethered to an institution to which I would have to return each day. Though I was still living in a foster home, I could keep that a secret, too, by keeping my worlds separate, though it required vigilance. No one, literally, could get too close to home. If no one ever came home with me, no one would ever know where or how I lived or that the people I lived with had a different last name from mine. These were not people I would have wanted as parents anyway, so I was saved that embarrassment as well.

I immersed myself in after-school activities perhaps as a way of more fully defining a life that others might have done through family and friends. My school activities became surrogate family, and I developed a sense of belonging and camaraderie. In spite of my shyness, I got along well with my peers, as I had at every stage of my childhood. I became best friends with Bob, who was also interested in drama, film, and girls, which neither of us ever did a damn thing about. I was drawn to a world whose principal activity was activity itself and the creation of a reality, and where you received immediate acceptance and reward, even awe, for doing it well. Literally, applause. Theatrics, in all its manifestations: a real-life version of my clay model fantasies. Most certainly puppetry, "hidden performance"—the best of both worlds. I even built theatrical settings in shoe boxes. In these socially licensed activities I could participate without fear of judgment or even theft.

I was not only the new kid on the block but also new to the world at large, feeling fragile and self-protective. I had begun to pick up the pieces again, and to try to put them back together. I was in the liquefied state of self-invention, and my foundation, though built upon granite bedrock, needed time to cure. Affirmation and acceptance, for myself as myself, as an equal, were essential. I did not need to be handicapped, I did not need pity, and I was not disadvantaged. I did not want to be different, because being different in this way made you less, not more.

Throughout high school I would be successful at keeping my school and "home life," such as it was, separate, so perhaps I would have made that good file clerk, after all. What I didn't know was that some teachers already knew, but even if I'd known they knew, I would have kept myself from knowing. One teacher had to have known that I lived in a foster home because it was written right there on a four-by-five index card inside her little tin box, probably right next to "90." Everyone in her little tin box had a number. That 90 was for IQ, and it meant borderline average. Whether I'd seen it or someone told me about it, I can't recall, but it was there, and I even knew where it came from—the IQ test I'd taken at Pleasantville High the year before. I recall this quite vividly, and have no doubt that my low IQ score, coupled with what I didn't know she already knew about me, are what defined me for her. She had you pegged even before she'd met you, and I was not a contender. She had her favorites, too, of course, and they were equally preordained. But while I was still in search of myself, I knew I was no 90.

The fact that she didn't think much of me to begin with really didn't surprise me, given my own self-doubt, but I resented her for it anyway. I was torn among fear, loathing, and wanting her to like me. And the way she walked from her office to our classroom just next door, with that disciplined authority, you'd have thought she was somebody. And God bless her, she was.

Mildred Windecker was not only my speech and drama teacher, she also was chairman of the Speech Department. A taciturn woman, she did not suffer fools easily, and if you got Miss Windecker for speech, you were unenvied. Of course, I knew nothing of her private life, but I couldn't help wondering about it, so apparent was her dedication to teaching and so opaque was she about everything else. She was past middle age, seemingly a confirmed spinster and even, as her name suggests, a throwback to the old-fashioned schoolmarm. Her colors were your basic black and white, though always tailored, and my sense was that she transcended fashion. This was still the late fifties, right before the Big Bang, so anything from then might seem old-fashioned, but I suspect Miss Windecker was old-fashioned even when old-fashioned was new. A woman so committed to her life's work naturally expected a full return; the best of the best. Whatever else she might have had going for her, though, I concluded that nothing else came close to her dedication. In that regard, respect was in order.

I figured I'd be lucky if she just took notice of me, but maybe luckier still if she didn't. I was one of about twenty-five students in her class. She had me seated over to the left—stage right, her right. (This was just a classroom, of course, but she made it feel theatrical.) Stage right was better than stage left because most of the time she looked stage left, where her favorites sat. They got most of the questions and assignments, and therefore better grades and prime roles in the school plays (I thought about being in the school play, but not really). I had no choice about where I sat anyway, so the good news here—and remember, I always found the good news—was that she wouldn't look at me at all. If this kid could find an upside in poverty, then I could undoubtedly find one in invisibility. How lucky can ya get? Then one day she looked right—stage right.

To be honest with you, being called on was better than being ignored altogether because I instantly recognized that being ignored altogether was preferable only when it was the only available option. If I had exposed anything, if I'd taken any risk at all, it was that I had willed that my presence get noticed, as I had so many times before when I badly wanted something. Even silence can create a presence if it's knowing. I wasn't afraid, outside of a little stage fright maybe, and after all, that's show biz.

The class had been assigned to prepare a short monologue from a play, and mine was John Patrick's *Teahouse of the August Moon*. I was ready just in case Miss Windecker called on me. The scene is a telephone conversation between Captain Fisby and Colonel Purdy (played by Glenn Ford and Paul Ford, respectively, in the movie). I played Fisby, talking into an invisible phone—the sort of thing the comedian Shelly Berman did so brilliantly in the fifties and sixties. I liked making believe I was talking to someone who wasn't there. I talked to someone who wasn't there all the time, which is another way of saying I talked to myself.

When you have a puppet on your hand you're talking through a block of wood, which is even worse than talking to yourself, where there is no expectation, because wood doesn't talk back. And when you're good enough to convince someone else that it does, then you've undoubtedly convinced yourself first, and you get attached. And if you get really attached, that makes you even better, and the wood is even more believable, because you've become a believer yourself, and all acting is believing. I was into my alter ego long before I ever knew what that meant, so I had no problem believing that I was actually having a conversation with Colonel Purdy.

She always sat in back because she wanted to make sure you were projecting. I was in command now of my own existence, and I saw her head gradually lift. An expression now of surprise and even satisfaction crossed her face, satisfaction born of unexpected revelation. As I went on, her head lifted higher still as she became more confident that I could sustain it; a wisp of a smile, her lips puckered in contemplation, edging past that 90 that wasn't mine. She lowered her head again and made her notes. She had overruled the four-by-five.

I had just joined the first club ever that I didn't have to invent for myself. From that moment forward, I had a believer, a mentor, and I had the sense always that she was proud of her discovery. And just as I could be counted on when I walked that little boy across the street to school for a dollar a week, I would not let her down, either. I needed the affirmation and recognition. I understood somehow that discipline was a requisite for completion, and until completion there were no applause. Woody Allen famously said, "80 percent of success in life is showing up," and nobody ever had to show me how to show up. If I could smell the cheese, or even if I could so much as *imagine* smelling it, and even, frankly, if I had to *invent* the cheese to imagine smelling it, I'd be there.

Invariably, the cheese showed up, too. From that moment forward, because of one teacher's belief in me, a belief that turned on a moment in time, a life came alive. *One person* can do that for a kid. Never forget that.

9

I Don't Dance

BUT THEN CAME Coney Island. You take the "el" (the elevated subway) and get off at Stillwell Avenue and you're there. Last stop. End of the line.

It was going to happen sooner or later anyway, except I wasn't going to be the one to do it because I wasn't going to complain, and besides, I had nowhere to go. But it really wasn't anything I'd done. In fact, it was probably because of something I hadn't done. I was this kid lodger living in another family's home. I asked for nothing and I had nothing to give, least of all myself. I cloistered myself in my room after school, but in the morning, as I prepared for school, I spent a lot of time in the bathroom looking at my acne in the mirror. I say "a lot of time," but I really have no idea how much time.

My social worker, Mrs. Bernstein, asked me about the bathroom thing, one thing led to another, and I must have said something about my bed being too short for my legs. She was nonplussed: "Why didn't you tell me this before?" It would never have occurred to me to complain. And I wasn't complaining now, either. It just came up. So it seemed nobody was happy and my social worker asked me if I'd like her to find me another home and I said yes, and that was that. Maybe I'd been there six months. I don't even recall saying good-bye or anything. I simply checked out of my room and left the key.

Anyway, you get off at Stillwell Avenue. Last stop.

If Boro Park was nondescript, Coney Island felt decayed. I walked past it every day on my way to the subway to school and back. At least Alan Freed had come to Boro Park. I don't remember anybody coming to Coney Island. Coney Island was literally the end of the line and at the end of Mermaid Avenue, at its very end, was a cul-de-sac, and that's where I lived now until they could find me a permanent home.

As a kid I saw things and lived places, but those things and places didn't seem to matter so much because I was completely focused on who I wanted to be, where I wanted to go, and how I was going to get there. I didn't notice the things around me, or if I did, I didn't pay them much attention. The future was the best thing I had going—the only thing, really, a distant promise I couldn't get to fast enough. The trick when you get there, if you get there, is to stop living for the future. If you don't, it never shows up because you've missed all the present and all you've got to think back on is a past that isn't there. That I can remember any of this is probably because I saw all the things I didn't want to see, and felt all the things I didn't want to feel, but put them away somewhere. If there is an answer to the question of my child psychologist friend as to why I was neither dead, on drugs, nor in jail, then this is it: where I can go now, I could not have gone before. And by not having gone before, I somehow survived.

It may not have been Flatbush, but Bensonhurst wasn't such a bad neighborhood, either. Bay Thirty-fourth Street between Bath and Benson avenues was essentially a street with middle-classish two-family homes and was just a few blocks from the main thoroughfare, Bay Parkway, and an easy walk to the Famous Cafeteria, where Bob and I hung out. My foster parents here were again elderly, with a grown son who had a family of his own. Aunt Sadie (not to be confused with Auntie in Flatbush) exuded a sort of unhinged cool, and Uncle Meyer, who I thought of as Pope Meyer because he looked like Pope John XXIII, was a gentle, kindly man who had a women's handbag business ("Every Bag a Gem") that had fallen on hard times. He could have been the model for Willy Loman in *Death of a Salesman.* I cannot forget that image of this small, elderly man slowly walking home from a long day in the city, slightly bent over, pushing his vertical suitcase on caster wheels down the broken concrete block. That he had lifted that suitcase up and down the stairs of the elevated subway line breaks my heart now, though as a teenager I saw what I saw without sensitivity. He was a proud, quietly determined man who knew somehow that there'd be better days ahead. But there were small clues here, like watered-down milk or the limits placed on my access to the refrigerator, to their need for money.

Uncle Meyer's hobby was cutting pictures from magazines and pasting them as collages in leatherette scrapbooks. With a pair of scissors, a stack of old magazines, and a bottle of glue, he could while away hours at the kitchen table, whistling and pasting as the world went by. I never quite got it, frankly, but he reminded me a bit of myself molding clay cameras and sets. And like me, if you got too close while he was "working," his sidelong glance would show discomfort. But if ever I thanked him for something, even if only for answering a question, he'd appreciatively respond, "Don't mention it." Though my interest might only be feigned, it suggested a recognition of his work that I knew he liked. "Thank you." "Don't mention it." He didn't even have to know what you were thanking him for: "Thank you," for any reason, elicited "Don't mention it," the conditioned response of a lifetime salesman, the salesman perhaps who gave every customer just a little something extra to go with that beaded bag, and "Every Bag a Gem."

Unlike me, however, he did not need to conceal anything, except from Aunt Sadie, who disapproved. I knew what was coming whenever Aunt

Sadie traipsed down those stairs (her sister, Esther, and brother-in-law, George, lived upstairs), sashayed into the kitchen, and caught him with the scrapbooks on the table. "Meyer—what the hell's the matter with you with all this crap?! C'mon—give me my table back!" "Leave me alone already." "Never mind leave you alone. What're you going to do with all this?!" "It's for the children," he'd mumble, meaning his grandchildren. Sadie would mock him for even thinking they'd want it, and then she'd saunter off just as easily as she'd sashayed in, switching off like a light with absolutely no residual anger or annoyance, as if the cameras had suddenly stopped rolling. Uncle Meyer, unfazed, would go back to what he was doing until, in about fifteen minutes or so, she'd do it again, and he'd pack it in, mumbling protests as he went.

This was their routine, and it was almost vaudevillian, but you knew, somehow, that these two were as incapable of any real misunderstanding as they were capable of demonstrating affection. They were an old pair of shoes and simply put up with each other, and whatever depth their relationship might have had in earlier days, I saw none of it now. He had undoubtedly won her over with what must have been his early business promise. He was the salesman, after all, and she this sashaying dame—an obvious allure for little Meyer, but with her, I suspect, always in full control. Sadie, Sadie, married lady. Don't mention it.

Uncle Meyer was pretty much to himself and Aunt Sadie could be as mocking of herself as she was of him, like the day she looked at herself in the full-length mirror after squeezing into her girdle and proclaimed "I look like a stuffed pig!" I'd left her a note once: "Dear Aunt Sayde . . ." And she lightheartedly corrected me: "My name's Sadie. Not *Saaay*-deee." And sociable? Once a week the "girls" (not one under sixty) came over for mah-jongg in the dining room, usually after I'd gone to bed, and I'd hear the clacking of the ivory tiles as I lay in bed, which, for some reason, always felt comforting: "Ssssh," she'd say, "the kid's trying to sleep." The kid was up.

I was comfortable with the emotional space here, and the absence of any expectation or requirement was just what I needed. I was free to come and go as I pleased, with no undue demands put upon me. Whatever the rules, I had no trouble figuring them out. For once I'd gotten lucky, and I would live here for the two-or-so-year balance of my high school education. And I still had Miss Windecker, New Utrecht, and Bob.

In the late fifties New Utrecht was fundamentally a mix of both Jews and Italians. Bob was Italian. Our favorite movie was *Marty*, about an Italian butcher from the Bronx. Paddy Chayefsky, its author, was a Jew from the Bronx, which shows how this generation shared each other's values, particularly familial values. And even though I never had a family of my own, I somehow intuited what this felt like, particularly the sense of belonging and continuity that family and friends provided. Chayefsky really knew these people. And he made me feel I knew them, too. I think I put him somewhere in the classical period with Shakespeare and Chekhov, neither of whom I'd ever read, either, but it would never have occurred to me that a writer named Chayefsky could actually have been a contemporary person living in the fifties. Paddy Chayefsky was only thirty-four years old in 1955 when he won the Academy Award for best screenplay for *Marty*. I was still at Hawthorne at the time of the picture's initial release. The picture itself won four Oscars, including one for best picture. I thought Chayefsky was so great that he was dead, and I'd still put him in the class with Shakespeare and Chekhov, both of whom I've since had a chance to look at. For me, writers who spoke from wisdom were dead people, which undoubtedly expressed my feeling about writing generally.

"I got hurt enough" Marty tells his mother when she tries to coax him to try to meet a girl at the Stardust Ballroom, "I don't wanna get hurt no more." I knew how he felt when he phoned and asked the girl: "Maybe you recall me . . . ?" and got rejected. It took a lot for him to override that fear a second time when he saw a girl whose own rejection he'd witnessed, firsthand, and whose feelings of unworthiness, like his own, he both understood and was emboldened by. When he followed her out onto the roof she even cried on his shoulder. When he asked her to dance, he was able to offer her words of comfort and inclusion: "You see," he said, "Dogs like us, we ain't such dogs as we think we are."

If I'd met him, he'd have been my best friend, too. In fact, Bob sort of reminded me of Marty, and maybe he saw a bit of himself in the character as well, which may be why he liked the movie, too. I think Bob and I gravitated toward each other due to a sense of mutual dislocation socially (especially when it came to the girls) as well as our common theatrical interests. In those days he wasn't sure if he wanted to be an actor or a priest. I thought he was a terrific actor. Bob always struck me as a well-read intellectual—something I most certainly was not. He wore black-rimmed glasses that he would take on and off to punctuate a point in conversation, his eyes in that sidelong glance of introspective thought, but without a hint of affectation.

I admired the broad scope of his knowledge—he always knew something about everything. When I asked him one day, "How do you know all this stuff?" he responded that he really didn't. He gleaned snippets from *Time* magazine, he said, and was able to piece together just enough information to make it sound like he knew more than he actually did. I'm not sure I ever believed that, though, and took it more as an expression of modesty, or perhaps even his genuine lack of awareness of just how brilliant he really was. His idea of snippets was far greater than my whole volume of knowledge, and I was impressed. It would never have occurred to me to subscribe to *Time*, though. I hadn't a clue what was going on anywhere except in my own head, and that had to do with my own life, and what was on TV, especially the quiz shows. But now that I know everything that's going on everywhere, all the time, it doesn't seem to matter much anyway, except that I wonder now if it takes me away from doing all that good stuff I must've been doing back then when I was a kid.

I remember Bob invited me back to his house one day. It may have been that he had to pick something up, or drop something off, I can't recall, but I waited outside. I didn't go in for fear that I would have to invite him back to my house. His father came out, though, and I could tell he didn't like me. He wasn't friendly and looked at me disapprovingly. When Bob introduced me he barely said hello. Maybe he didn't like me because I was a bad influence, or possibly even because I was Jewish, something not unheard of even in the generation that had lived through World War II, as Bob's father had. Or maybe it was because I never invited Bob back to my house. Amazingly, Bob had never once asked me about my family or even where I lived, and if he had, I would have artfully deflected it. I never went back to his house again. I didn't have to know the reason, but I would've guessed it was because his father saw me for who I was. I was still second-class. Bob stayed my friend, though, which was all that really mattered.

Bob graduated a year before me and I never saw him again. It was as if in leaving high school he'd somehow left the planet, and strangely, I don't even remember wondering about it. Until now this was as unexplainable to me as was the fact that he was the only real friend I ever had in high school. He'd been talking about going to Brooklyn College, though, and I was thinking New York. You have to understand that when you're from Brooklyn, every place else is out of town, and "New York" especially is a world away. And so we never kept up. He never called me, and I never called him, except later, *years* later, as I was waiting for my blind date to come down in the elevator I called him from the lobby of a mid-Manhattan hotel. I don't know what overcame me; I even disguised my voice. He knew it was me. "If I'd known then, I would have been a better friend," he said. Sometime after graduation, Bob had been told by one of our teachers that I'd lived in a foster home.

I had insisted always on a level playing field, long before we called it that. For precisely this reason, I'd known enough what not to display, what to keep distant. If I had a friend, or if I were in any way to be liked, it would have to be for who I was and for no other reason. If I needed confirmation, though, that I'd had a friend, this was it. That's all I wanted to know. There was no conversation. I hung up. I could not go back there. And perhaps I know now why. There could be no consideration given. I would not accept it. The elevator door opened: blonde, blue-eyed, flew for American.

Bob and I in the Famous were the guys in *Marty*'s luncheonette on a Saturday afternoon: "Whaddaya feel like doing tonight, Marty?" "I don't know, Angie, whadda you feel like doing?" Walking along Bay Parkway en route to nowhere on a Saturday night, Bob and I recited these lines with a sense of anticipation that, at any moment, anything could happen, including the appearance of two gorgeous girls who would magically jump from out of the shadows and throw themselves into our laps. Where these dreams came from I'll never know, but Marty and Angie and all the rest of them guys, who were a whole lot older than us, harbored them, too.

But now that I mention it, Linda Altman did throw herself into my lap on "Sing Night," which was our annual interclass sketch competition, performed in the school auditorium. Everybody came. I remember I was a sophomore at the time and someone had written the spirited tune "We Are the Sophs!" verses of which alternated with sketches acted out by students playing teachers. I played Mr. Goldenberg, our popular history teacher. I sat at one end of a conference table, placed center stage in front of a packed house of some fifteen hundred seats, and a very blond and beautiful Miss Altman (there was no Ms. yet) sat at the other, dressed to the nines in black heels and a tight gold lamé dress, playing herself as a student. I've even got the picture to prove it. The sketch was about how to get good grades and influence teachers, and as I'm getting into my teacher spiel, she suddenly stood up, made her way to my side of the table, and literally writhed her way into my lap. This was her idea of method acting. Bob and I had been talking just the day before about what a great piece of ass she was, never knowing, of course, the fate that would befall me. Fortunately or unfortunately, as the case may be, girls wore girdles in those days, although I don't recall Marilyn Monroe ever wearing one in a movie. This undergarment of fifties sexual repression not only stood in the way of a great deal of fun, it also symbolized the contradiction and hypocrisy of the outward expression of sexual allure and enticement, and a do-nothing Congress. "Sing" was my coming out, in more ways than one.

It was all about getting laid. You just didn't deal with it right up front like that, at least not that I knew of. You danced around it, you toyed with it in your head. But even if you could have said something, *I* could not have. Hell, Marion flaunted it right there in front of me in her house one night and I didn't respond. How I got into her house, I don't recall, but it wasn't anything personal, at least not for me. Her entreaties, though, were unmistakable. Nobody else was home, either. Great body, too, but still I couldn't deal with it (I'd have had a tough time getting past her braces, anyway). To this day, I'm still not sure if it was the innocence of the time or *my* innocence of the time. Both, I suspect. I'm still not sure what I missed, and I don't want to know. But the times they were a-changin'.

The risks were either getting stuck in the fifties, heading full-blown into the sixties, or somehow having one foot here and one foot there, which I suspect was more me than not. That left me completely out of synch and alienated (personally, I think it all caused pimples). But what I'd still like to know is, what the hell were *we* doing anyway, and how'd I miss out?

∞

BECOMING A MEMBER of the stage crew kept me engaged in theatrical and social activities while allowing me to keep my distance at the periphery at the same time. After all, the stage crew was, by definition, behind the scenes. When the prom dance was held in the girls' gymnasium, we set up the P.A. system and hung around all night until it came time to take it all down. I would spend the evening standing around off-court somewhere, just watching everyone else dance, taking in the experience vicariously—inclusion without intimacy, closeness at a distance.

Unlike Marty at the Starlight Ballroom, I was the dog who didn't risk being rejected, because I wasn't there to dance in the first place, and not only did I know it, everybody else also knew it. I co-opted rejection. I was stage crew. I had a job to get done. Standing around with my arms crossed expressed authority, but it was really the body language of insecurity and self-protection.

The pain on the inside no doubt kept me on the outside except for performance, which permitted transcendence through role-playing. But I was full of ideas, so instead of becoming a writer I became an "instigator," the genesis for which long preceded Hawthorne, although it was undoubtedly one of the things that got me there in the first place—always putting "ideas" in other kids' heads. I don't remember what the ideas were exactly, but I do remember "Don't be such an instigator!" Not standing up for the American flag, for example, was a bad idea.

Still, nobody ever went to jail for my ideas, and some of them might even have been pretty good. Like the time, when I was about eleven, when I thought up the idea of putting ice cream in soda and maybe selling the idea to a soda company. I even remember making the call and telling the idea to whoever answered the phone. The guy at the other end told me he thought it was a good idea, too, but nothing ever came of it. I was a font of ideas. Always inventing my way into something. I remember going down to the unfurnished basement of my last foster home in Bensonhurst thinking of how it might be possible for me to set up a movie studio down there by throwing blankets over the pipes on the ceiling and imagining them as sets, much the way I'd imagined my clay structures. But no matter how I figured it, I couldn't figure a way to get the camera, lights, and film.

Invention, for me, was survival. In one form or another, I'd been doing it all my life. And while my ideas may not have been always good ideas, the idea of having ideas was the right idea, and it's undoubtedly one reason why I gravitated toward the game shows on television. If I could make up ideas like that, I could be in a TV studio. Movies were a long way away, celluloid was mythical, as was Hollywood, but television was "live," and just over the Brooklyn Bridge.

When you're a kid instigator you're a bad influence because you're putting nonconventional ideas into other kids' heads, if that's possible, or ideas that threaten authority, which is very possible and which sounds like me. But when you're a grown-up instigator, and you're doing exactly the stuff you were doing as a kid, you're a "self-starter," an entrepreneur, or maybe even a "producer." Anything's possible.

I would eventually be made captain of the stage crew by one of the younger teachers in the department, Mrs. Grau. That kept me apart and, at the same time, allowed me the pinnacle of inclusion and engagement, as well as the "spotlight." Leadership and authority gave me control, of course, but control has as much to do with self-protection as it does with self-determination. For an artist, it safeguards a creative vision, but for me it was a protective barrier from hurt, and that self-imposed barrier is antithetical to real freedom. I wasn't Marty. He could bring his girl home to meet his mother. I couldn't bring her home. I could never risk this. Marty could make the leap; he could transcend it, working out his dance steps in advance, so he knew he could rise to the occasion. I couldn't. And I never danced.

> *I could have danced all night*
> *I could have danced all night*
> *And still have begged for more.*
> *I could have spread my wings*
> *And done a thousand things*
> *I'd never done before.*
> —Alan Jay Lerner,
> "I Could Have Danced All Night," *My Fair Lady*

As the chandeliers flew in from above, the stage at the Mark Hellinger Theater on Broadway transcended its earthly foundation. I leaned forward from my seat high up in the balcony, and my eyes must have widened in astonishment because at that very moment, as I turned to Miss

Windecker to share my wonderment, her anticipatory nod and tersely pursed lips curved into a knowing smile, a smile that took affectionate pride and satisfaction in the knowledge that the introduction had been hers, as if to say, "Aha. Yes. I thought so. . . . I thought you'd like that." The woman who had at first dismissed me, and who now had me seated next to her on this class outing, had become my mentor and perhaps something more. She was, after all, a spinster, and I was a foster kid, and so the relationship of student/teacher, speaking primarily from my vantage point, took on conceivably broader meaning. But she carried propriety with her, a standoffishness that volunteered nothing of her personal life, and demanded nothing of that nature in return. While she was unrelenting in her standards for excellence, she demanded nothing more than performance.

There is little doubt, however, that my desire to meet her expectations had as much to do with my winning her favor and acceptance, with all of its rewards of compensation and self-worth, as it had with my need to excel. Given the confidence she had placed in me—in itself rewarding—I believe she would have viewed my accomplishment as hers, as well. While we shared this commonality of distance, I inferred the restriction, respected the boundaries of her authority, and took comfort in both.

My Fair Lady, starring Julie Andrews, Rex Harrison, and the inimitable Stanley Holloway, was to be my first Broadway experience. It doesn't get any better than that. Act 1, scene 2, ends on Holloway's singing "With a Little Bit of Luck," and at the very end of the number, just as the curtain closed, he grabbed hold of it, almost draping it around himself, and traveled with it, instantly acknowledging that we were there, but teasingly shutting us out, making his way, I imagined, to the pub from whence he'd come. He swung as if he were the bouncing ball hitting all the notes, magnificently synchronous up to the musical button. I was ignited by his precision and the audacity of that moment of shared intimacy. Goose bumps. One could embrace an audience, receive its joyous approbation, and walk away scot-free, with them loving you all the more for it, and all on your own terms. The rafters shook with applause.

Suddenly the silent eye of a nonjudgmental lens that engaged and charmed you without risk to itself had a competitor. Full frontal risk before an audience. Not just dancing with one person, but with all fifteen hundred of them all at once. There was safety in a crowd. Intimacy at a distance, still. Being seen was better than not being seen anyway. Even the girls would be impressed. I could appropriate the approbation of the puppet. Very strange, though, especially for a kid who didn't dance. Except this kid could've danced. If he'd only had a way to get close.

10

Utensils

THERE IS SOMETHING that Jiminy Cricket once said that I never forgot: "If your heart is in your dreams/No request is too extreme/When you wish upon a star, as dreamers do" (Ned Washington, "When You Wish Upon a Star").

He gets carried away with the star stuff, perhaps, especially for those who need practical real-world answers, but I believe there's something there nonetheless. It is not something to think about so much as take to heart. And I can't explain it, any more than I can explain where passion comes from, except that I suspect Mr. Cricket would say that it comes from the heart as well. It makes no sense at all, I know, but as an accountant once said to me (he was actually an accountant turned author, which may account for how he could have said this), Who says it has to make sense?

Whatever it is, it usually drops in uninvited, unannounced, at its convenience, not yours, and never goes begging for takers. And since life's a merry-go-round anyway (stand still and you're still turning), you should lean toward it at all times, just in case, and reach for it as you would the brass ring (some people might say you can will it to you, and there might be something to that, too, especially if stars hear wishes, but you didn't hear it here). Should you catch some "luck"—"mazel" in Hebrew—then it's "mazel tov!" which means "congratulations" and also "thank God," which I somehow find more appropriate to my case.

Anyway, mazel showed up in Jewish Science at the Steinway Hall building on West Fifty-seventh Street in Manhattan on a Sunday morning. Enter the furrier.

Morris Jacobs, then probably in his late sixties, was one of those larger-than-life human beings—gregarious, outgoing, with big bright eyes and a warm, winning smile that could light up a room. He exuded an aggressive energy, a powerful life force that was both generous in its nature and eager to make itself available in any way that could help, especially, I sensed, for a kid. I had been introduced to him by my Big Brother, Fred, whom I would still meet on occasional Sundays in Manhattan. He and Morris both attended Jewish Science lectures, and I'd show up at the tail end of the morning lecture, which I gathered had more to do with a philosophy of living than anything religious per se.

As I was walking in one Sunday, Morris saw me, grabbed hold of my arm, and brought me over to a short, balding man, sixtyish, who looked me in the eye. This was Harry Salter, a bandleader who had created a popular television game show called *Name That Tune*, which I watched regularly. The show aired live on Mondays at 7:30 P.M. from CBS Studio 52 in Manhattan. Morris, as was his way, had taken an interest in my interests, and proceeded to sell me to Mr. Salter. Salter took another quick look and told me to show up the next afternoon at the studio. I would have shown up, gotten in my 80 percent, just to smell the studio. Anything that got me that far was worth the price of admission.

With one arm pushing me back and the other now around Salter's shoulder, Morris walked him to the elevator, and I could see that he was still selling him something, and I knew it wasn't a fur. I could only imagine. So can you. After Salter had gotten into the elevator, Morris came back and gave me that big-eyed smile of his. He never said a word. But if you can picture the cat that swallowed the canary, whole, with cheeks smiling wall-to-wall, that was Morris. *Naches.* That's what he felt. He'd helped a kid who could use some help. That was *his* reward. And I will never forget that smile.

> *Fate is kind,*
> *She brings to those who love*
> *The sweet fulfillment of*
> *Their secret longing.*
> —Ned Washington, "When You Wish upon a Star"

The next day, after school, I took the subway to Manhattan and the television theater—it was an actual theater that had been converted for television. I walked in the main entrance to the rear of the theater. The stage was straight ahead and, as usual, everything looked much smaller in person than it did on TV. Part of that had to do with all the wonderful equipment that was crammed up there: three television cameras on heavy pedestals (just as I'd built them in clay), at least one boom microphone, and lots of heavy coaxial cables, as well as the personnel for it all. There was a music stand with a black-and-white test pattern sitting on it, which the cameramen used to calibrate their cameras. The cameras each had four primary turret lenses to show the stage in varying degrees of depth, and hence a bigger appearance at home.

I was again struck by the agile yet economic use of space. The stage itself was very brightly lit, which is what black-and-white television required at the time. It looked hot, and it was. I was standing behind rows of empty theater seats, except for the front row aisle seat to the right, where Mr. Salter was sitting, watching a television monitor. There was magic in the air, and I stood transfixed. I was watching an actual camera rehearsal, which I'd never before seen.

The show's host, George DeWitt, was rehearsing with a contestant just twenty feet or so to Mr. Salter's left. Salter's focus, however, was clearly on the monitor, not on the reality of the stage just a few feet away. The *real* reality *was* the monitor. Everything outside the camera's viewfinder was irrelevant. I knew this because that's how I did it with clay. And not just with clay but also with every camera I'd ever had. Creation, after all, sprang from reality carefully framed and constructed, and game shows were the epitome of invention. I was looking simultaneously at both the chaos *and* the synthesis, the combination of which had always excited me. But this was no longer my imagination.

I was witness to a birthing. The show was being "choreographed." It was all about timing, movement, and rhythms, both in front of and behind the cameras, and an onlooker had an overview that would be lost to any one of its intimate participants. It was as if cameras were dancers, technicians their partners, and stagehands gymnasts—a balletic ensemble. And hence, my dilemma. It wasn't just about Holloway or the chandeliers, and it wasn't just about getting seen and getting close, either—it was about being in all places all at once. Impossible. Tell it to an eighteen-year-old.

I remembered being at that broadcast of *Caesar's Hour*. During the commercial breaks all hell broke loose—sets were literally torn apart and new ones erected. They had two, perhaps three minutes to make complete scene changes, and the studio audience would applaud the stagehands for *their* performance, which always seemed miraculous in its split-second timing. And at the precise moment when the last stagehand left the stage, the stage manager called out "Ten seconds!" Planning. Pacing. Movement. Timing. *Overview*. Shivers.

I walked down the aisle now, approached Mr. Salter, and reintroduced myself. He almost immediately passed me on to an employee, who turned out to be his brother and who instructed me about my job. I would hand out the sneakers to the contestants so they wouldn't slip when they ran down the stage to ring the bell to name that tune. That was it. Sneaker boy. And one of my first customers was an unknown young girl named Leslie Uggams. Soon she'd be singing.

During the broadcast that evening, as I stood at the far corner of the stage, I couldn't take my eyes off the pretty woman named Goldie who was standing right next to the lens of the camera. But it wasn't "pretty" I was watching. She held the cue cards. The show was on the cards. She held the show. I'd actually noticed her during the afternoon rehearsal. When the camera moved, she moved. And sometimes she moved ahead of the camera, to the next camera, because it had all been planned and she knew what shot was coming up next, and she had to be there for it or the host wouldn't have had his words. She was, quite literally, the walking script, and I liked her moves. As I watched her from behind the cameras, it looked as if the whole show moved with her, and she even had an audience behind her watching *her*. Boy, I liked that. Then I realized something else: Goldie didn't write the cards. A guy who smoked a pipe did that, with large metal felt-tipped markers. Really thick, refillable professional markers. I wondered why she would hold the cards and not write them. I could've done both.

And so as the weeks went by, I started talking to the guy with the pipe. I found out all about Bert and he found out a little about me, mainly my concerns about "hot spots" of light that were hitting the set and needed adjustment, or some other production element that I thought could have been improved on. As good as the show was, it could have looked even better. The Barry-Enright shows—*Twenty-one*, *Tic-Tac-Dough*, for example— looked great. Slick. Beautifully paced. Dramatic. The reflective flooring and backlighting on *High Low* were brilliant. A few of my ideas even made their way to others. Bert was an independent contractor, actually, and he provided cue card services for a number of shows. Eventually he even let me use his felt-tipped markers—just for practice. Here's the best part: I didn't have to work my part-time Western Union messenger job to pay them. They paid *me*. Fifteen bucks for the night. I was in television (and my printing was getting better and better all the time). Soon I'd be dancing.

Afoot and light-hearted I take to the open road,
Healthy, free, the world before me,
The long brown path before me leading wherever I choose.
—Walt Whitman, "Song of the Open Road"

Miss Windecker had chosen this poem for me to read at New York University's annual high school Poetry Reading Festival. It was my senior year, and perhaps she was offering it as a gift of encouragement. I do not believe it was an arbitrary choice, though; there was little about her that could be seen as arbitrary. I'd never read a poem before in my life, let alone recited one out loud. Still, she had chosen me, along with two of my peers, to represent New Utrecht High School in this citywide competition, which offered a scholarship to the winner.

Unrelated to this, I had applied to New York University for admission into their liberal arts program with a major in television and motion pictures, for which NYU was, and is, regarded as one of the world's leading universities. It was as relatively expensive in the sixties as it is today, and I had applied for a scholarship as well, notwithstanding the simple fact that my grades were only average. The thought that this might have been a determinant in their decision-making, or a detriment to me in any way, given my budding success, including my sneaker position at the CBS Television Network, had clearly not deterred me. And besides, I would never have let the facts get in the way of a dream.

It was now the early spring before my graduation and I was on a roll. I had been cast in our upcoming Varsity Show production of *Arsenic and Old Lace*. You may have seen the movie starring Cary Grant and with Raymond Massey in the role I was cast for. On Broadway, Boris Karloff played that role—Jonathan Brewster, a wanted murderer with a face that looks like Frankenstein's monster. I won't say I didn't think twice about this. I thought of Karloff, and I thought of Frankenstein, and of LaPenta getting to play the Cary Grant role, but then I thought, "Oh, hell, I'm an actor." I even bulked up with sweaters and a jacket to avoid

East Twenty-ninth Street, Flatbush, Brooklyn.

When I went home to take these pictures in the early '90s, almost nothing had changed, except the block was smaller and the street where we played stick-ball narrower. If you look carefully at my house (right) you can even see the flat brown aerial wire coming out of the living room window, and running up alongside of the house just like it did when our new TV came.

I remembered the front door being a bit wider, but of course I was a bit smaller. Maybe that's why Auntie had to step back so I could come in.

Left: The entrance to Hawthorne Cedar Knolls Residential Treatment Center for emotionally disturbed children where I spent almost three years of my childhood. It's as beautiful inside as out. No bars anywhere; control everywhere.

Left: A "happy" me at age twelve (a set-up job). I'm not only aware of the camera, I own it (an Argus 75, 620 film, twelve shots to the roll).

Right: Age thirteen. Bar Mitzvah. (More me than not).

Below: This is the clinic where I saw my social worker. George Frank's desk is just inside. The candy bars are in the middle drawer.

Above: Coney Island, 1953. A Sunday outing with a Big Brother for those of us who didn't have other visitors. Food was the one thing that came between me (center, right) and the camera.

Right: My "good boy" award.

Hawthorne Cedar Knolls School

Citizenship Award

Joseph Jacoby

For Outstanding Achievement in our Community

Left: Miss Windecker's speech and drama classroom on the fifth floor at New Utrecht High School, Boro Park, Brooklyn. Her office is just outside the door to the left. The only thing that's different is that our seats were nailed to the floor (movable chairs came in in the early '80s). I took this picture in 2001.

Left: Miss Mildred Windecker, chairman of the Speech Department. (New Utrecht High School archives: Photo: 1954)

Below: New Utrecht High School's main floor corridor that leads into the auditorium. The honor rolls, which date back to the 1930s (right wall), have been defaced. Mysteriously, they stop in 1960. Otherwise, it all still looks the same. (Photo: 2001)

Right: New Utrecht's auditorium, then and now. A thousand seats downstairs; five hundred upstairs. (Photo: 2001)

Nothing's changed.

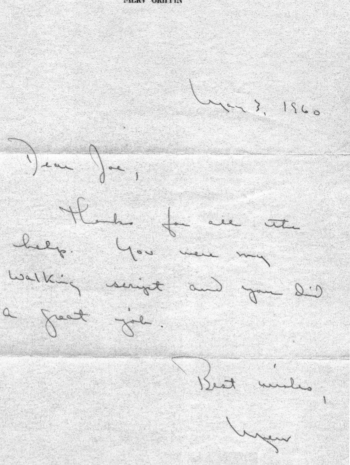

Mar 3, 1960

Dear Joe,

Thanks for all the help. You were my walking script and you did a great job.

Best wishes,
Merv

LITTLE THEATRE
240 WEST 44TH STREET
Bet. B'way and 8th Avenue, New York

MUTUAL OF OMAHA presents
KEEP TALKING
America's Hilarious Comedy Game
VOID IF SOLD   SEE REVERSE SIDE

TUESDAY
DEC 29 1959

DOORS OPEN
9:30 PM
DOORS CLOSE
10:05 PM

The independent contractor who wrote the cue cards for *Name That Tune* hired me to write and hold the cards for *Keep Talking*. Merv Griffin was its young host and I was, as always, the shy observer. I was instantly struck by his self-assuredness, his walk, and genuine interest in people. I would not have had the job long if he hadn't approved. He even kicked out the guys who were trying to sell him a new-fangled contraption called a Teleprompter. He pointed over at me during rehearsal one afternoon: "I got my guy," he told them (and I printed bigger letters, too). He gave me that silent nod of his, a tight-lipped smile of approval. A million bucks. That's how it felt.

Left: Morey Bunin, whose puppets, Foodini and Pinhead, I watched as a child. Morey invented a unique live animation process known as Aniforms. We did an Aniforms trade show together in the early '60s in Bermuda, where I took this picture.

Right: I was Morey's first trade show Aniform operator. It was new, I was there, and I worked cheap. (McCormack Place, Chicago, 1963)

Above: I am able to look through a two-way mirror and call out the names on the passersby's badges. I have a monitor and can see what they're seeing on the TV atop the booth, and I'm also able to hear them. Suddenly they're talking to a "live" cartoon! That was the uniqueness of the Aniform for which Morey later received a patent. (Note: The hand controls I am using are wrapped in black velour against a black velour background. The black and white image is seen in reverse polarity so that whites become black and vice versa and the controls become invisible. The effect is not really that of a puppet, but of a live animated character.)

210 fifth avenue, new york 10, new york • murray hill 5-7118

the bunin puppets

Dec. 14, 1963

Dear Joe:

Forgive me for not writing and sending this re-print sooner.
I have been terribly involved with getting ready for the
Garry Moore show and also in following up our Chicago convention, etc. etc., ad nauseum.....all of which you are familiar with...no?

I know you don't like the expression on your face in this
photo, but, but all of us do. You will note that you have
a credit as per my request.

We taped the Garry Moore show last nite. Since you can't
see it I'm sending a battered but readable script. You will
not find the writing particularly stimulating. It came off
cute and charming, but not with the guts I had hoped. Apparently they wanted to introduce him gently and if it didn't
come off they could drop it easily with no paing. I do
not know if they will do another as yet, but suspect they
will and this time I shall insist on a character delineation
and try to get some real comedy in the damned thing.

Marvin did the legs...and did very well. He will work out
O. K. He plods along until he gets it, but he doesn't have
your spontaneous spark. Yeh...I think you have spark Guiseppe.
Aurelio did the important arm, and charles did the other,
while I did the complicated head. The head turns from left
to right and the eyes are universal in action. He has a left
and right mouth and a big central grin. Pretty sophisticated
action really and he looked good on the monitor on playback.
Too bad you can't get to a set on Tuesday nite. Can't you
do it somehow....or is a buck private in training the complete
nonentity I think he is.

We're still wrestling with the $ problom at Aniform. Lots of
followup work to do on the amusement show. RCA is very very
interested in using Aniforms at the World's Fair. They have
the exclusive on closed circuit TV at the Fair and will do
everything in color. We may be part of it. I'll know soon.
They also are using MC's and will try to get the MC's to double
at Aniform operators. Hmmm....gives me an idea. Maybe when
you get back and we ARE working with them I can get you a crack
at it. Wow! That would be terrific experience and you have
the advantage of being an expert (?) Aniform operator! Morey and
his schemes! Sometimes they work though!

Aurelio can't work with us any more, so if we have more shows to
do on the Garry Moore program xx I have to look around for an
Artist Aniformer combination. know anyone? Aurelio is finally
getting busy on world's fair work

We are all look forward to seeing you at Xmas furlough. When
exactly do you get in. Florence moves today and tomorrow, so
you got a home!

We are all well, and why go into any more details when we'll be
seeing you soon.

                    Love from all of us to our
                favorite Joe!

                Morey

Above: I was in basic training at Fort Dix, New Jersey, when I received this letter from Morey.

Above: I play Carby Carburetor opening the show; everything revolves on a huge turntable containing four stages, each timed to begin and end at the same time for each of the four stationary 625-seat theaters, architecturally blended as one huge structure. There were four crews, each doing twenty shows a day, seven days a week. We worked a six-day week. I never thought of it as work.

Left and Above: I also did the Grease Monkeys, one on each hand, no extra charge.

Left: The New York World's Fair, Flushing Meadows, Queens (1964–65). The Chrysler "Show-Go-Round," at the Chrysler Pavilion. We performed in this theatrical venue.

Right: My first theatrical feature, *Shame, Shame . . . Everybody Knows Her Name,* opened at the Rialto II on Forty-second Street in New York City in August of 1970 and I sent Bil Baird a note. I don't know if he ever saw it, but his wonderful Christmas cards never stopped.

Bil Baird's Marionettes
59 barrow st · new york · 10014 · yu 9-9840

October 5, 1970.

Joe Jacoby
817 or 819 West End Avenue
New York City

Dear Joe,

Thanks for the flak. Will be seeing <u>Shame Ditto</u>.

Call me sometime -- I need the cooperation of

someone who knows the differences among such

terms as "internegative" - "buyout" - and "gaffer."

Nuts about you, *(old song)*

Bil

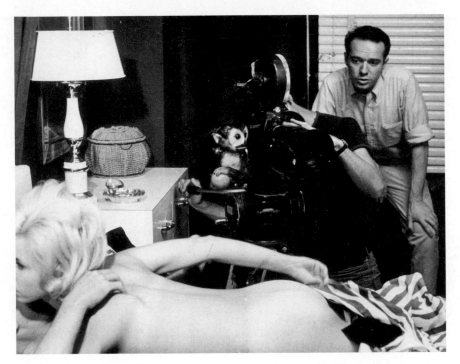

Directing my first theatrical feature, *Shame, Shame . . . Everybody Knows Her Name.*
This scene was photographed in an apartment in Manhattan. My cinematographer is
Stephen R. Winsten.

The Upper West Side of Manhattan. For the opening scene of the film, I wanted a rainy day
and got lucky. My recollection is that we moved a few things around to grab the right shot.

Northwest corner of Forty-second Street and Times Square. August, 1970.

Theatrical One-Sheet Poster for theater display.

Top: April, 1968. Riverside Park, Manhattan. Cinematographer Stephen R. Winsten (left of camera), me (facing camera).

Below: The Village Purple Onion, West Third Street, Greenwich Village.

Left: August, 1971. Shooting a scene from *Hurry Up, or I'll Be 30* behind the bar at Dr. Generosity's, a saloon at Seventy-third Street and Second Avenue in Manhattan. Left to right: Crew member Michael Barrow, Director of Photography Burleigh Wartes, me directing.

Below: The New York City theatrical advertising campaign for the release of *Hurry Up, or I'll Be 30,* in November, 1973.

Below: Movie mogul Joseph E. Levine in 1963 (age fifty-eight). In 1967 he sells his Embassy Pictures to Avco Corporation. When I meet and do business with him in 1972, he is perpetually miserable under the yoke of a corporate parent, notwithstanding the fact that it has made him a wealthy man. One day he complains: "If I want to buy a broom I have to call upstairs." For a lone wolf, gambler, and a man of independent mind (albeit a constantly vacillating one), I begrudgingly find respect.

Joseph E. Levine Presents

A Joseph Jacoby Film "Hurry Up, Or I'll Be 30"

Below: Opening scene at McDonald Avenue, Brooklyn. Left to right: Director of Photography Burleigh Wartes, me at the camera, Danny DeVito.

U.S.A. FILM FESTIVAL

Bob Hope Theatre, Southern Methodist University

is proud to have chosen

"Hurry Up Or I'll Be Thirty"

as one of the best U.S.A. citizen-directed films of the year.

March 25, 1974

Above: Judith Crist film selection. USA Film Festival at Southern Methodist University, Dallas, Texas. March, 1974.

Left: Spring 1976. Filming *Remember Those Poker Playing Monkeys* in a Baptist church in Madison, Georgia. (Released as *The Great Bank Hoax,* Warner Bros.).
Left to right: Burgess Meredith, me. His role was based on someone who had victimized each of us separately. As Jack Stutz—Israel Katz in real life—Burgess is plotting the robbery of his own bank. Katz would have said, "Trust me, and we'll sort this bloody thing out later."

Left: The poker-playing scene filmed in a private home in Madison, Georgia. Left to right: Director of Photography Walter Lassally (behind the camera), me, Burgess Meredith.

Above: Discussing a scene at the Baptist church.
Left to right: Michael Murphy, Ned Beatty, Walter Lassally, and me.

Left: A Hollywood trade campaign, sponsored by the Georgia Film Commission, that ran after completion of principal photography in the spring of 1976.

Davy Jones' Locker, starring
The Bil Baird Marionettes, 1995.

Top Left: Slugger Ryan (a rod puppet
operated from beneath) at the piano.
Crabbie's listening.

Top Right: Left to right: Captain
Barnacle, Patch, Joey.

Center: The pirate ship is fifteen feet long
and five feet wide. The original sky drops
are forty feet long and eighteen feet high.
While blocking this scene I must've been
thinking: "I came back. And I don't know
how."

Right: Since childhood, I'd been
enthralled by the overview, beginning with
my clay models. I stepped all the way back
one day and snapped this. I'm as enthralled
now as I was then.

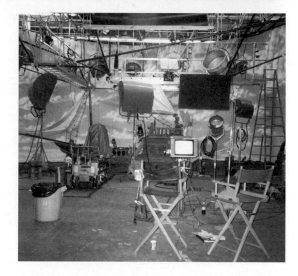

As I'm untangling Joey's strings, an ornery Davy Jones (the guy in the clam shell) squawks: "I hope you don't mess up your lines the way you screw up your strings."

Davy Jones' Locker premieres in December 1995 at Laemmle's Monica 4-Plex in Santa Monica, California for Academy Award qualification. Peter B. Baird (above), with whom I collaborated on the screenplay and who was the film's master puppeteer, as well as the voice for Davy Jones, was with me to share the experience. I believe he came to every show, first row center, and always with a bag of popcorn. He commented to me one day that he couldn't get over the joy of seeing the marionettes up there on the big screen, six feet tall.

Peter died of esophageal cancer on July 16, 2004. He was fifty-two. He considered this film his legacy.

My mother spent thirty-eight years in mental institutions. In October 1954, at the age of fifty-four, she was transferred to the Hudson River Asylum for the Insane in Poughkeepsie, New York (above), now known as the Hudson River Psychiatric Center. She would spend the last thirty-one years of her life here.

This original main Gothic building, designed by architect Frederick Clarke Withers, was completed in 1869 and is no longer in use, as is true of many former asylums. It was designated a National Historic Landmark by the National Park Service in 1989. (Credit: Joseph Jacoby)

As I recently discovered, photographs from Gary Jacoby's 1965 Bar Mitzvah album shed surprising light on my own quest. His father died in 2001. He was ninety-five years old and lived with his wife, Laura, in Forest Hills, Queens. His name was Benjamin Jacoby, the same name that's on my birth certificate.

Top Left: Benjamin Jacoby, Gary Jacoby.
Top Right: Joseph Jacoby.
Bottom: Benjamin Jacoby, Gary Jacoby, and Laura Jacoby.

that disappearing profile. It was awfully hot under those lights, but anything for the art. Moving from behind the scenes to in front of an audience must have been an act of willful assertion because I don't recall that I ever declared my availability, any more than I'd declared myself the morning I'd acted that scene from *Teahouse of the August Moon* in Miss Windecker's class. But in the wanting, I had brought it to me. An early incantation of my "self-levitation act," with all due homage to Jiminy Cricket.

Given my own insulated nature during those years, as well as the years that would follow, I am struck by the dichotomy of my social activity and the aloneness of my life otherwise. The scrapbook of those years seems to say that I was neither a recluse nor antisocial. I was an active participant in student government, having been cochairman of the planning committee, and was voted "Best Actor" in the celebrity section of our senior yearbook for my *Sing* and *Arsenic and Old Lace* performances. It didn't take a whole lot, I suppose, to get noticed.

I had been present in absentia, feelings of alienation that would resonate through my college years and beyond. Perhaps this sense of dislocation was a defense against hurt, for sure, but more than that, an expression of lack of self-worth and the expectation that discovery would lead to rejection. It was made bearable, paradoxically, by an evolving self-reliance that sprang from the absence of a family at the earliest stages of my life. If anything, the revolving foster homes reinforced this self-reliance, confirming "the permanence of impermanence," which led to keeping intimacy at a distance and thereby avoiding the risk of inevitable loss.

I did not win that scholarship, incidentally, though I would go on to the semifinals, competing against thirty-one other students who scored highest in the preliminary readings. And they turned down my scholarship application, too. But here's the good news: my application for admission was accepted. I was starting my freshman year in the fall.

∽

MY SOCIAL WORKER at the time, Mrs. Bernstein (Jean, but of course I never called her by her first name), had always been supportive and a terrific listener. Whenever I'd come visit her on Court Street, I'd have a story to tell. I *always* had a story. Her eyes would brighten, and a nice smile went with it, and then I smiled back and she liked seeing that, too, and that was always encouraging, and the next thing you knew I was conjuring full speed. My stories, though, were true, either about school or the game show or some idea I'd dreamed up for a new game show. I would bounce ideas off her, and sometimes in the bouncing off of ideas, new ideas would pop up, even as I was talking. My excitement must have showed through, because there was that smile again.

I was selling, for sure, but storytelling also was performance, and my enthusiasm sprang from that as well, and in the telling of these stories my ambitions shone through. But here's the catch: I'd sell at a loss if I had to, because in truth, it was all about approval. Stories for me were a sort of survival food, always a first and last line of defense. Selling something was my survival mechanism for as far back as I could remember, even if it meant shining shoes on Eastern Parkway for three cents a shine, at a probable loss, given the cost of polish and orange gook. Selling offered both approbation and penance. But whatever the story, there was passion, and a component of that passion was a plea for acceptance. It was the openness of this passion, the simple offer of wanting to share it— a sort of payment, if you will—that made her smile. If I were the theory, she would have signed off on the proof.

One day, as Mrs. Bernstein was escorting me out of her office to the narrow elevator at the far corner of the floor, Ida Freedman suddenly appeared from among the desks and file cabinets. I had not seen her since that rainy early morning about six years earlier, when we drove up Sawmill River Parkway to Hawthorne. Ida Freedman was Mrs. Bernstein's supervisor now and apparently needed to discuss something with her. She seemed her authoritative cold self, preoccupied. She then looked at me: "Hello, Joseph. How are you?" An acknowledgment that I was there but spoken as if I weren't there at all. It was the sort of avoidance I'd recalled in the car that morning. I had no stories for Ida Freedman. I detested this woman, but I feared her even more. She had lied to me before and could do it again. I don't know what Ida Freedman saw on my face at that moment, but while I am pretty certain I concealed the hate, I could not have concealed the fear. I stepped back, perusing the surrounding furniture. Freedman understood she had interrupted, and I caught a glimmer of awkwardness in her as well. She had to have known I didn't like her. She had to have known I didn't trust her. And she had to have seen that I feared her. She did not have to deal with any of it. But maybe she did.

Now that I know about Dr. Hulse, I understand why she wouldn't look at me in the car that morning. I think I understand now, too, why her answers had always been cold and abrupt. She herself needed rationales, and I suspect they were as elusive for her as any real understanding was for me. I had always wanted to know why they were sending me away. I could always rationalize it as punishment, but I never really understood it. And I don't think she fully understood it, either. The problem with doing things you don't believe in or understand is that they catch up with you somehow. I never even understood clearly what Hawthorne was and who it was for. I'm still not sure, although I'm sure it wasn't for me. And I had always felt, as a child, even then, that she knew she was doing the wrong thing.

∞

THE JEWISH CHILD Care Association of New York gave me a partial scholarship to go to NYU in the fall, and I was able to get a state student loan as well. Jiminy Cricket doesn't like to get into these things, but I don't think he's big on compensation. My sense with him is that there's a simple and direct through line between desire and attainment, without the murky business of setting things right. The power within you is really all you need. The power of the will and luck, while seemingly separate, have been known to work hand in hand. Personally, I don't care who gets the credit. But I still think I earned it.

Mrs. Bernstein worried about my survival, though. How was I going to live, and where? I told her I'd find an apartment, although I wasn't sure where. If I needed to (and I needed to) I could always find a roommate. She warned me there'd be many things I'd have to buy: furniture, dishes, utensils. I knew that furnished apartments could be found, and I could always buy dishes. I had a hard time grasping what the real concern was. The best part of the deal was that I could eat what I wanted to eat, when I wanted to eat it, and the milk would never get watered down again. I could come and go as I pleased and never have to report to anyone again. This wasn't defiance; this was simply unbridled enthusiasm for the freedom I had never known. This was going to be one great adventure. I had not a scintilla of fear or uncertainty, nor could I imagine how anyone could ever feel otherwise. I did not understand then where this concern came from, except as a projection of one's own experience. But the implicit genuineness of this concern did not escape me. Utensils, though, were a cinch.

I'd gotten the gold medal for stage crew and dramatics at my high school graduation, and then when Aunt Sadie had a sudden heart attack in the middle of the night and died, it was time for me to cross the Brooklyn Bridge anyway.

On the first day of fall orientation week, I was standing in front of NYU's Loeb Student Center across from Washington Square Park when a guy came up to me and stared. And kept staring. I think I stared back. Then he took a step back, as if to examine the merchandise more fully, just to make sure he'd had it right, and held that stare in disbelief. I probably took a step back, too. And then, smack out of nowhere, he just blurted out, "You're Joe Jacoby. You're the kid who kicked Mrs. Silver in the stomach. You were the school clown. It's me. Joe Israel."

And when he said that, *exactly* that, with that quizzical look of astonishment that I was actually standing there, on terra firma, no less, right in front of him, I looked at Joe Israel and wondered, "How'd he recognize me?" I wasn't sure I recognized him, but—boy!—I knew the name, all right. A lifetime of pain and uprootedness had transpired in the intervening years. How could it be that for Joe Israel, this could have been so vivid and ready a memory? Could I have left *that* much of an impression?! A "clown"? Maybe. Something of a "terror"? Okay, and most certainly "difficult" and "unhandleable."

In truth, I no longer felt like the Joe Jacoby he remembered, although I was still struck that I'd left an impression. Had I changed that much inside that I just couldn't be sure I recognized myself in his memory? Was this because this was a past I felt bad about, or was ashamed of? Or did I feel a loss of the kid he'd known back then? Had they succeeded in knocking something out of me, something I'd admired in myself? There was that moment of hesitation. "I was still me," I thought. "I must be. How else could he have known? I'm still here. I'm still the kid I remember being." I thought I'd changed so much, at least physically, but something there still showed through. This was such incredible news; this was such an extraordinary feeling, that all I could think to say was, "Yeah. Still here."

Part Four

Freedom

Patient is oriented, has some insight. She felt the whole

world was after her, due to the death of her mother.

11

"You Should Be a Producer"

"YOU SHOULD BE a producer," Harry Salter told me after I'd been fitting sneakers for a token living, and at that moment, I almost thought he meant it. After all, I'd been producing me, in one way or another, all my life, and here I was languishing backstage handing out sneakers and corduroy briefcases filled with Whitehall pharmaceuticals, the show's sponsor. I'd even taken one of these cases back to New Utrecht just to show them who I was now, which, of course, was a tip-off right there. But as evidence of my position in show business, or as some symbol of personal glory, this prized arrangement of Anacin tablets, assorted potions, emollients, and astringents just didn't impress. And mind you this was the same stuff "as seen on TV." My *Rootie Kazootie* cap, even *without* a feather, had more going for it than all these bottles put together, and you'll recall nobody knew me from that, either. I'd even gotten them to take out an ad in our Varsity Show playbill—"Compliments of *Name That Tune* on CBS." Nothing. I was still a nobody. What the hell did I have to do to get recognized? At this rate I'd never make it. And so I started dreaming up my own game shows.

Harry Salter's brother was a ne'er-do-well, a mean-spirited, embittered man who lived in the shadow of his brother's success, and under whose authority I worked on Monday nights. He'd been secretly scheming to prove himself the equal of his brother and had come up with a game show of his own. Well, sort of. I can't remember what he called it, really, but he'd sworn me to secrecy, in any event, lest his brother got wind of this treachery lurking in the shadows, and if so, I'd be a goner. There was never an idea attached to any of his thoughts anyway, unless you considered the wooden frame with the Plexiglas inset he had assigned me to build, an idea. In those early days of television, popular game and/or quiz shows had sets with lots of doors that opened and closed. They were called "isolation booths." So if you had the idea of an isolation booth and you plastered the sponsor's name all over it, you might've thought you had something. I was proud of that frame with a latch that authentically "clicked" when it opened and shut. You could write, and erase on the Plexiglas. I'd painted the frame battleship gray because everything in those precolor days, you'll remember, was battleship gray. Very professional.

Late one night, after everyone had left the office, he inveigled me into the deeper chasms of this conspiracy by slowly and stealthily unwrapping and revealing the photostats he'd made of Winston cigarette packs floating in the sky with clouds (not to be confused with *Lucy in the Sky with Diamonds*, which was still eight years off). These were *actual* Winston cigarette packs. I was impressed. Suddenly this thing was beginning to look like something, especially with a real sponsor's name on it, and I imagined they were somehow involved, which, of course, was the whole idea.

He searched my bright-eyed enthusiasm until it dawned on me that it wasn't my approval at all that he was after, it was instructions for what came next. He had as much of a clue about this as I did. All *I* knew was that you wrote something on the Plexiglas panel and it snapped shut: "click." And then you opened it: "click." That was it. That was the whole megillah. I thought *he* knew the rest.

A scowl crossed his face. I'd somehow disappointed. But deep down he knew, he *had* to have known, that he didn't have a show. I never told him there was nothing there. Now I had the sense that he was waiting for me to put something there. Something about me told him I could do that, or dream it up. I was this kid (something he resented, but something that held promise) who had failed his expectations and he just got meaner and meaner. I never asked for the money I'd laid out for the wood and the Plexiglas and the hardware. I never cared about that. What had meaning for me was that I was building a show, that I had been given an opportunity, and that my ability had been sought and trusted. It was the same old me, still. I needed the acknowledgment. I'd felt empowered as well, and I think that showed, and that was not a good thing. In my reach for recognition, I had showed a youthful hubris. I had not only outworn my usefulness, I had also shown myself undeserving of the opportunity I'd been given. So when Harry Salter said to me, "You should be a producer," what he was really telling me was that I was fired.

Fortunately, I'd met Bert. He was a self-employed independent contractor, and his company, Television Graphic Arts, supplied cue card and graphic arts services to independent television packagers (i.e., producers), and most of them were game show producers whose shows originated "live" from New York. I had just entered my freshman year at NYU when Bert called to tell me that his business had picked up and asked if I'd like to work for him on *Keep Talking*, a Tuesday night network game show that had moved from CBS to ABC. Boy, would I!

When *Saturday Night Live* debuted in 1975, "LIVE from New York" was a big deal, not only because it was coming from the city of high stakes, but also because live TV entertainment was, by then, a thing of the past. Live had everything to do with *risk,* the certainty that there was no certainty, that anything could happen, that anything could go wrong, and that by going wrong some things could go righter than planned, especially when you were dealing with cutting-edge satire and brilliant ensemble players. Chevy Chase could actually break his ass tripping down those stairs. And God only knew what Belushi would be up to, he flirted with danger—Joe Cocker or no Joe Cocker. Contemporary audiences are drawn to this for some of the same reasons I'd been drawn to it. Life in the moment is the medium's forte. Some of the best moments of live television for me, as a child, were the "mistakes" that happened, and that you waited for. Like the "frozen" Dr. Pauli on *Captain Video*, whom the camera caught talking to the stage manager, and who quickly refroze when he realized what had happened ("What, me not frozen?"). Or when a door opened and a camera dollied by. What the hell was a television camera doing on planet Eos, anyway?! The riggings behind "reality" were exciting stuff, and comforting, too, for a kid who saw reality as a construction, and a medium as the mirror image of life itself. The world was indeed a stage, and you could make it up as you went. And succeed.

Sid Caesar said seven simple words at the top of his show each week that, for me, heralded a thrilling event: "Good evening, and welcome to our show." That was it. Just those words. I saw and heard him say them live at the Century Theatre in Manhattan. You felt you knew him, and I wanted to let him know I was there, which is how you feel when someone comes into your home every week. When it's live, it's personal. It's a home visit, especially so when whoever it is in front of that lens exudes a certain unquantifiable honesty, if only through human foibles. He made the human equivalent of Dr. Pauli unfreezing. He coughed a lot. He jumbled up his words. You don't fake honesty; not through the lens you don't. And as childish as it sounds, you forget he doesn't know *you*.

"They think they know you," Danny DeVito would say to me years later as we were walking up the street and people approached or pointed at him, as if to say, "I know you" (and he good-naturedly pointed back, deflating their friendly folly). I thought I knew Sid, especially since, like all those shows I watched as a kid, he went where I went. They were my touchstone. But I never applauded beforehand. It would've gotten him nervous, and he would've started coughing again. He would have expected more of me.

"Ten seconds," the stage manager called out flatly, and Caesar did his nervous best to quiet the audience with hand gestures. You could hear a pin drop. The orchestra had abruptly stopped tuning. "Five seconds." He coughed once or twice; cleared his throat. He needed to cough (I think it was nervousness). And then, suddenly, like magic—the off-camera singers: "*Caesar's Hour, Caesar's Hour*, welcome to *Caesar's Hour.*" And the camera swung over, the spot hit him straight-on (and he coughed maybe), and he said the magic words (not always in order, but he said them): "*Good evening, and welcome to our show.*" Orchestra go! It was all over for me. Everything moved! *Goose bumps.* The announcer (Hugh Downs) jumped in, Caesar jumped off to change for the first sketch, and it was nonstop *electric live* from there. A Broadway show every week.

They could not—they *could not*—do that today.

In his final show, in May 1957, Sid Caesar did a light opera based on *Cyrano de Bergerac*, and his nose fell off. He turned a fallen nose into a nose job! And given his brilliance, nose or no nose, he *still* looked like Cyrano. Hail Caesar! indeed. *Saturday Night Live* rekindled the danger that had always been the magic of television. It was "managed risk" long before we'd ever heard of such a thing, and I'd been watching and practicing it since childhood.

So when I reported for duty at the Little Theatre on West Forty-fourth Street on Tuesday nights, I'd already imagined myself there, anyway, and I just did what I'd already imagined myself doing.

On one cold winter night, standing in front of a radio store window with my mother, I saw for the very first time a television set—a bare metal chassis upon which sat a picture tube surrounded by lit vacuum tubes. On this

*particular picture tube there were two dancing marionettes bouncing up
and down on roller skates. I was ignited.*

I was now on the other side of the window.

∞

HE WALKED A certain way. It was a sort of purposeful bounce, self-
assurance in each step. I liked that. Though he was only in his midthir-
ties, something told me Merv was going to be very successful. I saw
something I admired: an attitude, a manner, a certain professional
mien. I took it in. I was making myself up as I went along, and I was
now in the presence of winning role models. I'd been making me up all
my life, anyway. When I wanted to be in a club, I made up the club and
made myself chief. Besides, show business was all make-believe, anyway.
This was familiar turf. Even some of the people were make-believe.

I was the show's walking script. This was an awesome trust, and I
understood that. And just as I'd read the people around me, I suspect
they'd read me as well. I was full of focus and passion, and I could be
counted on, and I think that's what Bert saw, and the rest of them saw
it, too. It's very simple. Passion can be trusted. The cue cards were what
mattered, and my holding them at the right camera at the right time.
I jumped over coaxial cables and ducked under cameras as I made my
way from one camera to the next and back. I had memorized the shot
list. I knew every cue and what came next. If a camera went wide I knew
when to stand back, and how far. And when she moved in, we ren-
dezvoused. I'd found my dancing partner, and the image orthicon tube
with the turret lens was no less a heartthrob for me than was Alice Blue
Bonnet for Johnny Fedora. I never lost sight of the audience behind me,
either. *I* was "performance art" long before the phrase was coined. The
machinations of behind-the-scenes production had always been performance art for me, and I was part of its ensemble. This was puppetry,
after all: manipulation, control, timing, and movement—*live* television,

and always up against the lens—not even six degrees of separation. I courted millions with no one any the wiser. And for the studio audience, where I'd once sat and for whom I now danced, I was invisible for all to see. There was power in this. In holding the cards, I held the show.

Merv had a tendency to squint, and since he didn't wear contact lenses, my cue-card lettering was extra big. And when I'd catch his eye, he'd nod in satisfaction, but I never bothered him with words of my own, any more than I had preapplauded Mr. Caesar. This discipline, I believe, came not only from my early observations of professional decorum, but also from a need to fill the vacuum in my own life with fantasies I considered sustainable and realizable. I had an inborn and practiced awareness of cause and effect, a knowledge that the attainment of a goal required a kind of tunnel vision—stubbornness, if you will, another bad quality from childhood that transmuted into an adult asset. I'd learned early on that an action produced a reaction. Even "destructive behavior" and testing produced results, results that at times stunned even me. Self-empowerment fueled by passion, uncontrollable in any event, produced the best results.

"ABC's looking to do a half hour news show for kids," Bob Prescott, our burly, mustachioed sound effects man, bellowed at me at rehearsal one evening. He came to me, I suspect, for some of the same reasons Harry Salter's brother had. Bob was a jovial Santa figure and one of few of a then-dying breed from the old radio days, a live sound effects man. He sat with two small gray boxes between his knees, like bongos, and his job on *Keep Talking* was to sound the bell or buzzer when cued by the producer, who simply tapped him on the shoulder when he thought the time was ripe to move on to the next team. Aside from having to get on and off the air at the precise split second, this was as precise and high tech as it got. I remember taking the old NBC behind-the-scenes tours as a kid, and next to looking at the cameras, the sound effects demonstration fascinated me most. And so it was my passion, again, that probably gave me away, and my interest in all things production: "But they think only fifteen minutes of news will hold them. We need something for the other fifteen minutes. Any ideas?"

"What about the Bunin Puppets?"

"Do you know them?"

"Sure."

"You think they'd be interested?"

"I'll call and find out."

Maybe Harry Salter was right. Without even knowing it, I was already acting like a producer. I lied. Well, I didn't *really* lie. I *did* know them, but not the way Bob thought I did. Of course, I said it so he'd think it. After all, I'd watched them throughout my childhood, which had only been ten years ago—every day after school. *Foodini. Pinhead. Jolo the Clown, and Hostess, Doris Brown.* They were my friends. It's just that they didn't know *me.* But I wasn't going to let a minor technicality get in the way of a good idea. Besides, I'd sent away for their stuff: a set of cast pictures. How would they know they *didn't* know me? Puppets don't remember anything anyway. I had a hell of an alibi. And I knew they hadn't gotten any older. So if they appealed to me they'd appeal to kids today, too.

I had license, after all—I was working on an ABC show, a legitimate source had come to me and asked for an idea, and so I had every good reason to call. I'd always wanted to meet Foodini, anyway. Don't ask me why. I'd never really thought about him. There was no game plan here. I didn't want to be a puppeteer. I just pulled it out of thin air. The worst that could happen was that I'd call and get turned down, and that would be the end of it. This kind of rejection, just like Harry Salter's firing, I could handle. Besides, this could be the opportunity I'd been waiting for, and that would've overridden any fears of anything anyway. So I looked them up in the phone book, asked for Mr. Bunin (who answered his own phone, by the way), said I was working at ABC, and could I come down and talk with him about a new show we were putting together? "Sure, kid. When do you want to do it?" It couldn't have been easier. I had to listen carefully, though, because he spoke softly, almost in a mumble.

We set a time at his studio at 210 Fifth Avenue. And I remember thinking: "He doesn't sound at all like I imagined," and then it hit me. I'd just gotten off the phone with Foodini. At 210 Fifth, I entered a narrow building, walked down a narrow hallway, and got on a narrow elevator that slowly and painfully made its way to the fourth floor. The elevator door opened and closed with a bang, much amplified by the empty anteroom in front of me. It was not something you would not hear. He had the entire floor. I walked a few feet. An open door on the right looked down a long, narrow hallway that led to a machine shop in back. Inside the open door to the left, perhaps no more than fifteen feet in from the doorway itself, was a lone figure sitting at a wooden desk: a bald, bespectacled, middle-aged man in a white open-collared short-sleeved shirt, seemingly immersed in paperwork.

As I approached, he glanced up, rose from behind his desk, smiled a tight-lipped smile while removing his plain-rimmed glasses with the white adhesive tape attached to one of the frame's arms, neatly folded them into his shirt pocket, and with his head bowed, came around to greet me: "Hi. How're you?" he asked in a soft-spoken, understated way. I saw shyness, a withdrawn kind of warmth, but warmth nonetheless. He was a muscular man who stood about five-eight, and even though he'd walked only a short distance from behind his desk, I noticed a slight limp in his gait, which struck me as more of a halting body language than an injury. He seemed older than his forty-nine years, although when you're eighteen anyone over thirty is almost dead. But even in retrospect, he seemed older, tired. And he was.

As I entered his spacious office area, my eye caught the glass cabinet against the wall at the far left. I just stopped. Just as that bygone movie studio had felt like a cathedral with the dust-filled beam of light coming down from the skylight, what I felt now was just as magical. I had just run into my childhood. Inside the glass cabinet were all my friends: Pinhead, Jolo the Clown, the Dowager Lady and her butler, Hotchkiss, and, of course, Foodini the Great. I stood silent. I looked at Morey Bunin and he smiled at me. "Would you like to put one on?" I doubt I could have answered, but he already knew. He went to the cabinet and opened one of the two glass doors. He reached for Pinhead and Foodini both. I was struck by their smallness, perhaps twenty inches, though they were larger than any puppet I'd ever put on. They had always filled my set. They had always filled my life. They were *bigger* than life. I had never seen them in color, either. They were black-and-white people. It took a moment getting used to. I would have preferred to have seen them in their natural black-and-white.

They were motionless, now, but not like they were sleeping. Their eyes were open wide. Large eyes. All the Bunin puppets had large eyes that didn't blink. It made me uneasy to see them this way—static, vacant. I had gone backstage at *Rootie Kazootie* and saw him hanging upside down on a brass ring. But Foodini, Pinhead, Jolo, and all the rest were not so indecently exposed. Their heads rested upright on wooden dowels just under their jaw. They were dignified, stoic in their repose. Morey handed Pinhead to me. "Go ahead," he said gently. "Put him on." The rest is a blur. I doubt I performed right then and there. I would not only have been intimidated; it was almost a sacrilege for me to be holding him like this. I was trespassing on the very illusions that had sustained me through much of my childhood.

There was a puppet stage in the corner with a dark velour front and collapsible wings, left and right. The stage was of a custom-made lightweight metal on wheels, easily portable, with a velour curtain that rose up and down in the center, but with no proscenium, no scenery. It felt not so much like a theatrical stage as it did a utilitarian platform for presentations, perhaps the kind of stage you would use if you were performing on the *Ed Sullivan Show* or as a novelty act. It commanded your imagination, though, as did Burr Tilstrom's Kuklapolitan Players Kukla, Fran, and Ollie, where all was character, banter, and story-driven, with scenic vistas in the realm of your mind's eye. The physicality of Foodini on television, however, was a different matter entirely.

Although primarily driven by character, more so than, say, Bil Baird's marionettes, which were, and are, the personification of theatricality, Bunin's settings were minimal, fitting to a puppet's life in ways that Ralph Kramden's apartment did to his. You never saw the Kramden bedroom, for example, but you imagined what it looked like. So defined were Morey's characters that they could sustain themselves in limbo, without sets, if need be.

Seeing the stage, I realized now that he performed standing up. How I coaxed him I can't recall. Whether by outright request or through indirection, misdirection, one magician to another, I don't know how. I told him I'd watched his show as a child when I came home from school every day, but he knew that. I must've had a million questions, too, and I told him I'd sent in my drawing of Foodini's laboratory but that I'd never heard anything back. I did not see him leave, but all the while he knew what I was asking for. He got younger, too. And then, as if from nowhere, the other side of Morey suddenly appeared before me, looking down now from center stage: "Hmmm. What have we here?!" Foodini's eyebrows lifted in astonishment, his moon eyes piercing right through me. I was as stunned to see him as he was me.

"Gadzooks!" His eyebrows rose still further; his eyes showing ever greater amazement. (They were not articulated eyes—they could not move—but you would not have noticed.) "We have a guest! It's Joe Jacoby. A friend of Bunin's, no doubt." As his hand rubbed up and down against his cheek, his head shaking in consternation at having been caught so completely off-guard, the eyebrows lowered once again and he suddenly bellowed, "DUNDERHEAD!" Looking down now into what must have been his laboratory in the basement (Aha! *That's* where it was), lambasting Pinhead: "Why didn't you tell me we had a guest coming?! I could have prepared something. What a predicament. What a predicament." He paced now, left, right, left, right. . . . "Woe is me . . . Woe is me."

The quiet, shy, mumbly man who had been standing here just moments ago had gone. The Great Foodini of my childhood had remembered me. And as he conjured, I'd forgotten why I'd come. But I was home.

∽

ABOUT A YEAR would pass. My sound effects friend over at ABC never did get that kids' show off the ground, even though I'd told him the Bunin Puppets were available. Aside from my cue card work, I was a fully matriculated student now at NYU, with a full day schedule, but I kept contact with Morey anyway, occasionally calling to see if he could use me in some way. He would tell me that things were "in the works" and to "stay in touch, kid," always leaving me with the hope that some kind of work might develop. At the time I'd met him he had fallen on hard times, something I would not become aware of until much later. The puppetry of the fifties that had been so much a part of my life and that had put him and his puppets into the national limelight was no longer fashionable, having given way to sixties animation. Television is a business of fickle trends, economy, and speed. He knew he would have to adapt to an evolving medium in a way that could compete. The "limited" style of animation, such as the animation done at the Hanna-Barbera studios in California, was increasingly popular, and easier to execute than the costly Disney-style full animation, often referred to as "drop shadow" because of its three-dimensional detail. Morey was then at the early stages of melding puppetry with live video in a way that presented the puppet form as animation. It evolved from its initial trials as a rubbery upright puppet form into one that made use of video, essentially a two-dimensional flexible form that appeared as a line drawing of a cartoon character on a TV monitor. He would eventually be awarded a patent for it. The character, manipulated like a puppet, interacted with passersby who looked up at a monitor sitting atop the booth, as the operator, sitting inside the booth, engaged them in conversation, looking through a small, one-way mirrored window. A two-way conversation with a cartoon? Impossible! "Hey, Harry—come over here. Ya gotta see this! He talks to you!"

I became Morey's first trade show Aniform operator. I would pull stunts, like the time a guy named Harry walked by and the cartoon spoke to him through the TV monitor. Harry couldn't believe his eyes and ears and called his friend Sam over to see this. "Talk to my friend Sam here!" he said to the monitor, and the character froze. Sam thought Harry was nuts. "Say something!" Harry implored of the cartoon. Still nothing. Sam gave Harry a look and walked away. Now the character sprang to life and challenged Harry to call someone else over. Morey caught it and thought it was hilarious. Profitable mischief.

I once did a show for American Standard, manufacturers of toilet bowls, working from a booth behind their latest models and surrounded by pebbles as part of the decor. I overheard one woman whisper to her friend, "I wonder where the john is around here." (Talk about the power of suggestion!) The Aniform sprang to life: "Use the kitty litter!" pointing to the pebbles below. Laughter all around. Only a puppet can get away with this.

When I met him, Aniforms, Inc., was in its early infancy and would, in time, evolve into a viable business, effective primarily for live industrial presentations and trade shows. I never had the ambition to become a puppeteer, although performance was something that drew me. Beyond my love for puppets as a child, something shared by most children universally, the puppets I watched on television were, for me, a connecting link to something more profound, and a refuge from the world of uncontrolled and *uncontrollable* chaos that I had experienced as unreliable and unpredictable. They were a continuity, surrogates for the love I'd left behind, the trusted remnants of my abandonment. In finding my "friends" from a time past, I could reconnect to a love without fear of rejection and at the same time seek continuity.

Two marionettes dancing on roller skates as I peer through the radio store window, my mother at my side, setting my eyes on the first television set I have ever seen.

After my freshman year I found a furnished studio apartment on West Eighty-ninth Street, between West End Avenue and Riverside Drive in Manhattan. I purchased a few utensils. Unbeknownst to me, the Bunins lived across the street. In time he; his wife, Charlotte; his two daughters; and a young son, David, became my surrogate family. I learned puppeteering from a master. As a means of sustaining himself during the difficult years of Aniforms' development, he booked dates during the summer months at such places as the Kentucky State Fair in Louisville—right behind the baby animal farm. And I played Pinhead.

Were I to put this in a book, nobody would believe it.

12

Present in Absentia

THE SUMMER AFTER my freshman year was also marked by a relationship, my first real relationship with a woman (or a girl, as we would say then), which even at this writing I was prone to gloss over. It had a profound emotional impact on me, in part, I believe, because of its direct linkage to events of my early childhood.

Her name was Maryann. It was the summer of my freshman year at NYU. My dorm roommate knew a girl he thought I'd like, and thought she'd like me, too. She was my age, nineteen, lived with her mother in a suburban home in New Jersey, and I was instantly smitten. She had been a beauty pageant contender and desperately wanted fame as an actress. My roommate was taking acting classes, which I think is how they met. Perhaps he told her I'd be a big producer someday (I wouldn't have minded). The burn of her ambition echoed mine, and that shared passion may be what drew her to me, but even now I am somewhat puzzled. She was quite a beautiful and sophisticated girl and I bad-complected and anything but. I was working in live television and maybe she believed that I could somehow advance her career, sooner than later, or perhaps just the idea that I was working in the entertainment business at all held a certain allure. As hard as it was for me to accept, even now, maybe she just liked me. Maybe it was just me that didn't like me. Half of that is certainly true. But the thought of her liking me, just for me, would have to appear last on my list.

Believing in me, or where I might be going in life, would have been invigorating. The encouragement one feels from another's belief in you, especially when you're both very young and in love, even if that encouragement is driven by one's own agenda, particularly if it is driven by one's own agenda, has got to be genuine and therefore affirming. Given my history, I was discomforted on one level but surely affirmed on another. After all, she had confidence in me.

Other than my years with my mother and the ones in my first "permanent" foster home in Flatbush, I had not known emotional intimacy or accessibility. No family, no siblings, no friends in the first seven years of life. If familial networks are like neural networks, wired early on, then I was emotionally stillborn, disconnected, and isolated, save for my relationship with my mother.

I was easily threatened, but I also had an inner refuge, supported by an imagination grounded in and propelled by my passion. So while wide-open exposure would have led me to anticipate dire results, I could suspend my doubts, override my fears, and allow for something I had never known before, even if she had an agenda. Besides, I had no control over this. An agenda, in fact, would have been justifiable compensation to her for her interest in me, anyway. I could overlook my undeservingness and accept my good fortune, but I could never not know better. Perhaps my passion itself was my compensation to her. If you are looking to atone, what is created from within can be given away as payment. It is an offering whose primary rewards are acknowledgment, recognition, and acceptance.

Enter the mother.

Maryann lived alone with her mother, and the woman was a powerfully controlling force in her daughter's life. Nothing was ever going to come between them or in any way disrupt the agenda her mother had set for them both. Maryann had actually made this quite clear to me early on. This struck me even then as a stereotypical "stage mother/daughter" relationship. I suspect her mother believed that Maryann's feelings for me were genuine and hence all the more threatening, both to Maryann's ambitions and most certainly to their relationship. She undoubtedly also understood that my career was too far off to justify any confidence her daughter placed in me as "a comer." To the contrary, I was a disruption. I met her only once, as she stood silent and judgmental midway down the stairs, getting a look at me now for the first time. Hers was not so much a greeting as a deflection, as she gave Maryann some instructions of one sort of another before heading back up.

I knew instantly. The denouement was foretold. So this very brief summer romance would come to an abrupt end, in a way that is every young lover's worse nightmare: we got caught. One summer night we started on the couch on the screened front porch and worked our way down onto the linoleum floor, when we heard her mother's footsteps coming down the stairs. Not speeding down, mind you, perhaps even giving us due notice. Fortunately (or unfortunately) nothing had begun, and we hurriedly got off the floor. The woman sensibly stopped at the stairs inside, and Maryann rushed to her. I stayed on the porch, of course. It was a horrible feeling to know there was nothing I could say or do. She knew what we were up to, and she knew it would happen again.

I was deeply in love with Maryann, but I would never see her again. The pain of this rejection was almost unbearable. I called incessantly. In a voice of total and complete detachment, she told me her mother had forbidden her to see me ever again. She told me never to call. No matter what I said, there was not so much as a trace of feeling or hope in her voice. I simply could not reconcile this with the girl I knew the night before. She might as well have been another person; she may, in fact, have been another person. This was now the mother's voice I was hearing. My fears and suspicions had been borne out. I had shown that I was not deserving. Her mother's rejection of me, as much as hers, was confirmation of any mother's rejection of me, and not just my own, and while I could not perceive the full dynamics of this at the time, her mother's disapproval of me had to have struck at the heart of not only my unworthiness, but also my unresolved feelings about my own mother, the two being inseparable. Maryan had shut down completely, though. But consider: she was an only child; the father had gone; her mother's recognition and approval provided the most meaningful relationship in her life; and finally, she could disconnect—put behind anything that threatened. My roommate was right. In so many ways, she was the mirror me. There are understandings and attractions that speak to us mysteriously.

I have her picture, still, a picture I took as we walked by the lake in Central Park. I see a radiant warmth in her smile that is either asking for or offering love. Perhaps both. And a wiser man now sees, still, what the nineteen-year-old saw then. And if it came my way today, I would fall all over again. But then, I did fall again.

Up on the screen, the English actress Athene Seyler, playing an eccentric dowager in one of those British screwball comedies, *Make Mine Mink*, was screaming "FIRE! FIRE!" It's the only damn thing about the picture that I can remember, in part because Seyler's hysterical delivery was so funny, but mainly because the flame sitting four seats over to my right was so cute that I could not help but not see the picture.

∞

WE'D EXCHANGED SMILING glances the day before, crossing each other at opposite sides of the light on Washington Square Park. She'd been with her friend Val that day and I'd somehow arranged for Val to let her know that I liked her and I suspected the feelings might be mutual (it really does only take a moment), and so Val the matchmaker came along, too, just for safety's sake. I'm not certain how I knew Val; she was probably in one of my classes, though, and I believe she was

Carolyn's roommate. What Carolyn was doing sitting four seats over, I'll never know. I must've kept it vague. One of those "I'm interested, but not really interested, but bring her along anyway." However this thing got engineered, my thumbprint was all over it. If there was any rejecting to be done, I'd handle it. Intimacy at a distance. Four seats away.

My perception of those days was that if a girl liked you she didn't just come right out and tell you that, but she'd let you know it—a smile, a glance, no different really than it's ever been. But then it was up to you to do something. You didn't just sit around waiting for her to call. Girls today will go the distance. But we were on the cusp, remember. Guys called girls. Back in high school, I at least dialed the first six digits before hanging up (oh, yes, many times). Besides, Carolyn was shy, just as I was, and I think that's part of what instantly drew us to each other. It was that lovely, shy smile that bit me and, of course, her acknowledgment. She was a scholarship student from Baltimore and lived at NYU's Judson Hall ("the Judson"), idyllically situated on Washington Square Park, and when you came over to pick up your date, you waited in the "sitting room" downstairs. We may have just passed the age of innocence, but there were vestiges, remember. In film there is a thing called a "dissolve." At a moment in time, both images exist simultaneously, one superimposed over the other, until the outgoing image vanishes entirely and the incoming image is solidly before you. The very early sixties were midpoint in that dissolve.

I was a sophomore and she a freshman. She was not only smart, she was also warm and she liked me and that was just overwhelming. When I introduced her to the Bunins, Morey later told me she reminded him of a Danish girl he'd once dated whom Charlotte lovingly referred to as "Morey's Danish pastry." So successful was I at burying my past from myself that I had equal success in burying it from everyone else in life, including Carolyn. While I must have alluded to my foster homes, and perhaps even said my mother was "sick," I don't think I ever went beyond the most minimalist of answers, and I suspect I sent out enough protective flack to divert any heat-seeking questions. Nonetheless, ours was a relationship that quickly heated and pretty soon Carolyn was sleeping in late in her room at the Judson and cutting classes and we knew she was putting her scholarship in jeopardy. She was so smart, though, and so well read, that even I thought she'd find ways to get around it.

However, the idea of my cutting classes or losing my scholarship, one based essentially on need and not academic excellence, like hers, was unthinkable. For me, survival and goal attainment dictated discipline. It's not something I thought about. I just lived it. And so while her discipline faltered, mine could not. I could not have allowed anything to get in the way of my school performance, and hence the loss of my scholarship. The only backup I had in life was myself and my goals, and the discipline to assure both. Often, I wouldn't even know that she'd slept in or skipped classes until the day was over, and I'd call her after my own classes.

In the Department of Television, Motion Pictures, and Radio, otherwise known as the "TMR Department," focus, discipline, persistence, and ambition put you on the fast track. The speed at which you excelled was in large measure defined by what you came in with. My focus was television. It was live and immediate. I had the sense that television was still making itself up as it went along, and that spontaneity and seat-of-the-pants invention—really a mirror of my own life—had resonance. I worked in it part-time. I had access. It made sense to put my focus there.

While I had always loved movies, they were too far distant and out of reach, and there wasn't the immediacy and adrenaline rush of a live broadcast. Besides, movies were about telling stories, and I didn't have any stories to tell. Or rather, to tell the stories I might have told would have meant exposing and exploring what I'd spent my life hiding, avoiding, and running from. And what's more, my stories, even if I could've told them, would have been labeled a *Shandeh*—stories to be ashamed of, truths to be swept under the rug. Student filmmakers I knew and respected, those who took themselves and their craft seriously, wrote what they knew, even if in the form of thinly disguised fiction. They reached into themselves and their life's experience for inspiration and content. There weren't too many bona fides, but I can think of one: Scorsese. Marty's passion for cinema and discipline were so interlinked that it was impossible to separate them. I either did not have the content, or whatever content I had was in discontinuous pieces, impervious to examination. I was in the process of self-invention or reinvention. I could not have overseen my own deconstruction so early.

Marty and I were street kids from New York, and since the TMR Department wasn't that big in those days, and since we both had the same grade adviser, it really is no mystery that we connected. He was always impeccably dressed, and more than once he tried to get me to come down with him to see his tailor in Little Italy. I had neither the money nor the style of dress he had. He didn't have any money, either, but he dressed well anyway. For me, his impeccable dress and manner always connoted his discipline and self-respect.

For a while I hosted a quiz show I'd created for WCAG, NYU's closed-circuit radio station that "broadcast" into the Loeb Student Center on the Washington Square campus. It was called *Music Quiz Style*. I asked Marty if he could put together the music; he had a large record collection, especially classical music, which I was completely unexposed to. His knowledge of music seemed as endless, even then, as his passion and knowledge of film. One day he showed up precisely on time—*always!*—nattily dressed—*always!*—with his attaché case at his side. He opened it and pulled out a stack of four-by-six index cards with the questions and answers, and he had the records, too. I would read a question to the contestants, the music would play, and if they didn't give the correct answer, I supplied it. I hadn't bothered looking over the cards, and found I couldn't pronounce "Giuseppe Verdi." I mangled it badly. Marty was standing four feet away and couldn't help but show a kind of low-grade giggle, but not a mocking giggle, a compassionate, understanding sort of "I agree with you. I don't know why they gave him such a ridiculous name that nobody can pronounce anyway" giggle. Shades of the director right there.

This was the sixties, a turbulent time, a great time to reinvent yourself. Greenwich Village in the sixties was on the cutting edge at a very special time. John Kennedy came one day to campaign, and a kid yelled out, "We want Nixon!' And Kennedy fired back, "Well, you're not going to get him!" And the crowd roared. He spoke to us. Just for a moment. An indelible moment.

But don't be fooled: I may have shown up for class, and I recall the bits and bites, but I was actually absent most of the sixties (I haven't a clue where I went). To say that I was out of synch would be an understatement. I was out of time with my own generation. I did it all by rote, and if I was improvising, I wasn't aware of it. Here I was in the heart of Greenwich Village and I barely paid it a visit. I found that I was more in lockstep with the ungrateful dead of the past than the here-and-now of the present. I couldn't kick the "goodness," damn it. Hawthorne had instilled the fear of doing anything wrong, and the sixties were all about doing the wrong thing. I'm always there, always included, but present only in absentia. There were just enough remnants of my past—the compensatory damage, the feelings of unworthiness—to keep me always a tad out of tune. I barely inhaled. I'm the Woodstock generation but I missed that, too, and I wasn't smoking anything, either, because I didn't do drugs. An NYU film student, Michael Wadleigh, made *Woodstock*; I got the album.

But I got by. The few friends I had were themselves observers or loners, and strongly inner-directed and ambitious, although Marty was both, a keen observer and disciplined hands-on participant. No loner he. I've often wondered how many others felt like me. Alienated. Excluded. Not from the culture, but from the *counter*culture as well.

But at NYU I wanted to go fast, notwithstanding the fact that I didn't know the where of where I was going. Merv had always struck me as someone genuinely interested in people, with a producer's keen acuity and instinct. During a break one day, he focused his squinty gaze at me and asked: "What do you want to do?" I remember I couldn't answer, although I probably wanted to say, "What you're doing." Recognition meant more to me I think than the substance of the work. I was running to something and from something at the same time, discovering and losing myself all at once. But where I was wasn't so bad at all, and in so many ways it was informing *me* as I went. But going fast, doing fast, was a compulsive disorder. And one that paid off.

What made the most difference for me were my career aspirations and my optimism for the future. I'm not sure where this optimism came from except that anger is a survivor's tool, and anger fueled my optimism because optimism was a way of showing them they're not getting to you. Achievement stuck it to the naysayers and doubters and was at the same time empowering. Naysayers are a natural resource in great abundance, perpetual fuel for the optimistic plowshare because they produce anger. I needed the edge. I needed the fix. A doubter was my endorphin rush. What synergy!

But I was optimistic for simple reasons, too: I had passion for what I wanted and saw no reason not to have it and, in fact, I was having it. The exhilaration of absolute freedom was intoxicating. George Frank was right when he said it got better as you got older. As long as you stayed under thirty. We didn't trust anybody over thirty.

My grade adviser and film professor, Haig P. Manoogian, a dedicated and brilliant teacher and a giant in the annals of academic film lore, whom we all called Prof, tried to get me to focus on film. He made you feel special, and if he spotted something in you, he didn't want it going to waste. He tried steering me away from television, which I sensed he was dismissive of. But more importantly, he was passionate about film and wanted you to share in that. In class he spoke with disciplined rapidity, and with a smile. He loved the stuff he was teaching. He suffered no fools and took no prisoners. His knowledge of the medium was all-encompassing, whether of film history or the physical nuts and bolts of picture-making. He melded theory with action. My sense always was that he did not have a whole lot of stomach for Hollywood picture-making, and I once asked him why he hadn't become a Hollywood filmmaker in his own right. The answer, I recall, was words to the effect that it just wasn't for him; he seemed not to have the stomach for it. He apparently had no objection that it might be for us, though. His prize student, Scorsese, matched him in dedication, focus, and discipline. Prof got it right. Scorsese filmed rocks for geology class. Many years later I asked him what happened to that film. "It's been amalgamated with some other stuff," he said. And he knew. It was right there at the tip of his tongue. It also got developed.

But television was accessible, and I was as passionate about the medium as my college friend was about film. From April to June 1962 I not only did the cue cards but also got my first on-screen credit of associate producer on a game show called *Window Shopping*. A very nice fellow by the name of Bob Kennedy was the host, and the idea was to look at a rear-screen projection of a window filled with merchandise for about thirty seconds. It would wipe. The three contestants would have to recall what they'd seen, and the one who got most right, won the prizes. Alan Gilbert, who was related to Herb Wolf, produced the show for Wolf Productions, and then went to Los Angeles to write for *Let's Make a Deal*.

I was still inventing game shows. Morey had a financial partner named Frank Abrahams, who had worked on the staff of both the Goodson-Todman organization and Barry-Enright Productions. He said to me about Goodson, "Mark could look at a show idea and tell you within a few minutes why it wouldn't work. And he could tell you how to make it work"—assuming there was something there. I showed Frank a few of my show ideas (actual physical presentations I put together because that's how shows got pitched), one of which was for a show called *Once upon a Tune*. One day he said he'd like to show the presentation to Oscar Katz at CBS, and he even had the perfect host in mind, a Brit named Michael Jackson (not that Michael Jackson, and no relation). He'd hired

Jackson to do a radio show somewhere out of New York City once. I met Michael when we did some rehearsing for the pitch to Katz at the then Nola Studios at Steinway Hall on West Fifty-seventh Street. Michael was not the stereotypical game show host by a long shot: English accent, a bit chubby at the time (albeit with hair: without hair you didn't have a prayer in the pretty boy days of the three-network universe), but unique and extraordinarily engaging. It's all timing, and the time wasn't ripe—David Frost later proved it.

I couldn't follow Haig's lead. Perhaps in seeing that abandoned movie stage on Avenue M, I had inferred the inevitable. It was gone and it wasn't coming back. Things you loved never did come back. It was like the time I tried extending my projector's electrical cord with twine and even stuck my finger into the wall socket just to make sure everything was working. I'd learned that lesson.

13

Rejection Redux

Hello, I must be going
I cannot stay
I came to say
I must be going
I'm glad I came
But just the same
I must be going
La-la (good-bye)

I'll stay a week or two,
I'll stay the summer through.
But I am telling you
I must be going.

—Groucho Marx in *Animal Crackers*

IN A REVIEW I read of *Animal Crackers*, Groucho is supposed to be showing contempt for the Long Island society woman (played by Margaret Dumont) who is throwing a gala party in his honor. He's all facade, of course, playing the noted African jungle explorer Captain Geoffrey Spaulding, returning from safari. Groucho as Theodore Roosevelt? Hardly. He's as transparent an impostor as ever there was, and he knows it. Why the rest of them don't see it, "I'll never know."

But if he really didn't "care to belong to any club that would have me as a member," then perhaps the basis for his character's contempt for anyone who thinks him more deserving than he does is genuine. It would not be farfetched to imagine Groucho's writers cutting a swatch from their actor's fabric and weaving it into his screen persona (writers have been known to divine such things, you know). And though Mrs. Rittenhouse simply adores him, still he hedges:

> *I'll stay a week or two,*
> *I'll stay the summer through.*
> *But . . .*

Is her adoration ill-informed, not to be trusted, or is it real?

Of course, he could always pummel her to the point of rejection, and in so doing, create the very truth he fears lay hidden, and in fulfilling expectations, confirm the worst. Why is this familiar?

I could conjure their complicity in any playlet I'd devise, take control of the moment, and effect a predictable outcome. . . . I felt license to both express and elicit the behavior that would fulfill my expectation of punishment and rejection. I would actually dare that they lift the phone and call the Home to take me away. Success came at each and every turn. It was a complete lose-lose.

If I'd written his dialogue:

> I know I don't belong here, but here I am anyway. You can always kick me out later, of course, but there won't be a later because I'll kick myself out first, and then what will you do? And besides, if you don't kick me out I'll kick you out. As a matter of fact, I'm kicking you out right now. I never did trust you, you know—putting up with me like this. Who do you think you're kidding, you or me? Don't answer that or we'll both be in trouble. Either way I lose. Do I care? Of course I care, but I never loved me anyway, so we're even. Now get out.

It's great fun unless you're acting this in real life. And if you were selling tickets, you'd have an empty house.

My relationship with Carolyn was tortured. I distracted Carolyn on my fast track to wherever I was going, but I wouldn't be distracted myself. There was selfishness in this, too, you understand, because I'm sure I aided and abetted the very thing we worried about. I could always steal her away from her studies, and did. We were so utterly new to this. I would not say her discipline was lacking so much as her motivation dissipated.

I could not let Carolyn in. I could not have let myself in, let alone anyone else, and that's the rub. Access. I do not believe that meaningful learning can be forced or conscripted from without, and learning about self is the hardest of lessons. You need to be there. And you need to have reason to be there. And you need to give yourself that reason. It can be catalyzed from without, but it must come from within.

I could never have accepted her acceptance of me, notwithstanding my feelings for her and hers for me, any more than I could accept myself, and Groucho helped me sum it up. The social workers, Hawthorne—nothing had made any difference at all. From the fob-watched German psychiatrist to the experts born of parchment, they'd all had their go at me and in the end none of it mattered. What was there at the outset had simply transmuted into adult form. I have always believed that these people play by rules that do not exist except for the fact that they've invented them. And the difference between their "science" and that of the Marx Brothers is that the Marx Brothers make us laugh, and laughter has been known to cure.* Hail, Freedonia!† I'd forced rejection in two early foster homes in which I'd invested myself emotionally. Whether I would ever have been capable of investing myself again is an open question, given the fear and caution that had been instilled. When I came close to emotionally connecting with Carolyn, I approached a place of danger, a place with which I was familiar, and my instinct for survival drove me to defense. It is said that the best defense is a strong offense—and so "Groucho" kicks in. It takes on its own life, almost in spite of you, born of and fed by memory and fear of repetition. And if you abuse someone, or test someone to unbearable extremes, then either you get kicked out or she leaves. Either way, it's rejection. And regardless of who's doing the kicking, or who's doing the leaving, the end result is that you are left standing alone. And when it's real life, it's real pain.

I find it impossible now to recall details about my relationship with Carolyn even though we were together for more than a year, and I'm uncertain why, given my vivid recollections of so much that came before. Emotional engagement strengthened with time, and the threat of loss increased concomitantly. With increased intimacy grew the threat of exposure, or discovery, and the consequence of discovery was

* Dr. Hajime Kimata, Unitika Hospital, Japan: "These results suggest that the induction of laughter may play a role in alleviating allergic diseases." Norman Cousins: "What seems clear . . . is that laughter is an antidote to apprehension and panic." Groucho Marx: "A clown is like an aspirin, only he works twice as fast."

† In *Duck Soup* Groucho plays Rufus T. Firefly, prime minister of the small nation of Freedonia. As Joe Adamson writes in *Groucho, Harpo, Chico, and Sometimes Zeppo: A Celebration of the Marx Brothers*, "Shortly after the film opened, it was revealed that Freedonia was a town in New York. Its Mayor felt obligated to address a letter to Paramount saying, 'The name of Freedonia has been without a blot since 1817. I feel it is my duty as Mayor to question your intentions in using the name of our city in your picture.' Groucho felt it was *his* duty to write back, 'Your Excellency: Our advice is that you change the name of your town. It is hurting our picture. Anyhow, what makes you think you're Mayor of Freedonia? Do you wear a black moustache, play a harp, speak with an Italian accent, or chase girls like Harpo? We are certain you do not. Therefore, we must be Mayor of Freedonia, not you. The old gray Mayor ain't what he used to be.' "

loss. The push-pull of these conflicting emotions—engagement on the one hand, the fear of loss on the other—created an anxiety that, it turn, had to resolve itself. There was only one resolution and that was the demise of the relationship itself.

In an otherwise intimate relationship, when I was defensively controlling and increasingly pulling back, there was a transmutation from close-on participant to manipulator, which was my way of controlling the threatening intimacy, which was a fear of hurt and rejection, and so I threw up a veil, and the stage was literally set for acting out, with no protective barriers; no protective puppets to hide behind. One represents oneself in these matters. This pattern of Sturm und Drang was beyond my control and certainly even more difficult for Carolyn to deal with. I set up a threatening rejection, a defensive barrier—for instance, asking her to leave after some insignificant argument or dispute that I had undoubtedly instigated. It was a merry-go-round in which I was heavily invested, and with each successive spin it spiraled out, increasingly difficult to get off of or control. Inevitably it flew apart altogether; the hard-wired circuits prevailed. And since these were my utensils, I'd be the one who would do the kicking: "Get out!" And voilà! She did. Huh?

Childhood redux. Or as Yogi would put it, "Déjà vu all over again."

After Maryann and Carolyn, I was prompted to seek help. I was twenty-one. It had been fourteen years since I'd last seen my mother. Not that I thought that my mother had anything to do with any of this anyway. How could she? I had torn up her picture at Hawthorne eight years prior. My mother was dead.

My past and just about everything else that went with it were dead as well, and I never looked back. Decoupling myself from it was my way of burying and surviving the pain. That's how I got from there to here. My childhood had never been mine to begin with, so there was really nothing back there worth remembering or holding on to. I had no roots, which I found liberating. Like a snake that sheds its skin, I slipped out new.

I did not know, though, the extent to which the remnants of my past shadowed me. The me that had crossed over the Brooklyn Bridge may have left certain years behind, but certain years behind hadn't fully left me. Like hanging up the phone only to find later, when you go to dial out, that the other line hasn't hung up. I had a second line for life's other calls, but I just couldn't make a new connection on line one.

Every year during my four years as an undergraduate at NYU I met with Dr. Abraham Krugman of the Jewish Child Care Association, who approved my partial scholarship and my overall progress. After my sophomore year I asked him to arrange the therapy. I spent about a year and a half with Dr. Alan Levy in twice-weekly sessions that lasted forty-five minutes each.*

I was more interested, though, in knowing who he was and how he did what he did, than I was prepared to know about me in spite of my best intentions. I spent a great deal of time "psyching out" his methods and what he knew about me. My deflections were about self-protective control, my fear of discovery, particularly self-discovery, which in turn precluded emotional intimacy, the former reigning in the latter. The very conscious symptoms of rejection were no match for their underlying causes.

Dr. Levy's demeanor somehow conveyed that he knew more about me than I did, and I sat there in my leather chair waiting for him, sitting in his leather chair, to tell me more about me. He was the doctor, after all—a real doctor, an M.D., and a doctor should know more about his patient than his patient does. I didn't come to the doctor to examine myself, after all, but I soon realized that this was closer to what Dr. Levy had in mind. He specialized more in questions than answers, and while many of my questions prompted his, his were, not so coincidentally, eerily similar to mine. Swapping a question for a question, particularly one that belonged to me in the first place, took getting used to. But I really had to admire a guy who plagiarized my material and then put me up to answering for it. In those rare moments of inspired understanding,

* I am deeply indebted to both Dr. Levy and Dr. Krugman.

when my questions yielded answers that only I could have provided, I was dazzled by his insight. I didn't realize I'd been interrogating myself. I genuinely liked Dr. Levy, though, and did my best to help him out. I didn't want him to feel he was wasting his time. And so even in therapy, I was proving my worth.

Although there is a superficial resemblance between Dr. Levy's questions and the ones I was assaulted with at Hawthorne, these were two completely different experiences—one premised on a lie, the other open and honest. At Hawthorne, the social workers (George Frank excluded) hurled insinuations and accusations, not questions, and my responses were naturally defensive. While Dr. Levy must have had some background on me, my sense was that he was discovering me for the first time, just as I was discovering him. It all comes down to a fundamental honesty and willingness to explore and understand rather than a need to confirm someone else's preconceptions.

I was not an open book, though, least of all to myself. Besides, I liked being in control, which, after all, had worked so much more for me than against. There's security in predictability. Usually the things you didn't know about brought bad news, like when my mother spoke Yiddish. At least Dr. Levy didn't speak Yiddish (as far as I knew). The most deeply secreted parts of me were the hardest to reach. The ones that put up the greatest resistance perhaps have the greatest meanings to offer. The trick was to gain visceral insight by contact with the "other" you. It may only have been a fleeting contact, but in retrieving a remnant or sampling, even one that is minute, before the door slammed shut, I might piece together something bigger. It's really a war where one of you wears the other of you down. My conscious mind would literally shut down when it put up resistance to unconscious revelations.

But if you can't stay awake, you can dream. The dream state seemed to catch the two of us together, even though one of us rarely made obvious sense. The interpretation of dreams was something Dr. Levy readily weighed in on, and as therapy went on, my dreams became more memorable and meaningful. I was tapping into the motherboard and it heard me knocking.

But the dreams never came neatly packaged. Even dream interpretation, and the piecing together of meanings, engendered resistance. Dr. Levy might retell something I'd said in a way different from the way I'd said it, offering an interpretation or suggestion—connecting the dots, so to speak. And in that retelling, I might come to some understanding, or I might expand on it in some other way, and that might engage more exploration, digging deeper still. Sometimes I would even get so close to something that I wouldn't hear it at all. He'd repeat what I'd said, virtually verbatim, and I still couldn't hear it. Or I'd hear it and then lose it. Some unconscious barrier blocked the meaning of my stream-of-consciousness thought from my conscious self. It is difficult to hear things you've kept hidden for so long, particularly from yourself, even when they're your own words, and specifically those things that touch the past presumed long dead and gone.

. . . the dream.

It is the night when I am seven years old and asleep. I somehow feel my mother's approach and open my eyes. She is approaching my bed in her pink nightgown in what looks like a trancelike, sleepwalking state. She puts her hands around my throat and starts to choke me and I can't breathe. Some people dressed in white are spinning me around. I hear the cry of a little boy's voice that has come from somewhere outside my head and he wakes me up. It takes a moment for me to realize that the child's voice I've just heard, still echoing, as real as if it has come from down the hall, is me at age seven.

I had dreamed a reenactment of a childhood trauma.

∽

DR. LEVY ASKED me who the people are in the white clothes that I reported "spinning me around" in the dream, but I didn't know. In retrospect, I believe it is the associative confusion and turmoil I was feeling between my mother's attempt to choke me and her institutionalization, with the white clothing representing the attendants I'd seen at the hospital the day they took her away. The motherboard had spoken. And so had the child who had woken me up: *"Mommy, Mommy, what did I do?"*

The dream opened the way to a question Dr. Levy might not have asked had I not provided the opening. In retrospect, it seems a belated inevitability given the year I'd already spent in therapy. There was an elephant in this room and nobody spoke of it. If I were ever to experience a single defining moment in psychotherapy, this would have to have been it. "Would you like me to inquire into your mother's condition?"

I took it as a suggestion. "But she's in her sixties now! She's old," I said, as if to say she's old news, and old news is dead news. The me in me, perhaps even the both of me, wanted her to stay dead. I'd forgotten I had a mother. I don't recall anger, I don't recall fear. I don't recall recalling. I had torn up her picture and I had closed the door. I didn't even feel like her son anymore. I was never her son; in fact, I had been her child. "Son" sounds to me as being more attached, somehow, and so much more grown up, and I was never her grown-up. Dr. Levy fell silent. He would never have attempted to sell me something I'd resisted. But the dream opened a crack in the door I'd slammed shut long ago and would have to open again to some resolution. The expression on his face was one of detached observation. But his silence asked that I look again. Besides, I didn't want to disappoint Dr. Levy.

I believe that he felt the moment had come for me to confront my irresolution, which, unbeknownst to me, had impacted all my relationships thus far in life, and which had led me here in the first place. While he might not have had it all down in detail, I suspect Dr. Levy got the sweep of me the moment I walked in on day one. But his was not an understanding that transferred to a prescription pad.

What was supposed to happen? I'd been coming so long I'd forgotten why. Seeing Dr. Levy twice a week was a touchstone; each session was one of potential discovery and there was a combination of avoidance and adventure in exploration. Had something already happened that I wasn't aware of? Would I not feel rejected ever again? Would I not set up the patterns I'd set up with Carolyn? That was the point, of course, for my being here. My life otherwise, academically and part-time professionally, could not have been better. Now in my senior year at college, I had the sense that we were coming down the stretch. Things had run their course, and I felt that Dr. Levy felt that way as well (although he never said it), so this sense of imminent closure may also have prompted his initiative regarding my mother. Even my dream, coming now rather than sooner, may have been an unconscious alert that the time had come to ante up, or the dream itself and its aftermath catalyzed the wrap-up. I doubt that I would have had the dream, however, had it not been for my coming here.

"Okay," I said, "find out."

He asked Dr. Krugman to write to the hospital. Dr. Levy read me the response, although I never actually saw the letter itself. I recall it to be a relatively brief letter, one that had a pablumlike disclaimer that she continued to improve (although I sensed it was an improvement that would take a lifetime) and she spoke of her two children. I was also invited to write her doctor to make arrangements to meet with him, if I so desired. "There are no two children. I'm the only one," I said. He explained to me that this kind of illness can produce delusional or false memories and that lucid and delusional thinking can be mixed. I was certain then, and now, that there could not have been a girl after me. I would unquestionably have had memories of her. However, my mother was forty when I was born, and I would have no way of knowing what might have come before me. Even by the sixties, I had yet to see my own birth certificate, and did not get a copy of it until the early seventies. It states no prior births, but it's entirely possible that information can be wrong. And while I still have no reason to believe so, doubt lingers.

It was a small step between Dr. Levy reading me the hospital letter and his suggestion that I might want to speak with her doctor if I was interested in doing so. This now had its own momentum, and I really had no good reason not to follow through, but it took me three months to answer the director, which I did in June. I have always responded quickly to most things in life. Action is something I've embraced, and I have always been attracted to high energy. Success has to do with action. I was three months from college graduation and probably preparing for final exams. For whatever the reason, I deferred a bit. But follow up I did.

The motherboard had spoken, as had the child, and my dream had opened the door a crack. Dr. Levy enabled me to open it farther still. All I had to do now was walk through. How and when I would do that was up to me. It was June and I was graduating from NYU and in November I would be inducted into the U.S. Army Reserve for six months of active duty. I suspect in light of the ever after that would follow, something instinctive guided events from this point forward. I had been a survivor, after all, and where this comes from I don't know, any more than I can tell you where passion comes from, but in my case I believe they were joined. Sometimes in life there are no good choices and no good answers.

Dr. Levy was going on vacation, as I recall, and a few sessions before his departure he told me that he felt the time seemed ripe for us to wind down my therapy. I remember feeling not only that I expected it, but also that it felt perfectly right. We'd gone just about as far as we could. And while he had signaled an end, I did not experience a sense of abandonment or disappointment. I don't recall my final session as being any different or any more memorable in any way than any other session, and he was no more revealing of himself than he'd ever been. I know, though, that through the years, whenever friends have found themselves in trouble, I've recommended Dr. Levy.*

---

* In March 2002, almost forty years later, I went to say hello to Dr. Levy. Same address, same office, same black-and-white tiles in the anteroom—from Pintchik, a famous home decorating store still in Brooklyn. How do I know this? He got personal. Somewhere in those closing moments, as I was walking out of his office, I noticed some family pictures sitting on a bookshelf, which was very telling because I hadn't remembered anything of a personal nature before. He had indicated to me earlier, however, that he didn't practice much anymore. He eagerly and proudly picked up the framed pictures to show me. There was a picture of himself and his beautiful wife. And there were pictures of his grown son and daughter (his adults, now, you might say). His daughter is now a practicing physician, though not a psychiatrist. I said something to him about my sense that he always seemed to know more than he let onto. He smiled and quipped that his daughter had once asked him, "Daddy, do you read minds?" What made her think that? I wonder.

I believe that so much of this process is about the chemistry between patient and doctor. A lot of that is potluck. For myself, I thought he was as good as they get. I still think it.

On my army application where it asks for next of kin, parents' names, etc., under mother, I wrote diagonally across that space "DECEASED." Where it asks for father, "DECEASED."

I never went up to the hospital.

Part Five

Discovery

I am of the opinion that good medical care and home

surroundings would quickly restore her. Such care I am

not prepared financially to supply her. Not being a med-

ical man, I still feel that she can be restored, given

proper care. I bespeak for her that a short time under

favorable conditions can restore her to normal condition.

14

Synchronicity

I HAD BEEN qualified 1-A by the Selective Service System, which meant I was a prime candidate for the draft and could be called up at any time. My choice was to serve two years of active duty or find a reserve unit. The reserves required six months of active duty and five and a half years of active reserve training, which translated into one four-hour meeting each week and two weeks of summer camp (Anacdutra—the U.S. Army's acronym for "Annual active duty for training"). I'd take it. You had to find a unit, though, that had an opening. I got lucky the day I walked into the armory on West Forty-second Street in Manhattan. The 356th Station Hospital had an open slot, and processing began.

Two months later I was sworn in. No sooner had I been sworn in than I received my draft notice: "GREETINGS." How could I be drafted if I'd already enlisted? I took the subway to the end of the line in Brooklyn, where I'd signed up with my local draft board when I was eighteen. Stillwell Avenue in Coney Island. I knew this neighborhood. I'd lived here, in my next-to-last foster home, but more than that, when you were from

Brooklyn, Coney Island was your summer playground. Now it felt like the same barren end-of-the-road place I'd walked through every day to and from school. It had all been temporary anyway.

I walked into the office of the local draft board. There were three middle-aged civilian women talking among themselves with paper coffee cups in hand, smoking cigarettes. They were not the Andrews Sisters, but they weren't nearly as bad as I'd expected. They might be mothers in their own right and I hoped they'd understand. It was as barren an office as I'd ever seen, made of what I think of to this day as "Coney Island/Brighton Beach" wood; the kind of wood the early roller coasters were made of, with the ricketiness built in. The place creaked. Termites would have had a tough time finding work here, but somehow everything stood up. Everything was painted battleship gray; a few typewriters sat on wooden desks, and there were carbon paper, forms, and such, but nothing of a nonutilitarian nature. To this day when I think of structures in Coney Island or Brighton Beach I think of wood painted gray. Even as a child I somehow understood that this was a last-stop place. Just a few feet more and you were in the ocean. And "over the ocean" was where all the poor children of Europe were, with nothing to eat. And if you complained too much, or weren't grateful for what you had, they'd ship you over there, too.

I showed one of the board women proof of my reserve enlistment along with my draft notice. She took the notice and told me I'd be notified. I didn't know if they liked me or didn't like me, and I didn't know if that mattered or didn't matter, but I hoped they did and I hoped it did because my life hung in the balance. A week or so went by. I tore into that envelope the moment I saw it in the mailbox.

Had I not followed my instinct and looked for a unit when I did, or had the unit not had an open slot, I was drafted for two years of active duty. There's a better than even chance that would have meant Vietnam.

At about the time that I decided to write this book, I began thinking of the way things unfolded in my life. I'm not sure there's a simple answer to the question of "Why now?" except that "Everything has its time," and if not now, when?

My draft notice crossing with my army reserve enlistment was a momentous event for me, though an isolated one. A *coincidence.*

The sound effects man on the game show I worked on had asked me for an idea for a kids' show and off the top of my head I thought of the Bunin Puppets. As much as I'd loved their puppets as child, I'd never dreamed of becoming a puppeteer. Pure *coincidence.*

I rented an apartment on West Eighty-ninth Street across the street from where Morey Bunin and his family lived, and ended up working for him—that, too. Morey and his family became my surrogate family. A *coincidence.* The fact that I was now performing the very character I'd watched as a child on television was fortuitous.

At age seven, seeing marionettes dancing on roller skates on a television set, and the passion that evoked in me, would *coincidentally* take me to places that became even more meaningful as time went on.

Perhaps the *coincidence* that resonates with me most deeply is walking up to a nondescript brick building on Avenue M to see that cavernous empty stage and that lonely camera crane sitting in the middle of it without a camera on top, and instantly recognizing it as a place where they'd made movies. When I think of a cathedral, I think of this space and that camera crane standing there by itself and the beam of light that was coming down from the skylight the way the beam of light travels over your head when you look up in a darkened movie theater from way up in the projection booth onto the screen, and all the dust particles that are swirling around inside and how the picture travels magically on that beam onto the big screen.

On Saturday, October 15, 1960, by sheer *coincidence,* I was standing next to a color television camera holding Merv Griffin's cue cards for a Saturday afternoon network show called *Saturday Prom.* It broadcast live from the NBC color studios in Brooklyn. On Avenue M. The watchman never knew.

These kinds of things happen to us all. The psychiatrist Carl Jung described such as events happening because of synchronicity—the simultaneous occurrence of events that appear significantly related but have no discernible causal connection.* We just don't think about them, or if we do, we're inclined to let them evaporate as unconnected coincidences. There's a story in these coincidences. But I can only tell you mine.

After my uneventful but dutiful active duty at Fort Dix, New Jersey, I returned to civilian life needing a job. The good news was that Morey Bunin had a performance contract with the Texas Pavilion at the upcoming New York World's Fair (just a subway ride away). He had created an Aniform character named Tex, a gun-totin' cowboy specifically designed for the Texas Pavilion, who would challenge passersby to a fast draw and engage them in spontaneous banter.

One night I went with Morey to the old New Yorker Theater on Upper Broadway in Manhattan to see François Truffaut's *The 400 Blows*. A film about a young boy who escapes from a detention center and keeps running, it resonated with me deeply. I blurted something out about "the story of my life." I wasn't aware that I'd said anything at all until Morey later asked me if I knew what I had said. He sensed I hadn't. I hadn't. He repeated it for me to hear. "I said that?" I'd given him something about me that I had not given myself. I suspect Morey knew most of what there was to know about me without my ever having to say it. It wasn't until I was ready to put the pieces together that a story emerged with connecting links I'd never fully considered.

Prior to the World's Fair and just before my army stint, I'd had the distinction of being Morey's very first Aniform performer at a trade show we did at McCormick Place in Chicago for the Scripto Pen Company. I played Bullwinkle.

Morey had never been able to pay me much, as he had gone through some financially straitened years, and I understood the difficulties, especially with a family. This was a star of my childhood, you understand.

* Jung advanced the "synchronicity" hypothesis in the 1920s, and gave a full statement in 1951, in an Eranous lecture. The concept of synchronicity indicates a meaningful coincidence of two or more events, where something other than the probability of chance is involved. . . . Synchronicity elucidates meaningful arrangements and coincidence which somehow go beyond the calculations of probability."

This was the Great Foodini. I was struck by the meanness and short memory span of the entertainment business, an invaluable lesson unto itself. Money had never been an issue for me anyway, and I gladly would have worked for whatever Morey could afford to pay me, including free. I was a student, after all, and I was being taught and trusted by a master whose work I had so much loved as a child. I felt then and now that it was a cherished gift just to have met him, and to have been given the privilege and opportunity to be his friend, to perform for and with him, and to develop skills that would serve me so well later.

Morey needed several Aniform performers for the fair, though, given that this would be a seven-day operation with extended hours. Of course, I would be one of them. And he offered me the same wage he was offering everyone else, something in the neighborhood of $200 a week. This was the sixties, remember, and that was good money. Just to give you a relative comparison, my monthly rent was $125. And I lived in Manhattan!

I didn't think it was fair, though. Why should I get the same as everyone else? After all, I'd been there first. Passion transcended money, but this had to do with acknowledgment. I felt I deserved something more for the years I'd worked for so little, and occasionally for nothing, even just an extra $10 a week. His response was immediate: "That's it, kiddo. Take it or leave it."

There was no meanness in the way he said it, just a matter-of-fact implication that there were plenty of guys he could get. Nothing more than "I don't really need you, kid. Your call." I did not experience this as a rejection. Morey wasn't my girlfriend or my father. I took it as a diminution of the value he now placed on my skills, and as a betrayal, and I could not understand it. How could he have forgotten everything? He of all people. Notwithstanding my respect for him, I had respect for myself as well. This was not what I expected. I was angry now, and anger had always strengthened my resolve and propelled me. I was clear in my decision and I didn't give it a second thought. "Leave it." I was telling him "I don't need you, either." And I hung up.

Throughout my life, if I've felt abuse, unfairness, or disloyalty, my response is immediate, regardless of need, and without any consideration for alternatives. I was used to flying without a net. Risk was never something I thought about. It was synonymous with and inseparable from life itself, and inherent in the rules of engagement I'd intuited and practiced as a child. I never had stability, predictability, continuity, or security. I survived on an alternative template for life that became my internal gyroscope for self-guidance, stability, and control.

As an adult, I fully recognize that stability does not exist. By believing in it one gives power to others and lessens one's capacity for self-reliance, action, and true growth, for which a capacity for risk is requisite. My childhood engendered that capacity.

But I still had the rent to pay.

I called Evelyn Tinsley. Evelyn had been producer Herb Wolf's personal secretary when I was holding Merv Griffin's cue cards on Herb's game show *Keep Talking*, and I knew she liked me. She'd always been encouraging and even introduced me to her niece, whom I dated for a short time. Herb owned a number of shows I'd worked on, and I called to see if he had anything coming up. As it turned out, Evelyn was now working for the legendary television producer Max Liebman,* and he was producing the "Chrysler Show-Go-Round" at the World's Fair. It seemed like all roads led to the fair.

The Chrysler show would star the world-famous Bil and Cora Baird Marionettes, whom I also had watched as a child, though I'd liked only Slugger Ryan. I never felt the affinity for his characters that I'd felt for Morey's Foodini and Pinhead, but the Bairds were a much bigger name, with many more characters and a theatrical inventiveness that was grander than but not as intimate as Bunin's, built around broad concepts and themes rather than the few deeply etched characters that were

---

* Max Liebman, a pioneer television producer, produced *Your Show of Shows* starring Sid Caesar, Imogene Coca, Carl Reiner, and Howard Morris. Liebman would later produce *Caesar's Hour*, which I attended as a child.

Morey's. The Bairds were regulars on the early NBC *Today* show, and appeared frequently as a novelty act on the *Ed Sullivan Show* and other variety shows. Baird was the gold standard of puppetry in America. And while Bunin had peaked, Baird was still active and growing. Evelyn somehow remembered.

"You do puppets, don't you?"

"Yes, yes, I do puppets."

"You do them with the strings, don't you?" It wasn't really a question.

"Sure. Sure I do them with the strings." I had made them out of peanuts and papier-mâché, using sewing thread for the strings.

"Well, hurry up and go down to 59 Barrow Street right away! Bil Baird's looking for puppeteers. Tell him Mr. Liebman sent you."

I was down at Bil Baird's studio on Barrow Street in Greenwich Village within the hour, and I told him Max Liebman's office had sent me. He did a quick lookover at this kid standing before him. "What have you done?"

"I've worked for Morey Bunin."

"Morey doesn't have marionettes. Morey has hand puppets."

"I know, I know. But I can do marionettes."

"Uh-huh. Uh-huh." I would soon discover that whenever Bil did his uh-huh-uh-huhs, you knew he was thinking it over. He pointed me to the marionette bridge straight ahead. There was a marionette in the shape of a monkey wrench hanging against the brick wall at the far end of the bridge. It was one of dozens of marionettes that Bil had designed and built specifically for the "Chrysler Show-Go-Round," in which all of the puppets—marionettes or otherwise—represented either part of a car or a tool used to fix and maintain one. This would be one tool, now, that I'd have to get a fix on. "Okay. Okay. Get up there and let's see what you can do."

I'd never been on a marionette bridge in my life. And until looking at it right now, I'd never even seen one. But I'd imagined one, and I think that helped me get up there. With the bravado and sure-footedness of an old trouper, I climbed the ladder at the side of the bridge and walked confidently along one of the two wooden parallel planks—literally walking the plank—that constituted the bridge (each plank about sixteen inches wide, with about three feet of open space between them) and reached for the control mechanism of the marionette that was hanging against the brick wall. I'd already imagined what a real one would feel like: bigger and heavier than mine, and the strings were longer. That's all. I'd already made the "airplane control" from Popsicle sticks, so I knew what that was, too. I'd been flying this thing all my life, really. At least that's what I think I thought.

The strings were about nine feet long, and it was about five feet from the bridge to the floor of the stage below. No big deal, really. There was a huge mirror against the wall behind Bil that was tilted at a slight incline so a puppeteer could see his marionette. Bil dropped the needle on the record player, the music started, and I started dancing. I was a good dancer, too, by the way, as long as I was the marionette. I couldn't have been doing this for more than a minute or so when I quickly glanced up at Bil, and saw that he'd been watching my face and the marionette, both. He had seen the joy, he had seen the passion, and I'm sure he'd seen the need.

"Uh-huh, uh-huh," he said. "Okay."

"I can get this. I just need another minute or two."

"Are you a member of Equity?"

"No. But I can join."

"Uh-huh, Uh-huh. Okay. Go get your contract from Max Liebman's office. And then go over and join Equity. Rehearsals start next Tuesday at the fair."

"Leave it" led to this.

∞

DANCING GIRLS! THREE to the bar—strings attached, of course. Bil had me up on the bridge for the opening number. I was one of four puppeteers, twelve dancing girls in all, kicking up a storm in lockstep, as they made their entrance from stage right into the footlights. Every puppet in the show was designed and built by Bil Baird himself. I don't imagine, though, that too many people really cared what "part" of the car the "girls" belonged to, just as long as they kicked and swiveled. When Bil designed the female anatomy he wasn't going for high art.

There was, of course, extraordinary art in all of his work, to the extent really that a Baird puppet is as uniquely identifiable as, let's say, a Moore or a Picasso, so original is the signature of its line and shape. But Bil liked the ladies, and left well enough alone when it came to sculpting gorgeous gams. In fact, if you were lucky enough, he might grab your arm, pull up your sleeve, reach for his Magic Marker, and lo and behold, an original Baird nude would appear magically thereon. Every Christmas, for many years after, Bil would send me one of his large original woodcut greetings on rice paper, which I proudly framed. One year he wished me: "A naked Xmas and a happy Nude year," and the following year he simply drew an X-rated dancing girl, replete with strings, sans inscription. It was meaningful to me that Bil remembered and included me. I frankly never quite felt worthy of it, but inclusion was not something I was ever comfortable with anyway. Still, I had the framed evidence.

So here I was, having never danced a day in my life, kicking up a storm. No arms folded, standing on the sidelines, this time; no, sir. I was up there pulling the strings, for all to see. Cameras moved. Puppets moved. And dancers moved, too. And if nobody saw me, I could move. Cameras. Puppets. Dancers. Me.

The "Chrysler Show-Go-Round" was a minimarvel for its time. There were four theaters, each with 625 seats, in one huge structure. The show was divided into four parts, and each audience saw all four parts of the show in sequence as it revolved on a huge turntable. To keep it all synchronized, everything was prerecorded except for the live host at the beginning and end of the show. All we puppeteers really had to do was manipulate the puppets themselves. Since we didn't have to actually speak, I always felt that my performance was a bit of a cheat. But just as an actor can say things without words, so, too, can the puppet. In fact, the puppet has an advantage because the audience pays greater attention, there is greater focus on less, and the audience infers more. This is where childhood fantasy kicks in. The vulnerability of the puppet reaches out for our protection and taps into recollections of our own vulnerability, and the child in all of us identifies with this. Any empowerment we can lend to it is our empowerment as well. I believe this is the essence of the primal appeal of puppetry universally.

I would sit in back of one of the theaters during my lunch break on occasion, just to watch a performance, and after a few viewings, I usually could identify the puppeteer behind the puppet just through the puppet's movements. It's the puppeteer who brings life to an otherwise inanimate object, irrespective of voice. A puppet can move and still be lifeless. I enjoyed playing the guessing game of who was doing whom, and especially enjoyed watching certain performers: Bil Baird, of course (who didn't actually perform that much, mainly because he was down at his Barrow Street studio building puppets and preparing to shoot *The Sound of Music* in Los Angeles), Faz Fazikas, Wayland Flowers, Jerry Nelson, and Bill Tost. There were many others, of course, but these are the ones who stand out in my memory.

Attitude is expressed through movement, gesture, and often absolute stillness. The subtlest of gestures can engender profound sadness or even spark hilarity. It was all about physical inflection through movement and timing, and in many ways this was dance. Many of the puppeteers, in fact (we had about forty, given four crew shifts; there were eighty shows a day, with each crew handling twenty shows), were actually trained dancers, and dancers evoke emotion and reach out to us without speech. Cora, incidentally, had been a dancer herself before meeting Bil. How I ended up in a dance troupe . . . *I'll never know.*

While best known for his marionettes, Bil also had hand puppets, and Carby the Carburetor, the star, opened and closed the show as a hand puppet. I was capable enough on the bridge, but Bil's instinct was to switch me to the hand puppet stage, and I felt most at home there. So

I now had a "star" on my hand, quite literally, but Carby and I got along just great.

Remember this: if you need to put somebody away, get a puppet. Puppets get away with murder, and it's never a crime. They can say and do things and be held totally unaccountable. A puppet can proposition a man's wife, for example, right in front of him, and you can be standing there, too, with your mouth moving, and he'll howl with laughter. Try it without a puppet. Go ahead. I could tell a woman to use the kitty litter, and people would howl. Had I thought about it, I never could have said such a thing.

A puppet doesn't think. Such abandon. Such license.

Since the host was the only one with live dialogue, all Carby had to do was sit there and listen to him spiel. I didn't have anything against the hosts, and in fact one of them, Hal, became a good friend. Fatefully, he offered to put me up if I ever came out to Los Angeles, where he lived. But still, spieling is spieling, and one day I took matters into my own hands, so to speak, and decided—Carby decided—to pull attitude. Other puppeteers had their shtick, too, of course, and I had mine. It was a simple thing, really: Carby put his finger up to his rather elongated rubber proboscis and just wiggled it. The audience howled. I was encouraged. Not knowing what had happened behind him, the host spun around and Carby just sat there. Rigid. Eyes dead forward. A puppet on a shelf. A cigar-store Indian. As soon as he turned front and continued, Carby repeated his gesture, only this time adding a slow up-and-down "burn" with a come-hither head movement, as if to say to the audience, "Who the hell does this guy think he is?" You acknowledged them, you took them into your confidence; you made them your cohort in crime. Mocking authority was as sure-fire a way to win them over as raising the flag. This time the host spun around quickly, but Carby froze even quicker. Nothing deader than a puppet that doesn't move. The audience knew he was alive, though. They knew he was playing dead. There's where the life comes in, you see; there's the child who believes. Now you know how I got here.

And as the theme came up, and the stage started turning, Carby waved good-bye to everybody, the audience applauded wildly, the host was left with only half a spiel spoken, and I figured once the front office got wind of this, I'd be fired.

Six hundred twenty-five people in each of four theaters on a continuing roll, all day long, twenty times a day, six days a week, was the challenge. The risks of this incessant repetition were boredom and taking an audience for granted. All those shows all day long could be numbing, stretching discipline to its limits, so you had to invent, and conjure somehow, within yourself, a psychic Benzedrine. A prerecorded sound track didn't help any, except that it demanded your presence, quite literally, and threw you into a race with it and your own stamina, as you resisted falling into a rote, mechanized performance. A live performance that becomes rote is one that defaults to muscle memory and cannot inspire, keeping in mind that a puppet's life is about more than the fabric it is made of, and an audience will have no way of knowing what it may otherwise have missed. There is responsibility here.

Each audience was an original. The hum of the audience anticipating the show was not unlike the feel of an orchestra tuning up before the show begins. With the gradual dimming of the house lights and the sudden brightening of the footlights they all fell pin-drop silent, commanding your energy now to perform. Just a touch of laughter now was all that was needed to jump-start your transcendence and, boy, were they willing. There was no better feeling in the world than the laughter of so many people swooshing over you like a wave because of something you'd done, usually through some minute movement, keeping in mind that some of these puppets were no more than fifteen inches tall. I always marveled at how they caught it, just a beat delayed, in unison, but realized, too, that the eye, in a darkened theater, has a way of focusing and telescoping, even from a great distance.

The discipline mustered in rising to the challenge was a source of satisfaction in itself. It confirmed my stamina, reliability, consistency, and professionalism; in effect, my right to be here. Proving my worth twenty times a day suited me fine. The reach for approval is in large measure a performer's quest. And with each audience you gave and took something unique, and you were challenged to invent something new with every show. To get there, though, you needed that sense of controlled abandon, and part of that abandon did indeed spring from a need to transcend repetition and avoid the mechanistic. An ability to let go, and the fact of being physically hidden, went a long way in allowing that to happen.

Invention was all I had to keep this thing going. I'd gotten here through invention—how, I don't know. There were times, though, when I worried I'd gone over the line, especially when I was having fun (I wasn't getting paid to have fun—or was I?), and that some of my hijinks might even get me in trouble. Puppet heresy! There was something of the child that kicked in here, albeit this time with license: the school clown back in business. The mischiefmaker. The contrarian. Bil told me that when he was a kid going to school, rumor went around that he had marionettes, and all the girls worried that he might be contagious. Maybe Bil saw a bit of himself in me. That would have made my day.

I once asked him why he spelled his name with one "l" (you've probably been wondering that yourself), and he told me he didn't need the other "l" because "Nobody ever pronounces the second *l* anyway. Besides, my name's *Bil*, not Bi-lil-lil." A Chrysler executive had asked Bil if he would agree to change his marquee billing on the outside of the theaters to "The Bil & Cora Baird Puppets" instead of "Marionettes." They were afraid people wouldn't know what marionettes were. Bil agreed, with one proviso—that Chrysler change its name to "The Chrysler Car Company." He probably wouldn't have stood up for the flag, either, I'll bet, and had Bil been any younger they probably would have sent him to Hawthorne, too, and knocked the marionettes out of him.

Bil was approachable, playful, and open-faced. He always struck me as a mischief-making puppet himself. He even looked like his puppets, or they looked like him, depending on who you think created whom. His mannerisms and expressions, including his furrowed smile lines and especially his eyes and eyebrows, always seemed awestruck, filled with perpetual wonder, just like so many of his characters. His puppets even walked like him. And his female puppets, especially, were clearly modeled on Cora, with their wide foreheads and high cheekbones. Bil was a man in perpetual motion, invention brewing at every turn, and the extension between the artist and his art was unambiguous.

I never got to know Cora well. She struck me as a disciplined, nononsense perfectionist, which I undoubtedly respected but feared as well. Perhaps I was concerned that I would not live up to her standards, so I kept my distance. Cora ran the "front office," and I knew that I would not want not to please her.

She must've gotten wind of something, though, or maybe she was just curious. As I was getting ready to open the show one night, she sneaked up and hid herself behind the scrim that concealed some of our stage lighting to my immediate left. Even if I'd glanced over, the colored gels would have blinded me. I did my thing, though, got my laughs, and as the stage began to revolve and turn the audience out of view, I prepared to move out onto our finale stage, where I would close the show for the audience that was coming up. As I pushed back on my small wheeled stool and stood up, the lights behind the scrim gradually dimmed and I suddenly saw Cora looking directly at me. She'd seen it all. I knew what I'd done. And I knew I was fired.

"That was very nice, Joe. Very nice."

I thanked her, and as I hurriedly made my way to the finale stage, I ran into Bil, who was simply standing there. "It's a great feeling when you've done a great show!" I enthused.

Bil looked at me with that hangdog gaze he often had, his mouth wide open, like a leprechaun puppet hanging from a string. "Uh-uh. Uh-uh." What could he say, really? He'd have to agree, wouldn't he? I rushed on, noticing his gaze following me, his mouth still agape, his head bobbing up and down in puppetlike agreement.

My enthusiasm had nothing to do with enthusiasm. My enthusiasm was a sales pitch. I was the guy dancing up and down when his toes are being shot at. Full of energy and bounce, and driven now by the fear that I had not lived up to expectation, I was enlisting Bil as my ally. It was all deflection.

I worried that I'd been too cavalier, shall we say, and that Cora had caught it. I'd heard what she said, but I wasn't sure she meant it. Had I known she was watching I would have given a much more constrained performance. I'd thrown caution to the wind, overstepped my bounds. If Hawthorne was not in this somewhere, then I don't know what is. Even hidden, even with a puppet on my hand seeking affirmation (the puppet was seeking it, not me) and getting it (only making matters worse), I anticipated rejection. In seeking approval (he needed that, not me) I had exceeded my allowable bounds, bounds I would continue to exceed in perpetual need of approbation (his approbation, not mine), but not without a sense of guilt for doing so, and hence the expectation of being fired. Me. Not him. One chew on the steak, that's all, and a begrudging allowance, at that. That's all I deserved. This was with me, still.

The expectation that I would be let go, and my ongoing efforts to forestall it, stayed with me for the two seasons I worked for Bil and Cora Baird at the New York World's Fair.

⚭

ONE SUNNY DAY as I walked out the stage door for my lunch break, the rear doors of the adjacent theater opened, and the audience filed out of the show I'd just performed in. It was clear they'd enjoyed themselves, but I couldn't help but feel an ache of disappointment that nobody knew who I was. I wanted them to know who I was. It was a strange feeling, really, and I don't know if it was jealousy or resentment or what it was really, because how do you feel such things for a puppet? All I knew was that I did all the work and he got all the credit. And what's more, I was here at the behest of the puppet and not vice versa.

I had no design talents, no construction skills, and no alter ego to mold into a character of my own, although I certainly did inhabit, interpret, and bring to life someone else's characters. Most significantly, though, I'd never dreamed of becoming a professional puppeteer. While puppetry was something I loved, and though I most certainly loved performing, I had arrived here quite by accident, or, more likely, by way of Jung's acausal connecting principle. It all happened just as I've told it, and the fact that I would work for two of the masters of American puppetry while in my teens and early twenties is still a mystery to me.

I found myself looking up at the theater marquee confirming what I already knew: "Starring the Bil Baird Marionettes." There was no evidence of my being here at all, really. But what right did I have to these feelings? I was extraordinarily fortunate in having this job, and I couldn't have been more aware or appreciative. But this was about the future. I didn't like being the fly on the wall, and especially somebody else's wall. I wanted to stand out, be seen and heard. Suddenly I saw no future in anonymity. And I think it was right then and there, as I jostled my way through that joyful crowd, that I knew I needed the kind of recognition I would never get from puppetry.

Performance, though, was in my blood. I'd have to figure it out.

∞

POSTSCRIPT: NEW YORK City, summer 1979. A dinner party encounter between Bil Baird and Edmund Morris, the author of a Pulitzer Prize–winning biography of Theodore Roosevelt. He tells Bil that a former protégé of his has optioned his book for the screen. "Who's that?" Bil asks.

"Joseph Jacoby. He often talks about you."

"Oh, yes, Joe. He had the best pair of hands of any guy I ever worked with."

When Edmund told me this later, I was startled. "Bil said that?" Sylvia Morris, who was sitting next to Edmund, leaned in, and said, "Yes. I was sitting next to Edmund when he said it."

I had a tough time grasping it then. I have a tough time grasping it now.

15

To L.A. and Back

I MUST HAVE gotten carried away with memories of Jolson singing "California, Here I Come," and that energetic montage sequence in *The Jolson Story* of the steam locomotive chuggin' its way to California, where Jolson would make the world's first "talkie," *The Jazz Singer*, for Warner Bros. in 1927. I have no doubt this clarion call set me up.

And then there was *Dragnet* and Joe Friday's opening lines: "This is the city. Los Angeles, California. I work here. I'm a cop."* They all wore ties, dark suits, and fedoras. The black-and-white film noir grittiness identified a city that I instantly recognized as the streets of New York, just a little farther west. I inferred a lot here. Night scenes had blinding headlights, but my mind put everything in context: neighborhoods, streets, buildings, traffic lights, newsstands on corners, umbrellas when it rained, galoshes when it snowed, even sewers. City stuff. Even the underscoring got it

---

* One of the most famous crime shows in television history starring Jack Webb as Sergeant Joe Friday and Ben Alexander, featured as Friday's partner, Sergeant Ben Romero. NBC, 1951–59. Revived in 1967–70 (NBC) with Webb and Harry Morgan.

right. There was energy here: "Just the facts, ma'am. Just the facts." Friday spoke in clipped, fatalistic, deadpan tones, the kind of finality that tipped each sentence into a ravine. They all spoke that way. All a film editor had to do was butt the last syllable up against the first incoming and you had style. Concision. Not a frame to waste, ma'am. That's energy. That's New York. My preconceptions of Los Angeles were pretty firm, and altogether flimsy.

Nothing looked like what it was supposed to. I was looking out my window as we came in on final approach, and there was nothing down there but endless tracts of grass and flatlands. Only the cows were missing. My heart sank. I turned to Hal, my host friend from the World's Fair, and asked if this was it and he said yes, this was it. I asked what happened to the city, and he said it was downtown. "Hollywood's downtown?" "No, Joe," he said, smiling wryly, "Hollywood's where I live. Nobody lives downtown." It turned out that a lot of people lived downtown but nobody in the entertainment business lived downtown and when you were *in* the entertainment business everybody else was on another planet.

I wasn't sure what I was here for; I really hadn't thought it out, but if you wanted to put things on film, and I did, this was the place. What I would do exactly was undefinable for me then, even if I were allowed in. Maybe I thought something would fall out of the sky and hit me. This was as much a search for me as anything. While my objectives, like my credentials, were amorphous, my ambition wasn't. Taking action was always better than inaction and might reveal something. Jumping into uncertainty was far better than living with the certainty of a dead-end path, and that's what I was feeling after the fair. Besides, uncertainty had a certain ring to it.

I had brought an offering, though. It was in the cargo bay.

I had never stopped thinking up ideas for game shows, partly because this was the one area of live television I fit into and that had offered employment. Mainly, though, I constructed game shows because I believed I might actually sell a show of my own. I'd been dreaming up ideas ever since high school and had worked for a game show producer.

I'd watched shows being pitched to network executives, and I'd even pitched a few myself. Getting a decision was not a long, drawn-out affair, either: you either got an order for a pilot or you didn't, and you knew it within a day or two. Unless they really didn't like what you had, or liked what you had but hadn't a clue who you were (which was where I fit in), in which case you got an answer right away, and I got an answer right away.

I remember once that Herb Wolf had pitched a show in the morning and his phone rang in the afternoon and ABC ordered the pilot that day. As a kid with no patience, I liked this. I was always told I had no patience and that that was a bad, bad thing. I would tell any kid today not to have patience. Having no patience is a good, good thing. Patience is for people who don't have any passion or ambition, and don't want you having any either, because then you're liable to do something they'd wish they'd done but were too afraid to, and then they'd be scared and jealous. Don't be scared. Let them be jealous. But don't listen. And don't let them take yours.

Although you could conjure and structure a game, and plan for its contingencies (I'd always worried the contingencies; this was home turf), you couldn't really script it unless you fixed it because in certain game formats a contestant might choose any one of a number of available options and you had to be prepared for that, and more than that, you had to have thought through how the game would proceed given any particular decision. Everything had to be anticipated. Nothing could be left to chance. Not unlike a military strategist, if something were to happen you hadn't anticipated a solution for, your game wouldn't survive. What better a person to worry about a game show than a survivor? Game shows also required a skill for applied structure, inventiveness, style, showmanship, and theatricality, all talents of a kind, but you weren't dealing here with the high drama of the human condition. It could be great artifice, though, and that was good enough for me. Anything that would have demanded personal exploration, let alone personal exploration for public consumption, would not have been a good fit for a kid who ran too far in front of the past and never looked back. I had found my vacuity quotient, my comfort level, and it didn't run deep.

And so I had an offering.

"What's that you got in there?" Hal asked, looking at the flat, oblong box I grabbed off the conveyor belt. "A game show," I said. Something to open a door with. The few shows I'd dreamed up before this were all good shows, I thought, but none of them ever sold. At the time, Mark Goodson was the king of game shows. He'd been there at the very beginning, when television was literally brand new and nobody knew anything and they were all making it up it as they went along. I never knew Mr. Goodson (I would later meet him once, and only briefly), but I respected his reputation for thoroughness. The proof of the pudding was in the entertainment value and longevity of his shows. At this writing, *The Price Is Right* is still on the air. I always respected professionalism; I was in awe of the kind of precision and polish of a Goodson-Todman or Barry-Enright show. If you watched a game show in the fifties or sixties, chances are Goodson or Enright owned it. Morey once said that if my name had been Todson-Goodson, or Goodman-Todson or Todson-Godson or some combination of those letters, I would have sold something; he was probably right.

I was in Hollywood now. Hal's house was just off Beachwood Drive, right at the foot of the Hollywood Hills—underneath that famous "Hollywood" sign. As we drove up and I saw that sign, I figured I knew where I was even though I wasn't where I figured I'd be. I had expected energy and the feel of a city. Not a place, as Jolson sang, where "birdies sing at eve-ry-thing." The sign told me what I couldn't feel.

I'd also brought with me a few phone numbers. One of them was Michael Jackson's. He was then doing a late-night talk show on KNX/CBS Radio, and *Time* magazine had already hailed him as "the all-night psychiatrist" of Los Angeles.* He instantly remembered me and invited me to his home for lunch, where I met his lovely new wife, Alana, who was the daughter of Sue Carol and screen legend Alan Ladd. Michael asked what I was up to, and when I told him, he generously offered to introduce me to his agent, Noel Rubaloff.

---

* Michael Jackson was inducted into the Radio Hall of Fame in 2003.

∞

I CAN HEAR it now: "From what do you know from this?!" The word "encouragement" is not in the Brooklyn Jewish lexicon: "Better you should find a job, big shot." If you're a Jewish kid from Brooklyn, especially if all you had were dreams, you had better be careful what you stood up and said. Even if you felt it. *Especially* if you felt it.

I called my new game show *It All Adds Up*, and when I set up the board and showed it to Noel in his office, he was sufficiently impressed to have me pitch it again to the program executive over at NBC. Maybe I was naive enough to think that it might make a difference being out here, but even out here they'd heard of Goodson-Todman, so you know the rest. This would be my earliest exposure to "executive risk aversion," and their fear of taking chances, except with the proven, and only then because they needed to buy *something*, because if they didn't buy something by, say, Friday, they'd be broadcasting test patterns on Monday. And there was another factor: youth. A kid in his twenties then, while benignly admired, was a threat to the established order and certainly not to be trusted with the full reins of production ownership.

Seems like I was hoist on my own petard, though. Noel Rubaloff called: NBC was so impressed with the show they wouldn't buy that they wanted to know if I'd be interested in writing for *Let's Make a Deal*. Here I'd been the aficionado of game shows but had never watched *Deal*. I'd flipped the channels, of course, gotten a sense of it, but my interest had waned, just as I later let go of puppetry. To "write" a game show would have meant swapping a puppet for a pen, albeit a pen with invisible ink. I felt no joy about the offer. Selling your own show was a whole lot different from working on someone else's. My answer to Noel was simple enough: "I don't want to write game shows. I want to make movies."

Years later I heard a story about the diminutive actor, the late Herve Villechaize (three-eleven), who had achieved fame and financial success playing Tattoo on the TV series *Fantasy Island*. One day he called his agent and told him, "I don't want to play midgets anymore. No more midget parts!" That was me, but without the résumé.

Deal's head writer was Alan Gilbert, the producer I'd worked for in New York on *Window Shopping*, and when Alan found out I was in town, he asked if I'd be interested in meeting with the show's producer and part owner with Monty Hall, Stefan Hatos. The network executive approving. The agent saying that this might not be such a bad idea after all. This had all the trappings of a seduction. In having pitched them, I had sold me, both to them and *to me*, because if I was going to do something I really didn't want to do, I'd have to conspire against me, too. And so with a little help from my friends, I did myself in. Had I known myself better I might not have been so gullible. But let's face it: there are worse ways to do yourself in. I paid the rent. I even bought a car. I'll get to the car.

About a week later, when I saw my name come up on the closing crawl as one of three "writers," I wrote "home"—to friends and the Bunins—telling everyone how successful I'd become, and in record-breaking time, especially in a town where time stood still. And I wrote it on *Deal* stationery, too, which made it authentic.

As a child I'd created those paper slide shows by cutting vertical slits on a sheet of construction paper and then pulling a long strip of paper through it, like the individual frames in the Sunday funny papers. The first thing I'd crayon in was the credits. I had the title credits before I had an idea, and sometimes maybe the title gave me the idea. I don't remember what the credits said, frankly, but I suspect they heralded my presence in some way. A beginning presaged things to come, and if you had a beginning, and could identify yourself as being present, there was hope for something beyond it. Those credits undoubtedly confirmed *me* for me more than anything. Without me, without the credits, I'd have nothing to look forward to, and the search for me came after the credits.

If you were doing the pulling, though, one frame at a time, you had control over the story. You could make it up as you went along. Making it up as I went along was life as I knew it. It still is. Unpredictability was predictable. It still is. It's just that here I had some say. Why else do children build worlds? How else do grown-ups learn how to? The few who do.

I still have the photographs I took from way up in the bleachers during *Deal*'s rehearsal. Here I was, intimately involved in the production of a major game show, taking pictures like a tourist, and clandestinely at that (shades of clay models on a metal cabinet). Something about stepping back and taking it all in still enthralled me. Like sitting in back of the house at the "Chrysler Show-Go-Round" on my lunch break, wanting to see how it looked from out front. Like standing in the high school gym during prom night, on the sidelines. This wasn't fear, though. Something about the distance of things still held me. Perhaps being part of it took away the yearning to join; the plea for acceptance, once satiated, arouses discrimination. "Is this what I really want?"

Looking at this now in retrospect, I'd always wanted to be all the players, at all times, a physical impossibility. I never could make up my mind which position held fastest for me. And wherever I was, I was never where I wanted to be. It wasn't clear to me then; it isn't clear to me now. But the closest I'd get, which I hadn't gotten to yet, would be somehow most fulfilling. But I'd still want to be over there. Or maybe over here. Only one thing was certain: I always knew the game. And I'd gotten onto the field.

For me, life in L.A. was life in a bubble, and so geographically spread out that you really couldn't walk from one place to the next except from place to parking place. Even when I made my mad dash up to the Beachwood Market for a container of milk from my new apartment on Beachwood Drive at the foot of the Hollywood Hills, the equivalent of a few Manhattan blocks, it was hard work. I don't remember if it became hard or if it started off that way, but it happened fast. I could walk sixty blocks in Manhattan and never give it a second thought, but out here if I got milk, man, I got into my car and drove a block.

And so the car was very much an appendage you couldn't live without.

My appendage was a used Vauxhall, a British import I found through an ad in the newspaper. The old man who owned it offered to drive by, and when I took it for a spin it worked just fine. He seemed like an honest old man and told me there was nothing wrong with it. For a used car it looked well kept, but I knew nothing about cars, and although I had a driver's license, being a city kid, I'd never owned one, so I took his word on it. The price was $212.50. I ended up owning a lemon that had everything wrong with it within forty-eight hours of purchase. How lemons timed themselves to suddenly disintegrate like time-release capsules, I still don't know. First it was the brake fluid, then the fan belt, the carburetor, just one thing after another. I called that sonofabitch and told him to come get his car and give me back my money but he didn't wanna, and I heard a tone now that informed me. He *knew*. Sonofabitch. So much for John Lennon's "He's a nice old man, isn't he?"

Somehow, though, these wheels delivered me to where I was going each morning, where two other writers and I would sit in the office of Stefan Hatos, and noodle the deals of *Let's Make a Deal.*

As I drove to work that first morning and made my turn around the hill from Barham Boulevard onto Olive Avenue in Burbank, there in the distance I would see now what I had only seen in the movies as a child: those hallowed, majestic Warner Bros. sound stages over on my right. The awe I felt at that moment was Dorothy's first glimpse of the Emerald City in the distance. Those solid structures had history written all over them. As I say, film has permanence, something I never had, and those stages were a "home" of sorts. Belonging, however, is not something I ever felt entitled to, so there was yearning mixed with sadness.

It was one thing for Manoogian to encourage me in the abstract, but it would have been quite another had he been standing there waving me in as I drove by. What drew me? I think a large measure of it is belonging. And a love for the craft. And then there's the magic of it, reality as a construct born of illusion and fantasy. That remains indefinable. Now into my twenties, I still could believe. And as I drove past, taking it in slowly, very slowly, with the stages passing on my right, I was feeling now the feelings I had felt as a child. Then I went to work.

Stefan Hatos held court sitting behind his desk. The man looked and acted like Gene Hackman's character in *Superman*, Lex Luthor. Hackman does a brilliant job breathing life into that character, but Hatos's performance, while sufficiently overbearing and self-infatuated, somehow rang hollow even though he was playing himself.

Hatos: "Where'd we put the zonk last time?" The zonk was the booby prize. If you were unlucky enough to win this, you were generally given some token equivalent. The show, however, was obligated to deliver the actual item if you wanted it. On one occasion, a churchgoing couple won a cow. They had come from their church with two nuns, who were seated in the studio audience above the trading floor. It turned out they wanted the cow delivered to an orphanage in Tijuana, Mexico. It got delivered. As a sort of bonus, the cow was pregnant, so in addition to milk for the kids, they got an extra cow. So says Hank Koval, executive in charge of production.

"Door two," one of us writers says. Brief pause for reflection. A room of contemplative silence.

"Door two it is."

"Again?" one of us says incredulously.

Hatos, smiling with satisfaction, slamming his riding crop on the nearest available object: *"Again!"*

After a grueling morning of this kind of thing we'd break for lunch. And you thought *you* had it bad.

That stretch of dialogue is pretty accurate, actually, but otherwise I'm faking it. Just like I was faking it when I was doing it, and faking it, always, is harder than doing it. For me, these morning writers' meetings were meetings from hell, and in case you haven't noticed, I did not like the man who sat behind the desk. But the challenge being put to me now and my level of absorption in this daily process, when you consider the evidence, may in part explain my avoidance, complicated by the fact that I was having trouble enough finding *me*, let alone remembering where we'd put the zonk. It is truly remarkable, when you consider all the things I *do* remember, that I haven't a clue how we put this show together, how the deals were structured, who wrote what, what I wrote or didn't write. I had my own office, though, replete with dartboard, so I must have done something, but the only reason I know this much is because of an old letter I found where I talk about the dartboard and a few other things, but not a word about the show. The fact of my presence here was more meaningful, somehow, than the meaning of my presence here.

If I had an idea, which I suspect was rare, he would quickly shoot it down, but it was never anything personal because he shot all three of us down. And then, quite often, an idea would appear a few minutes later, usually his, even though it bore a striking resemblance to that dumb idea you'd had just a few minutes earlier. I used to look to Berni and Alan and try to figure out what was going on here. Both men were twice my age and veterans in the true sense of the word and had been with the show since its inception three years earlier (1963). I felt like I'd walked into the middle of act 2 without ever having cracked the play. I might not have known my lines (and thank God it wasn't one of those "naked" dreams), but somehow I had to find a way to look busy. Alan Gilbert was always eager and lighthearted (even his walk was jaunty), and if anything ever bothered him, I never noticed it. At age fourteen he'd appeared (mustachioed) in his father's vaudeville act "Bobby Gilbert and His Talking Violin." A dear man, and the man who'd championed me for this job, he could laugh his way past anything and did. My sense was that, for Alan, this was electronic vaudeville (not a far cry), and had an elephant walked into the room right then and there, he'd have jovially welcomed the creature and worked it into the deal. Alan's adaptive skills were boundless.

Berni Gould, on the other hand, was far more circumspect and laid back. In his youth he'd been an actor on Broadway in *Pins and Needles*. He was known for telling composer Alan Jay Lerner (who would write *My Fair Lady* just a few years after *Pins and Needles*) that if he wanted to adapt a comedy Berni had written based on the legend of Rip Van

Winkle as a musical, he'd have to do it exactly as Berni had written it or not at all. Berni won the "not at all" prize. "The one thing you have to learn in life," he later counseled me, his pipe piping, "is compromise. If you don't learn how to compromise, you're going to be very unhappy." Maybe not those words, exactly, but close enough, and as he spoke, I heard a man who had known disappointment. At the time, though, I knew nothing of Berni's history or the Lerner story, but if I were going to know disappointment I would have to live it on my own watch. (Besides which: disappointment? What disappointment?)

As the three of us sat in these daily meetings, Berni would be puffing away on his pipe, Zenned out, and I figured that the only way Hatos would know if anyone was there was through the smoke that belched from the bowl of Berni's pipe. It stood to reason, after all, that if you saw smoke coming from a chimney stack, chances were somebody was home. Alan once said, "Berni is the only guy who can go to sleep with his eyes wide open." Whether it was Alan's water-off-a-duck's-back laughter (with a backbone from vaudeville) or Berni's smoke signals, each had his way of getting the job done. I have no way of knowing if either man was content with where he'd landed, but I couldn't imagine it for myself.

I always showed up, though. You never knew what would happen if you showed up, but the consequence of not showing up was predictable. A professional showed up and the one thing I prided myself on, as far back as childhood—whether I was taking that little boy to school for a buck a week (the dollar bill was nice but it was never about the dollar bill), shining shoes on Eastern Parkway in Brooklyn at three cents a pop (you got the same worth regardless of price, incidentally, and still do), painting a slatted door green, or selling records on the living room trunk—was that I was professional. But my "invisibility" here was another matter entirely. Something else was stirring, stirred up by the World's Fair and by coming out here in the first place.

As we get older and supposedly wiser, we forget our "fantasized turns in," the moments that awe and inspire us; the things that tug us toward them, and kindle our passions, and by turning toward them, we bring them to us. It really only takes a moment. But as we grow up we learn to bury these passions in order to survive in the real world, perhaps to avoid facing disappointment, including, as my friend Berni had cautioned, through compromise. And for some, whose passions materialize in their life's work, they somehow lose their aura, their magic, something about them lets us down and there are feelings of "Is that all there is? "Now what?" Are they less than what we imagined them to be, or were the imaginings more than what they ever could have been? The childlike wonder that was there at the outset, the romance, fades. It's like carving your initials in the bark of a tree with your very first love and swearing to remember to come back to it years later. And while you will revisit the same park many times after, you've forgotten the tree. And you've forgotten to remember. Try to remember.

The expectations of what it means to be a professional make it unprofessional and unbecoming to feel the childhood sensations, now childish, that were there at the outset and that have taken us to where we have come. Commerce has entered. When I was a child it was only love and magic: the TV set in the window of a radio store, the camera standing idly on the corner, the projection booth of a movie theater, the building where they once made movies; the passions evoked by these "inanimate things" are forgotten. As a child, I could never openly display my passion for fear of embarrassment, ridicule, and having it stolen. As an adult I would get to practice much of what I dreamed as a child. There is synchronicity here, there is the power of dreams, it is not accidental, and it transcends rationality. There is that saying "Be careful of what you wish for in life, you're liable to get it," which I've always interpreted as acknowledgment of the powers within us but with a cautionary note that one must not deal trivially, preparing for and assuming responsibility for, both self-realization and success. The things you passionately want will come to you. The handling is in your care.

I had come to the right place. For the right reason. At the wrong time. I was present in absentia, and L.A. was not a place to come looking for yourself. Picking up from one side of the country and flying to the other was a good idea, perhaps, if you were looking for work and new beginnings, but not if you were looking for you. On the other hand, you could lose yourself out here just as easily as you could lose your car, but while you might be able to recover your car, it would be a whole lot harder to recover yourself, and more dangerous still if you hadn't found yourself in the first place. L.A. was a journey that had to be taken, though. At journey's end, just four months later, I knew I wanted to make movies.

Deal's production office was a few blocks farther down from the NBC Burbank studios where we taped a week's worth of five shows in two days. By the time I'd get to the NBC parking lot at about nine o'clock in the morning, hundreds of contestant wannabes would be lined up around the building; all hoping to be picked for the forty-one reserved seats on the trading floor from which Monty picked the traders and made his deals.

[THE PHONE RINGS. *It was after the taping day when he called. I jumped out of the shower and picked it up.*]

STEVE HATOS
Joe, it's Steve Hatos.

ME
Hi, Steve.

And so Alan, Berni, and I would divvy up forty-one plastic shopping cart numbers and fan ourselves out along the line and start interviewing. If you liked someone, you gave him or her a number. Pandemonium.

STEVE HATOS
Kid, I'm sorry, but I'm afraid
I've got some bad news for you.

ME
Oh?

If you wanted to feel what power felt like, all you needed was a dozen of these numbers.

STEVE HATOS
I'm gonna have to let you go.

For myself, I couldn't wait to get rid of them. I'd been the kid once who stood on line and wanted to get in. I knew the feeling. I wasn't comfortable with this. It was all arbitrary anyway.

ME [Placid]
Uh-huh.

STEVE HATOS
But I'm gonna give you two weeks severance.

ME
Thanks, Steve.

Besides, anybody with the moxie to get all dressed up in those crazy outfits and travel the distance some of these people traveled was entitled.

STEVE HATOS
And if I can offer you some advice . . .

ME
Sure.

Occasionally I'd spot someone with a notebook and pencil. These were the diehards who were convinced we had a system on how we decided where to put the cars and the zonks and that if we'd put a zonk behind door two last time, or a car behind door one, we wouldn't do it again the next time. Wrong. Hatos made those decisions on a whim. This kind of thing was right up his alley; he liked to confound. He'd get a kick out being predictably unpredictable. We never knew what he was going to do until the moment he did it, and neither did he.

STEVE HATOS
In this business you need a sense of humor, kid.
And I just don't think you've got it.

There was no system.

ME
I appreciate that, Steve.

STEVE HATOS
Good luck to you.
ME
Thanks, Steve.

I hung up. I was sitting now at the edge of my bed, still dripping wet. I could hear the shower in the distance. Reality was the running water. I wasn't sad, I wasn't feeling rejected, my feelings hadn't been hurt. A weight had been lifted. The man had been eminently fair; his tone reasonable, and, as always, direct and to the point. I didn't like him, but that was another matter entirely. He'd made the right call. Had it been me, I'd have fired me two months sooner. But I was free now to go home.

Years later, whenever I would tell people I'd once been a writer for *Let's Make a Deal* they would sort of frown and ask, "What was there to write?" I understood what they were asking, of course, which was confirming for me as well, but I never quite knew how to answer, except that the deals that Monty made were structured, and someone had to write that all down: if you buy a kit, and you open it up, you get a book of instructions inside. I always felt that the writing on *Deal* was an instruction book for Monty to follow—deal to deal—because as Berni once said: "You think

Monty came up with those ideas out of his head?" And you could structure and wind this toy up over and over, to run, in fact, for twenty-three years. It did. And so did Berni. And so did Alan.

I sold my Vauxhall. At a loss. Best deal *I* ever made.

16

Cut Goods

FRAGMENTS. PIECES. SWATCHES. Remnants. Maybe
life itself. All cut goods. I think of these words and I think of a tailor. A
Jewish tailor. I don't know why a Jewish tailor, plenty aren't, but that's
what I think of. I also think of the "rag trade," the *shmatteh* business in
Yiddish. Schmuel Goldfish came over by boat from Poland (via Liverpool)
and worked as a glove cutter, advanced to foreman in the cutting department of a glove manufacturer in Gloversville, New York, and ended up
as the sales manager of the Elite Glove Company at their office in Manhattan. And then one summer's day, on his walk home from work, he was
drawn to the Herald Square Theater on Thirty-fourth Street, not considered a respectable venue in those days, where they showed "flickers"—not
yet movies, mind you, just flickers. At the time they were showing the
silent *Bronco Billy* (1913). He had an epiphany, and by the time he'd gotten home he'd made up his mind. He was going into what was then the
beginnings of the movie business. He didn't have to ask anybody what he

thought. Nobody was in charge of anything except that he was in charge of himself. I can't help but wonder where that America went.

He eventually met up with a guy named Edgar Selwyn—a playwright, actor, and play producer, who put himself into a lot of his own plays (why not?)—an obvious source for screen material. The two of them formed a company to make pictures, *Goldwyn* Pictures; part him, part the other guy. And when they finally broke up, Goldfish kept the "wyning" piece of the other guy's name: And Samuel Goldwyn got invented. A piece of this, a piece of that. Cut goods.

Alice Rosenbaum did the same thing, from Russia. After escaping communism, she took the first name of the Scandinavian author of a book she'd read on the ship over (she'd made up her mind to be a writer at age nine and claimed to remember the day and time she'd made that decision), and her last name from the Remington-Rand typewriter she worked on in Chicago—a piece of this, a piece of that, voilà!: Ayn Rand. Cut goods.

I'd reinstated myself with my army reserve unit, the 356th Station Hospital on Forty-second Street as soon as I got back. During the summer months we'd spend two weeks training, and during a break one day I overheard a conversation in which one of the guys was talking about his plans for retirement. To keep a perspective on this, you have to understand that we were all in our midtwenties, and this was the midsixties and before IRAs and 401(k)s. A miasma of despair swept over me, perhaps because I hadn't thought about any of this, and hadn't dealt with something apparently real that perhaps I should have been dealing with but couldn't relate to. Denial. If I wasn't sure of my present, what future would I be planning for? How was it these guys in their twenties were thinking so far out anyway? I was thinking only the present, as if it and I were one, and I had to hurry because I realized that by tomorrow it would be past. How else was I going to get my first picture made if I was always a day behind because of the present I'd wasted on the future?

Denial. Besides, what if there was no such thing? A future, I mean. How could you know it would be there when you showed up? Or worse, what if *it* was there and *you* weren't? Did anyone ever come back and say, "Hey, this thing's great. You should come visit."? Anybody who did, though, would be living in the past, which I was always told was the *worst* thing you could do, and maybe that included the dead. Who knows? Besides, as Satchel Paige, a truly legendary black baseball pitcher who didn't get into the white major leagues until he was in his forties, once said, "How old would you be if you didn't know how old you was?" (Satchel didn't know how old he was.) I got up, walked away, and left it at that. I wasn't depressed anymore either. I even got my picture made. So much for denial.

I always seem to have made it up as I went along, putting life together as it went. Me making it up, or it revealing itself; I'm not sure what the difference is. Continuity had always been something I invented. Like taking different patterns, different swatches, stitching them all together, and making them look like me. Anybody looking at me would have hardly seen a seam, so expert was I at concealment. It was all about acceptance, not deception. But cut goods, still. With at least as many pieces as Alice and Schmuel. If you've kept all these pieces in disguise, though, you've kept a dirty secret, one that perpetuates an irresolute sense of guilt and worry about being found out.

This impostor guilt may even countermand whatever gains you've realized, neutralizing any sense of accomplishment—in effect, paying the price for your legitimacy and acceptance. My need for success and approbation was driven, at least in part, by my need to reconcile the good with the guilty. Acts of apparent selflessness, the giving of time, offering advice, *altruism*—these were often acts of contrition disguised as selflessness, beneficial to others and therefore to me as well. I had no need otherwise. Need made you vulnerable, and vulnerability was something to hide. Whole goods, no seams. Paradoxically, even my closest friends may have wondered why I would do so much, and I may have lost one over it.

You can deny your beginnings, but I don't believe they ever really leave you. And perhaps that is the ultimate paradox: the irritant in the shadow is the propellant for the pearl in the sunlight.

As I walked into the darkened screening room, the picture was already up on the screen. I hadn't come late; I supposed the work session had begun early. Ray, the son of the furrier who, you'll recall, had gotten me my first job in television, was talking to the lab technician at the control panel in back. I nodded as I passed, and quietly made my way along the sidewall to one of the fifty or so empty seats. What was up on the screen looked and sounded like a real movie. It *was* a real movie. It didn't have any stars in it, but that didn't matter. It was called *Aroused,* and was the kind of low-budget "exploitation" movie you'd see on a double bill at a sixties drive-in theater or New York's Forty-second Street: tits 'n' titillation. This seemed to deliver, and had a narrative to go with it, although, to be honest, I wasn't paying that much attention to the story. I was mesmerized: Ray had made a movie.

Then in his midforties, Ray had been a successful commercial photographer, and he had the same kindness of spirit his father had. I'd stayed in touch and was all the more eager to reconnect when I got back and heard he'd produced his first picture. So here I was at Movielab, Inc., whose logo read: "In the East It's . . . Movielab," which told me you could do here what you did there. Since Ray had already done it, and I was here to see it, it was like telling me the Dodgers were coming back to Brooklyn, which I'd frankly been expecting anyway. Still am, in fact. Brooklyn was the only real team the Dodgers ever had anyway.

I picked up on the conversation Ray and the technician were having in back as the footage counter rolled beneath the screen, and I was struck by their clinical detachment. The objectivity of that footage counter ticking along as the picture played above it, combined with the dispassionate commentary I was hearing in back, said something to me about the disconnect between the "reality" of the movies, which is frozen for all time, and the reality of the time and space that was discerning, controlling, and determining of the reality that was ticking by in front of me. And yet people bought into the reality that was up on the screen. Even a picture's "spontaneity," the parts that surprise us, for which one has to suspend disbelief in the cause of a good time, had to be measured, in the sense that it had to be believable within the context of disbelief. Both realities—the one we live day to day, and the one we make up, as in movies—are cut goods, with one determining and the other determined, at least to the extent that it's not all within our control. That's what I believe. If you wanted the film to come out good, whatever "good" meant to you, you had you and the film to rely on; theoretically, at least, you could determine the outcome.

If you wanted real life to come out good, you only had yourself to rely on, but things could happen that were not in your control (I knew something about this, you know). And if you got deep enough into this moviemaking thing, you could forget what you had no way of controlling anyway, and instead control what you have to control to make a movie. And so making a movie was at least as much an escape for its maker as it was for its audience. A win-win in an uncertain world. Why, then, would anybody want it any other way? And maybe you'd even get to be famous, and recognition was just what I was looking for. And they'd pay you for it, too, the distributors. If you had something to say, that would be sensational, but you didn't need something to say, you needed something to get away with. And if the audience were entertained, they'd let you get away with murder. In fact, that's just what was happening in front of me. That footage counter couldn't have cared less if they were kissing or killing. Clay models, redux. *Big* time. How much did this thing cost to get into? That was the only question I could think of.

When the lights came up I turned and looked back at Ray. He stood up, smiling broadly: "What'd you think?" I was awed by his achievement, by the simple fact that it existed and that it looked and felt professionally made. The realization that one man, having never produced a movie before, could do this, without Hollywood, and without anyone's permission, was inspiring. As we went down in the elevator, I began asking questions, none of them, I suspect, having anything to do with the picture's story. What was the next step? How was the movie going to get into theaters? And finally, the sixty-four-thousand-dollar question: how much did the movie cost to make? By now we were standing on Fifty-fourth Street in front of Movielab, and Ray lit up one of his big cigars and I could tell he was feeling like a real producer, which, of course, he was, and I remember feeling what a great feeling that must feel like. I didn't know if he'd tell me, because as a kid I'd never told anyone what my passions were for fear of having them taken away. "Twenty-nine thousand dollars," he said without the slightest hesitation. We were walking toward Broadway, and while Ray was talking, I was thinking about where I was going to get twenty-nine thousand dollars. On the one hand, twenty-nine thousand dollars was all the money in the world to me. On the other, it couldn't be impossible if he'd done it.

I asked Ray how he'd raised the money, and he told me that some family members had invested, and I suspected he'd invested some, given that he'd been a successful photographer. This was when six thousand dollars a year was a living (I don't recall ever needing more), and when my friend John earned ten thousand dollars one year, that was verging on genuine comfort, so you can imagine what twenty-nine thousand dollars must have felt like to me. But I knew what I had to do even if I hadn't a clue how I would do it.

It never bothered me that I'd never made a movie, though. I'd worked on movies—that is, I'd worked for Morey and for Bil on filmed commercials. It might occur to others that I'd never made a movie, but that was talkable. I'd made everything else up as I went along. Why not this? Besides, it never occurred to me that I couldn't. I'd been practicing in my head all my life. Making the movie was beside the point. Twenty-nine thousand dollars was the point. In a book, one sentence follows the next. In a life, two whole years can go by, and a reader would never even know it. They did and you do.

Movies are the ultimate cut goods. Photographed in small pieces and usually out of sequence, they are a virtual life form animated only when these pieces are "cut" together into a preconceived pattern. Creating reality piecemeal through storytelling, under conditions of controlled chaos, with me in control of both the chaos and the polished ends, was a lot better, and safer, than being in control of nothing. But it's especially true when you've carved out a life in the imaginary practice of these techniques, a life that might just as well have belonged to someone else, at least at its beginnings. Where it gets mystical is that the me who was on hold for the future now emerged, taking over from the me who mysteriously functioned, even excelled, while under the yoke of authoritarianism and after. Passion and the will to realize our dreams drive this; nothing less.

Now—an arbitrary but perfectly reasonable *now* (amid a confluence of certain upcoming synchronistic events)—was a potent time to get even (anger, smartly measured), to seize control, and to create reality in the way that Alice and Schmuel had. A kid whose only continuity in life came from his dreams and the characters he knew from television, who followed him from neighborhood to neighborhood, knew it, for whatever reason, when he saw it.

The power of the motion picture—as close to a religious experience as I had ever felt—confirmed for me that the reality you invent is as meaningfully real as any other, invested with mythic powers and powers of inclusion, including familial inclusion (with me at the head of the table). Mr. Goldfish would have his epiphany on Herald Square and Thirty-fourth Street. I ran into that enlightenment in a darkened screening room at Movielab, Inc., a film processing laboratory housed in an ugly, old, nondescript brick building on West Fifty-fourth Street in New York City— just twenty blocks up. Fifty-three years later. And this time, MIT sound.*

---

* Some scenes in movies are shot silent, without sound (i.e., nondialogue scenes), and sound is then added later. This has come to be known as shooting a scene 'MOS" (mit-out sound). I haven't the vaguest idea how this began, really, but if I had to guess, somebody must've had an accent. And so MIT would mean, well, *mit* sound.

I'd never seen *The Wizard of Oz* as a kid. I was too busy getting around, I suppose, my schedule being what it was. I knew that the road led to the wizard, but beyond that I was vague, except that I understood that Dorothy found her way home. I never felt any real desire to see it. "There's no place like home" just didn't reference me.

Still, I inferred the road's broader meaning and found it affirming, and I could follow it, providing, of course, I built it. I had no other choice really, and following was never something I was ever any good at anyway. The capacity to resist and survive authority does not imply an absence of self-discipline. Purposefulness is born of inner-directed passion and ambition, as well as at-a-distance, selective judgment and self-determination, all compatible with resistance. Punishment strengthens one's determination, which is a lifelong requisite for achievement and success in adult life. I learned in school that for every action there was an equal and opposite reaction, "opposite" being the operative word. Some hadn't learned the lessons they themselves taught. But no matter which road you follow; yours or someone else's, there are characters along the way. I know who wrote Dorothy's. Mine just seemed to show up.

Meanwhile, I needed to find a job to pay the rent. I called Dan Enright, whom I'd met a few years earlier through Morey's partner Frank, the same fellow who had set up the run-through of my game show for Oscar Katz at CBS. Enright was, of course, half of the Barry-Enright producing team of *Tic-Tac-Dough, Concentration, Dough-Re-Mi,* and the one that did him in (and the subject of Robert Redford's masterfully crafted film *Quiz Show*), the quiz show *Twenty-One*. (*Twenty-One* aired in prime time, one night a week, on NBC from September 1956 to October 1958.) Enright's shows depended heavily on their big-money lure, whereas Mark Goodson's shows were essentially games that stood on their own without money, and the reason why the Goodson-Todman shows escaped any taint of scandal.

To sit with Enright was to be with a slice of early television history, and a kid who'd lived these events through the tube and the headlines and who had admired his skills and craftsmanship couldn't help but ask the questions. I was hesitant at first, but to my surprise, he virtually leaped at the chance to talk, and was quite open and willing to answer any questions I might have, questions I suspected he'd anticipated and had already answered hundreds of times before anyway. I felt, though, that he was still seeking vindication for his own version of the truth, and probably from anyone who showed interest enough to listen. Who knows? Maybe through repetition he'd find it. Spit it out enough times and maybe you get rid of it; that's the value one receives through an act of expiation, although I doubt very much that this man lost any sleep from guilt. I found it discomfortingly flattering and odd, frankly, that he would so readily confide in me. After all, I was a kid looking for work. But I was also a kid who held his showmanship in high regard, and he knew that.

It had been eight years since Enright's empire had collapsed, literally overnight. And in the end, it had been his own self-interest that kept him from full disclosure of what he knew—a disclosure that, in my judgment, no congressional committee would have wanted to hear anyway, and nobody knew that better than he. To listen to him tell it now, though, he was still the embittered fall guy. When I asked if NBC knew the show was rigged, he said (and I paraphrase), "Of course they knew. How could they not know? They told us to do whatever we had to do. The show wouldn't work otherwise. They knew that." When I asked how NBC got off the hook, he said, "You don't think they were going to take away NBC's license to broadcast, do you?" In a closed executive session of the congressional committee investigating the scandals, Enright was asked if the NBC executives knew *Twenty-One* was rigged. He responded, "You would have to be very unsophisticated or very naive not to understand that certain controls have to be exercised."

Twenty-One simply couldn't work because the questions were so hard that no matter how smart you were or how well read or informed you were, you'd conk out early. But unless the home audience was able to establish a rooting interest in someone—even if it was the villain you love to hate—they wouldn't tune in next week. And so the fix was in: find an interesting personality, ask questions you know he or she already knows, and let that person stick around for a while.

I remember feeling that Enright's version of how things happened made sense, even though I always felt that anything this man told me had some shadow lurking behind it. And if there wasn't a natural shadow, he'd put one there. He just had that sort of conspiratorial personality, and even when he'd let you in on something, it raised a red flag. He was not an empathetic man, no genuine warmth, but rather he had a cunning, and even a streak of mean-spiritedness. One would have to have met Enright to fully appreciate how uncannily close actor David Paymer came in capturing the spirit and detailed nuance of the man in Redford's *Quiz Show*. The idea that NBC had told him to do whatever he had to do to make the show work was not only believable, and implicated the network in a conspiracy, it also was a factor that, in the end, Enright himself offered plausible denial for, in the hope, quite simply, that he would work again.

This whole quiz scandal thing was a charade, although it did bring about regulations and guidelines regarding the operations of quiz and game shows, and producers of these shows became extra-sensitive to adhering to strict codes of transparency. But in the end the network got off scot-free, and the committee's findings didn't amount to a can of beans in terms of any real consequence, except for one contestant and one producer.

Now, in late 1966, working for Screen Gems, Inc., in New York and producing shows in Canada, Enright was still persona non grata at the three American networks (there were only three then).*

---

* In September 1972, Barry-Enright Productions returned to the network airwaves with *The Joker's Wild*. It ran for two years on CBS, daytime, and entered syndication in 1976. After Jack Barry's death in 1984, Bill Cullen took over the hosting chores. In July 1978, *Tic-Tac-Dough* returned (CBS, daytime) after having not been seen in almost twenty years (it originally premiered on NBC from 1956 to 1959). Corporations have indelible memories. Dan Enright knew that. It just took a while.

"You can write," he said. I wasn't sure if he was asking me or telling me—this might have been *Twenty-One Redux*, who knew?—but he needed writers. If I could tell Bil Baird I did marionettes, I could tell Dan Enright I could write. The show was called *Magistrate's Court*, a five-day-a-week courtroom drama taped in Canada. All I had to do really was come up with a few sentences with themes and setups for cases to be argued before a magistrate. If they felt they could use it, I would then develop each idea to script form, with dialogue, with an average case running four to six pages; I believe they used three to a half-hour show. I was paid fifteen dollars per script. My rent was a hundred dollars per month. Seven of these a month and I had the rent money. And coffee, too. I did it for a short while, until the show was canceled a few months later. When I was twelve, Mrs. Williams up at Hawthorne had told me I could write. But she never offered any loose change.

Work otherwise was "catch-as-catch-can," as it usually is in the entertainment business, and especially if you were being "creative," a word that increasingly meant a life without structure. What other life was there?

17

Follow the Yellow Brick Road

I REMEMBER BACK in the sixties there was a billboard on Sixth Avenue not far from Times Square that read: "Why doesn't someone give Mogubgub Ltd. two million dollars to make a movie?" There was a name and a number. At first I wasn't really sure he meant it, or even if there was a Fred Mogubgub. Maybe this was some kind of cartoon character like a Gerald McBoing-Boing or a Mr. Magoo, or a prelude to a bigger ad yet to come. It was so simple and direct that it couldn't be what it appeared to be. And then I thought, well, anybody with a name like Mogubgub and the brazenness to hang it out there like that deserved a billboard *and* a movie. It was bold, brash, and in your face. I loved it. I was curious to know, though, what kind of calls he was getting, but I would never have taken the chance of calling myself. This might have been serious. This wasn't something to play games with anyway. You wouldn't play games in church, would you? I wondered, though, if he ever got the money. Remembering this vividly must've meant something. It was added encouragement, I suspect, and maybe I envied it a bit, too; who knows?

But taking it seriously spoke to me further about the possibilities. The idea was getting around. And it wasn't an idea anyone could steal from me, either. This was a legitimate pursuit, the real thing. If I needed sanctioning, this did it. This was kosher heaven.

Fred Mogubgub had an utterly unique approach to classified advertising: instead of offering a job, he offered an opportunity. Instead of offering money, he asked for it. And instead of looking for a job, he invented one. The implications were far-reaching and unique to my experience. Something resonated. I remembered that billboard. Of course, the cost of putting up a billboard was more money than I needed to make a movie, so that would never have been a thought of mine anyway. But you can imagine what all of Times Square would have looked like, lit up with billboards wanting to raise money to make movies. A billboard classified at the crossroads of the world.

∞

IN 1966, A Scandinavian import called *I, a Woman* played at Brandt's Rialto Theatre on the corner of Forty-second Street and Broadway. The Rialto was considered the jewel of the "sexploitation" houses, and was generally reserved for "upscale" foreign movies. There was something about seeing sexual content in a different language, and in a somewhat fancier theater, that made it more respectable somehow. Being foreign meant "art," and art gave license, and if you got caught going in you could always blame it on the subtitles coming out. *Playboy* magazine rose above the girlie magazines in the same way. What better place to read the genre fiction of Philip Roth or Saul Bellow? Why else would you buy it? Of course, the only person who gave a damn whether you came or went was you.

In truth, the sexual content of these films never lived up to their graphic billboards, and the "production values" of some of these imports had a way of sucking the sleaze out of things that, after all, were not what you were expecting, any more than you were expecting *The Ten*

Commandments. The canny street-smart could sniff this stuff out a mile away, while the guilt-laden paid the "arty" price of admission. It was all impulse buying. Sex is not something you put on your to-do list. The market for this stuff was insatiable, and the lure of the photo displays and the marquee titles above them did the trick.

In the Coney Island of my childhood the Mule-Faced Boy stood on a raised wooden platform with a canvas hood over his head and two moonlike circles cut out for him to see through, while the carny barker described what he looked like under the hood. A life-size painting behind him looked just like what he was describing, as he put away that fat roll of 50-cent tickets and took out, *for the next ten minutes only*—the 25-cent tickets. I felt bad for the Mule-Faced Boy and was torn between buying a ticket and not wanting to embarrass him by staring. He didn't seem to mind it, though. In fact, his eyes looking through those large, cut-out holes seemed a million miles away. Inside, when he took off his hood, he didn't look anything as bad as I'd imagined; nothing at all like his painting. He basically had a very bad case of buckteeth. And he wasn't a boy, either. He was a fully grown man. He looked just as bored by this as I was disappointed.

I realized that the better part of the show was the free part on the outside. The anticipation of him taking off that hood and my imagining what he really looked like underneath and looking at the giant painting behind him, those were what were worth the twenty-five cents.

I copped a Mogubgub. But instead of spending all that money I never had for a billboard, and asking for two million bucks, I put away the two-million-dollar tickets and took out the twenty-nine-thousand-dollar tickets and became my own billboard. I'd talk to anyone who would listen. I was making a movie. With or without money, that's how sure I was. But for twenty-nine thousand dollars (or any portion thereof, as a lawyer would say) you could own a piece of the pie.

The armory for my Reserve unit meetings was *on* Forty-second Street, just a few blocks west when you left the West Side subway and walked past the theaters, every one of them my billboard. Almost everything on

Forty-second Street said sex. By the time our weekly meetings rolled around, you were primed for the pitch. And I was the only one with the raffle book. I only had so many tickets left, and when they were gone, they were gone. My fellow reservists were as eager to see what was under that hood as I'd been: *"Lonely girl comes from Midwest to big city, hooks up with dating service, meets guys."* Very imaginative stuff. You take it from there.

ARMY BUDDY (an M.D.): How many guys?
ME: What would you guess?
ARMY BUDDY: Three?
ME: That's right. Exactly right. [beat] And they're all perverts.

This was interactive storytelling before we even knew what that meant. I was making it up as we went along.

ARMY BUDDY: What happens then?
ME: If I told you, I'd ruin it for you.

Nobody ever questioned I was making a movie. Nobody even asked to see a script. There was no script.

My problem was I couldn't tell the same story twice. I wasn't trying to be creative; I just couldn't remember what I'd said. And every time I talked, I got another idea. It didn't matter, though, because I was fitting the guy I was talking to into the picture. Cut goods, remember. Nothing off the rack here. Not that he was becoming a character, mind you; he became a "collaborator." You had to know your customer. And once he saw himself in authorship, he felt invested.

ARMY BUDDY: How much are you looking for?

Don't get me wrong. It wasn't all lickety-split one, two, three, just like that. This took time, and I had the rent to pay. There were a few freelance production jobs and even a few extra parts in movies and day-time soaps in between, but during this time I met my first lawyer, Jack Perlman. I met Jack through Charlotte Bunin (I still maintained cordial relations with the Bunins), and if there was ever such a thing as an avant-garde lawyer, Jack was it. A Harvard graduate, he'd gone to law school with Arthur Cantor, a successful Broadway producer, whom he represented, along with important avant-garde filmmakers such as Jonas and Adolphus Mekas. Jack was defending a bare-bosomed cello player, Charlotte Moorman, on an obscenity rap in federal court. It seems ridiculously innocent now, but a bare-breasted cello player was the proverbial tempest in a teapot in the late sixties. In one corner there was Bob Fosse, who had just completed his first theatrical picture, *Sweet Charity*, with Shirley MacLaine, and in the other Fosse's ex and star of the Broadway production of *Charity,* Gwen Verdon. The day I walked into Jack's office he was on one phone with Arthur Cantor, who was suing somebody for fifty bucks, and on the other with Verdon, who was castigating some movie critic for panning *Charity*. Jack was clearly a lawyer-cum-friend, -cum-confidant, -cum-shrink, all in one. He acknowledged my presence at the door with his head nodding back and forth, and his eyes rolling smilingly upward, as if to enlist my patient understanding. The phone receiver nestled snugly against his ear, he removed his black-rimmed glasses and motioned for me to come in and sit down. Removing his glasses somehow signaled a pending order of business—mine—and that he'd be with me in just a moment. When he got off the phone, he shared with me his bemusement with his quixotic clients, luxuriating in their *mishegas* (wacky nonsense or craziness). He moved his legal pad closer to himself now, and we immediately got down to business.

The fact that I was this enthusiastic kid who had blown in from nowhere, embarking on something that was somewhere between mainstream and taboo, appealed to Jack and his liberal bent. Anything he'd perceived as derring-do would have grabbed his interest. He was Timothy Leary in a suit, sans the LSD. Jack's enthusiasm and optimism were unbridled and perpetual. A proponent of liberal causes and a defender of artists' rights, he had an obvious love for the arts and a solid belief in an artist's right of free expression, whether he or anyone else agreed with it. I did not think of myself in the category of any of these accomplished people, but I got lucky anyway. When Jack heard what I wanted to do and that I'd gotten some of my army buddies to agree to invest, he immediately drew up some papers for them to sign (I didn't have the money to pay him yet, but he took the shot anyway), and I was off and running.

Meanwhile, I'd answered a want ad in the *New York Times* for a commercial production manager's job, and when I met the director's representative he quickly sized me up and told me flat out that he didn't think I would fit well with his client. I suspect my ambition showed through. Bob, the director's rep, asked what I'd done, though, and I told him what I was doing—putting money together for a movie I was making. He asked "What kind of movie?" and I was off to the races. I really hadn't said all that much when he asked, "How much money do you have? How much are you looking for?" Sex sells. Right then and there he called his friend Tony. Here I'd gone up looking for a job, got turned down, and made a date to come back to meet Tony, a successful graphic artist. That's when I asked Jack if he'd come with me, knowing that his presence would enhance my credibility, and lo and behold, I had two more checks. Jack was amused, though. "That's not the story you told me in my office." "It's not?" "No. But I like this one better." He came with me a few more times, too, and on the bus one day I said, "Jack, I really appreciate your taking the time to help me with this." He quipped, "Are you kidding? I love hearing you tell these stories. It's a different story every time!"

I began to worry about this, though. Here I was taking in all this money and I hadn't written anything. Not even Jack asked if I had a script. He just assumed I knew what I was doing. Either that or maybe they all figured these kinds of movies didn't need scripts anyway—and they wouldn't have been far off. I wrote a ten-page treatment and hired a guy, then in his seventies, to write the script. He promised to have it done in two weeks. I paid him five hundred dollars. Meanwhile, I was casting. How you cast a movie without a script, I don't know (but I knew the characters), any more than how you raise money that way, but nobody ever told me I couldn't. People would later tell me all kinds of things I couldn't, including things I already had, but I would soon learn to worry more about those who said I could. The "you can'ts," also known as the "noers," were either fearful, jealous, or both, and often just plain dumb. The fact is, as the screenwriter William Goldman has said, "Nobody knows anything." Nobody here would have known a good script from a bad script, anyway, and if they felt you knew what you were talking about, that was good enough for them. I suspect it all came down to something else, though: my passion. And my conviction. I couldn't have hidden those for no money.

gambit: n. (in chess) an opening in which a player makes a sacrifice, typically of a pawn, for the sake of some compensating advantage. (*New Oxford American Dictionary*)

In the spring of 1968, I opened the partnership's bank account. I called it the Gambit Company. I'm not sure how that word flew into my head, but when I checked, it said exactly what I meant for it to say. The picture I was about to make was not the picture I wanted to make but rather the picture I needed to make to do that, but had you asked me then what picture I wanted to make, I would either have told you that I was making the picture I wanted to make or that I didn't know the picture I wanted to make and was making this instead, which, of course, is almost like saying the same thing, except the second answer's more forthcoming. You were not a player until you had game, as we say now, and the clock was ticking, and a ticking clock was something I'd always watched—an extension of the observer I'd always been, the metronome against which the beat of life, including the lives of others, moved; an awareness that life had to be gotten on with, and in my case compensate for lost time, and otherwise. The day was finite. Making a picture, any picture, took dedication, resolve, and commitment, an obsession bordering on temporary insanity, the suspension of all else that is deemed "real" for a reality that not only engenders a life force but also one that transcends and scuttles the one we live daily. It becomes all-absorbing. It is both addictive and contagious. It is the very physical manifestation of one's passion. It was that palpable expression of the passion that had always been with me and that put $34,500 in the bank. And still, no script.

The sixties saw the emergence of a personal cinema not unlike that of the French New Wave, exemplified by a new generation of independent young filmmakers, my generation, with pictures that were autobiographically inspired. Whatever autobiographical essence l could draw from I was not about to divulge, even if I'd been aware, which I was not. I could not have looked back or deep. Forward was unidimensional, untrammeled, fertile, and wide open. Uncharted territory. In the thrust of going forward you went up, and that might take you flying. I was as much about self-invention as any picture I might make, and making pictures was the essence of invention, especially when you were dreaming both them and you up at the same time, with one informing the other.

I had done my homework, though, and was both inspired and encouraged by the dismal state of affairs in this genre known then as sexploitation. Not only were the stories inane to nonexistent, but also the camerawork, lighting, acting, all of it, dreadful. I could run rings around this. But I was as ambivalent as Chayefsky's Marty would have been, and he'd had a tough time asking the girl to dance *with* her clothes on. The requirement of success, though, trumped everything. I had no intention of standing still or getting swept away, and where I was starting was as good a place as any, even if where I was headed remained to be seen. With nothing to say, and all the tools to say it with, I was passionately directed to the distraction of moviemaking. I had game. But back then, we said I was doing my thing.

I'd hired everybody; shooting dates were set; even a budget was drawn to conform to the amount of money I'd raised; and the only reason I'd stopped raising money was because I'd exceeded Ray's twenty-nine thousand dollars. Two weeks later I had a script. Read a few pages. Dropped it. Went to bed. Passed out. It was that bad.

I didn't think the story was so bad—I'd certainly had enough experience telling it—but the script was awful. For the very first time now, I was confronting what was on paper. Nothing about any of this made sense. It's as if I'd been juggling balls, with all of them in the air all at the same time, and none of them ever landing. I had somehow suspended gravity. Of course, had I known the *right* way to do things, none of this would have happened. I was at the early stages of how things worked in life, and to this day I am suspicious of anything that makes sense. That wonderful actress Ruth Gordon said it beautifully: "Never face the facts." Me, she didn't have to tell. This was no different, really, than when I was back in Brooklyn with my mother, creating slide shows out of construction paper. As I pulled on the thing, it just sort of came out, like the swizzle of custard from the custard machine. Putting this together was like laying track; you just had to make sure things joined up somehow. I made my peace with the script. I had a workable story, after all. I'd get past it somehow. I'd enthuse it—don't ask me what this meant; I have no idea. If I could get this far, though, I could suspend gravity here as well. And I did. I started filming. It was shot entirely in apartments, a Greenwich Village disco, an antiques store, a place of fine dining, and the streets of New York, and ten days later I had the makings of a movie. Now someone had to cut the goods.

∽

ROSENZWEIG: "What the hell kinda picture are you making there?! My girls don't wanna touch the negative."

ME: "What the hell do you care what I'm making?! I'm not asking for reviews. Let them wear gloves!"

ROSENZWEIG: "They *wear* gloves."

ME: "I'm paying you by the foot. Let 'em use their feet!"

And I hung up. Just what I needed to hear. Everybody called him "Rosie," though. An old-time lab man at least in his seventies, he was always upbeat, always cheerful. Nattily dressed and compactly built, he'd be jaunting his way down the street without a care in the world, a perpetual smile on his face, the perfect balance of contentment and courtliness. Rosie was a posy. I'd been attracted by his sense of caring, too, which was reflected in his company's name: Quality Film Labs. When you asked Rosie about the quality of his work he would proudly put out his hands and say the words, just like the Allstate guy: "You're in good hands." He took pride. The grandfather I never had. He'd watch over you. He was actually operating a small boutique out of an office at Deluxe Labs, then owned by 20th Century-Fox, way over on West Fifty-sixth Street. That was fine with me. I had someone to talk to, a contact guy. But what this ruckus was about now, I couldn't fathom.

To hear him tell it, the "heat" in my negative was burning down the building. Forty-second Street was far "hotter" than anything I was shooting, but then again they were probably developing their stuff at a drugstore in Brooklyn. It must have been my topless dancer, or maybe my lead actress running back and forth between the window and the bed, bare-ass (wrapped in a sheet, of course), but the bed scenes, such as they were, were more about designer sheets than sex. I would never have let a little sex get in the way of a good story, anyway. After all, which would *you* prefer: a story without sex, or sex without a story? Never mind. I was caught.

It was a balancing act, all right. If you wanted to get beyond the grind houses, though, and into the drive-ins, which would actually increase the number of theaters you could play, you needed something more to hang your sex on. And not your hat, either, although I'd seen guys walking into these places with their hats *and* their raincoats on. I didn't want to be so respectable, though, that nobody would talk to me, but that's what was happening here with blushin' Rosie: his "girls" wouldn't talk to him. But that didn't mean they *wouldn't talk.* And in that respect, it was disrespect. Here I was reaching for the moon, and Rosie's screaming from the toilet. I called him back. You don't hang up on your lab guy. He's got your jewels.

ROSIE: "My girls don't wanna touch your negative."

ME: "Rosie—we did this already. Can't you see I'm in the middle of a picture?"

ROSIE: "A picture, okay. But this is pornography."

ME: "How the hell do you know what this is? Have you seen the picture? And what if it is pornography? Who put *you* in charge?"

ROSIE: "I was expecting you were making a picture. With a story. A beginning, middle, and an end."

I could hear it now in his voice. He needed reassurance. He was guilty through association. He had to face his "girls," after all, and particularly as an elder statesman, he had a "quality" reputation to uphold. The eyeballing of silent uncut footage of a scene, shot many times over, could create a false impression, but if there's a story . . .

ME: "I *am* making a story with a picture. Damn it! This *is* a story. There is a beginning, middle, and an end. How can you tell from the pieces? But I don't care what you're expecting. I'm paying you. Develop the film!"

ROSIE: "There's a story?"

Message delivered. Again I hung up. I imagined him running down now to the basement, or wherever it was they did this stuff, and proclaiming, "Girls! There's a story!"

And that made everything kosher, like a chicken blessed in brine. You could go home and eat it now, but still, watch out for the bones. Rosie and I absolved each other. We were lantsmen. I never knew a story could have such power, but I must have known something because I'd been making them up all my life, telling them as I went, and believing what I was telling, always. For Rosie's girls, and for me even, "There's a story!" gave license.

Let the yentas, the old gossips, complain. "From what do you know from stories?" "You had to go do this?" "You couldn't go out and make a living?" "You had to announce it so the whole world should know our business?" "Maybe you should put yourself in the picture?" "Why not? A Clock Gable we got yet." "Big shot!" (In 2001, an elderly legal secretary actually said to me, in a deprecatory tone, "So who's going to play you, Tom Cruise?") When they are good, they are very good.

But not my mother. She would never have said these things. She had given me all that I had asked, all that she was able.

There were no tracks in my dream that night in the hotel room with my mother when I was seven. They'd all burned down, and that's when I woke up. I don't know why I dreamed the tracks were gone, but I knew. And in the morning she'd be gone, too. I had to lay the tracks now. Even as a child, I had so many dreams. I don't know where they came from. I certainly had no right to them, given what I'd done. But I was not going to fall off. There was penance to pay here. Somehow I'd set this right.

∞

TWO YEARS LATER, August 1970, it opened. *Shame, Shame . . . Everybody Knows Her Name.* Forty-second Street and Broadway. Rialto II. I stood with my girlfriend, Jackie, looking down Forty-second Street all lit up as far as the eye could see. And there was the marquee of Forty-second Street's newest theater all lit up with the title of my movie. She asked me, "How do you feel?" in a tone of "You must be feeling pretty good." It had been four years since I'd had that epiphany at Ray's screening, and here I was now, standing in my own shoes, having achieved everything I'd imagined, and yet my expectations seemed so much greater then than anything I felt now. With my camera in hand, I memorialized the marquee, for no other reason, I suppose, than my omnipresent awareness of the temporal nature of things, capturing an accomplishment I could otherwise not feel. But I don't think I ever answered Jackie's question. I must have wondered, though, "Where's the rest of it?" It was all so anticlimactic.

Many years later I would read a good review of an old friend's movie in *Time*, a major film by a well-known actor-director, and I called him. As I recall, there was a picture of him sitting on a deck chair on the beach near his home. I congratulated him and asked where he was sitting at this moment that we were speaking, and just like in the picture, he was on the beach, facing the Pacific Ocean. I was curious, though. I asked him, "How do you feel?" His first word was: "Huh?" And I said, "This must make you feel great." He responded, "Now what?" "Huh?" I said, and he repeated, *"Now what?!"* I understood.

But here's one what. I'd met a guy who was then the lighting director on NBC's *Today* show and who also had worked on Stanley Kubrick's *2001: A Space Odyssey*. Being an ardent admirer of Kubrick myself, I invited him to see my picture. As we talked a bit afterward, he suddenly said, "I think Judith Crist should see this picture." He asked if I'd be interested in setting up a screening for her and lunch afterward.

By the seventies, Judith Crist was one of America's preeminent movie critics and probably the one audiences most trusted and listened to. Not only was she *TV Guide*'s movie critic, she was network television's first theater and film critic as well, reviewing movies for the *Today* show. I couldn't imagine why Judith Crist would want to see this film, but Jack thought she should, and I had nothing to lose.

I did not want to be around when the screening began, though, thinking that might be awkward, so I showed up just a few minutes before it was over. I slithered my way into the darkened screening room, saw a solitary figure seated somewhere in the middle, and took a seat in the last row. As the lights came up on the closing credits, I introduced myself. She stood up, greeted me, and in a very businesslike tone said, "Well, I think you've done some very nice things here but this is not a picture for my audience. Would you like to have lunch?" Thank God, I thought, she'll still have lunch with me.

My sense of Ms. Crist, almost immediately, was that she was totally in love with the movies and was interested in the people who made them. At lunch that day, she offered me two suggestions: one was that I should not hesitate to "toot your own horn," which I thought I was pretty good at, and now I was sanctioned not to feel guilty about doing more of it. Her other suggestion was that she'd like to see my next film, which encouraging assumed that there would be a next film. But I remember feeling, "What next film? Where is that going to come from?" The fact was, I was unemployed, with a very minor picture playing over at the Rialto II. I had accomplished most of what I'd set out to accomplish, but only if I got a chance now to make another movie, and only if that movie would make me feel something more than what I was feeling now.

My lunch that summer afternoon with Judith Crist was the most I could have hoped for. She had given me the opportunity to meet her. She had offered encouragement, too, and that lingered. But for reasons I could never have foreseen, and that I will come to, it would be the most important lunch of my life.

18

Hurry Up, or I'll Be 30

I WAS SHAVING in the mirror one morning and that title just flew in from nowhere. A swizzle of custard and no cup to catch it in. All I needed now was a story to go with it. I was on to something, though; it was just too good a title for there not to be a story behind it. *Hurry Up, or I'll Be 30* had anxiety written all over it, mine, but funny, too, and the kind of thing people would hear and smile at, probably because they recognized something of themselves. My own generation had already sent notice: *30 Is a Dangerous Age, Cynthia*, starred Dudley Moore and Suzy Kendall. Never saw it; didn't need to. The tagline said it all: "If you haven't made it by the time you're thirty, you never will!" Hmm. Troublesome. And then there was our omnipresent mantra "Never trust anyone over thirty." I didn't have much longer. The arbitrary imposition of a goalpost—a birthday, let's say—was catalytic in my drive for success, but also raised the bar just enough to keep it threateningly out of reach. In this case, a deadline by which to make good—or else. Or else it might not count, and if *it* didn't count, what about me? Just the threat of it was enough to steal the thrill of any thunder, but enough, too, to keep things moving.

Still living at home in Brooklyn, and with his thirtieth birthday looming on the horizon, my film's protagonist, Georgie, would be on a search for his own identity, aware of his loneliness and isolation, and very consciously trying to bridge a life from which he has grown increasingly distant with one that he has only vaguely heard about and knows little of firsthand. It is a conscious effort, a desperate effort, but heroic in its own small way, to transcend. *"Now what?!"* can embolden even the humblest, whom you might never have imagined. And there, I thought, was where I should start.

This time, though, I had it down on paper, five handwritten legal sheets, and a thirty-odd-page treatment and some other notes. I thought of Paddy Chayefsky's *Marty* more than once, and how my high school buddy Bob and I used to quote Chayefsky lines as we prowled Bensonhurst on a Friday night hoping to pick up girls, but ended up propositioning pigeons instead and settled for coffee and a roll over at the Famous.

In a homage to a film that had meant so much to me in my teenage years, Paddy Chayefsky's *Marty*, I revealed more of me than I ever realized. Even the suit of clothes the main actor wore came from my closet. The sensibility of the events leading up to the "romantic" denouement could not have been more me, and certainly not Chayefsky. My principal character, likable but otherwise forgettable, is as much alienated from his generational sixties culture as he is from the no-man's-land of his Brooklyn lifestyle. His attempt at romance, enjoined now by his circumstantial meeting of a beautiful aspiring actress, and for reasons that are as inexplicable to us as probably to him, foretells disaster. And when she meets a sophisticated producer at a party, he becomes instant history. Try as he might to reinvent himself for her acceptance, the inevitability that was foretold comes to pass.

Quite seriously, I never thought of any of this as being personal. It was too made up for that. I dismissed any suggestion of autobiographical intent. I thought of it as 'faux biography," carefully manufactured, and if you saw it differently, then I'd fooled you. The critical comparisons were absurdly generous. Georgie being taken in by some shyster "producer" seeing him as an easy mark, and being taken into a world of theatrical fantasy where not even the fantasy is "real," would form the basis for much of the story's bittersweet humor. The beautiful actress who ultimately rejects him you would have expected anyway; that was pure fiction. The fact that he would try to reinvent himself just to try to get her to accept him, that was a plot concoction. These weren't all my ideas anyway. I coauthored the screenplay, based on my story, with a playwright whose play I'd seen and admired, David Wiltse. We were finished by March 1, 1971.

All I had to do now was play "chickie." In Brooklyn when you played chickie you were the sentinel on the lookout, and if you saw someone coming, you whispered "Chickie!" and everybody scattered. I played chickie for the script, on the lookout for Georgie and the rest of the cast. And late one cold March night, as I was walking down Broadway on the Upper West Side to get the morning paper, chickie struck gold.

He couldn't have been more than fifty feet away when I spotted him bouncing up Broadway as I was headed down. As I often do, he was walking alongside the curb, in what we Brooklynites call "the gutter," to avoid pedestrian sidewalk traffic and speed the journey. I was mesmerized; here came Petey. Petey was the guy in my script who owned the car wash. How I knew this was Petey I don't know, but his sheer febrile energy was palpable even at a distance, and Petey was all about energy and body rhythms. I imagined someone small of stature but bigger than life. His scene was more about physical comedy than words, to be shot inside the confined space of a real car wash, with its giant brushes swirling, and the racket of the machinery drowning out whatever it was he'd be trying to say; sheer lunacy. I gave no conscious thought to any of this, mind you. And as he got closer I couldn't help but notice his blue canvas crepe-soled shoes. They not only struck me as being slightly out of season, but also as incongruous with the long tweed overcoat he was wearing. Maybe that's where his bounce was coming from: the shoes. He otherwise defied gravity.

Oblivious of me, he zoomed right by. My eyes never left him, though, as I magnetically spun around like a compass, as if connected by some unknown force field, and called after him, "Excuse me!"

He stopped and turned. I said it again and approached him. "Do you mind if I ask what you do?"

"*Huhh*?? WHO'RE YOU?!"

"I'm . . . I'm a filmmaker."

"Huh?"

"I'm a filmmaker."

"Yeahhhh?" A bit dubious, perhaps. "What kinda films you MAKE?"

"Well, ya know . . . I've made a . . . and I'm working on a sort of slice-of-life comedy. What do *you* do?"

"I'm an AC-TOR."

God, he even sounds like Petey. He probably figures I'm full of shit, and I guess I'm thinking, well, ya know, I mean what're the odds here? Both ways. It didn't really matter, though. I had my Petey. And there was something else about him that struck me as so familiar. "No, c'mon. Seriously. Whaddya do?

"I'm an actor."

"Are you really an actor?"

"Yeah, yeah. I'm really an actor. You really a filmmaker?"

"Yeah, yeah. I'm really a filmmaker. Would you . . . uh . . . would I know anything you've done?" I'm being polite. Still, it's a dicey question to ask.

"Yeah. I'm in *Cuckoo's Nest* Off-Broadway."

"Oh, yeah, I wanna come see that!"

"Yeah. You should come see that."

We loitered at the gated storefront of a chocolatier there on Eighty-sixth and Broadway, near the corner cigar store. We were communicating now through the sidelong glances of our reflections in the storefront window, the kind of thing you might do when you really don't know what else to say to a stranger, but you're trying to schmooze him anyway, and instead of standing there in the middle of the street staring at each other, you stare into the darkened window under the pretext of some other interest.

He was quiet now, in an observant way, very different from that volley of energy that had come at me. He reminded me of my friend at NYU. It was a combination of things: a laserlike energy, an unfiltered directness, a purposefulness that his body movements betrayed, physical stature, and a genuine warmth and openness. And they were both Italian, too, for whatever that's worth, although I suspect that was worth a great deal.

People I'd known through childhood and adolescence, Italians and Jews, both, most from working-class families, "the real people," were enriched by familial sustenance and values, something I'd been exposed to but could never make my own. As a child I had leaned over the fence and observed, but the fence was a seemingly insurmountable lifelong fixture. Even when I attempted to get around or over it, it would renew itself in front of me. Perpetually out of reach, the other side of the fence was accessible by association, an underlying sense of identity through familiarity, which offered sustenance and a sense of belonging, too. The activity of moviemaking is an activity of belonging. Though temporal and intense, it is an extended family experience, which I believe even those with families experience in that way, as well.

"What's his name?!" he insisted. I told him the name, and he acknowledged he didn't know him. I told him that in time, I thought he would. We hadn't been standing there all that long, really, but we were freezing our asses off and he'd been heading home anyway, and I wanted to get the paper, and so I told him I'd come see the show, and maybe we could get together afterward for coffee or something. I had a good feeling about this, though. I just did.

As I recall, the *Cuckoo's Nest* set had swinging doors on either side of the stage, with the primary action taking place directly in front of you.

The setting, of course, is a mental institution. He played one of the inmates of the asylum, and I waited for him to show up. All of a sudden, out of the blue, *BAM*! The doors on stage left come flying open and this Mad Hatter, dressed in a white hospital gown (shoeless!), comes flying out as if shot from a cannon, only to exit the doors at stage right, *BAM*! And from the split second when he appeared to the five seconds later when he disappeared, he had brought down the house. No dialogue, nothing. And then, a few minutes later, *BAM*! *again.* This time, the opposite direction. And again, the house comes down. This is what I'd seen on the street, magnified ten times. Chaplin did this. If I'd needed a sanity check, I found it at the cuckoo's nest.

We went over to the Bagel on West Fourth Street, corner table. I handed him the script, and met his girlfriend, too, whom he'd met just a few months earlier, and told him that it would be a very low-budget movie ("Great . . ."), that we'd work long, long days ("Great . . ."), crazy hours (Yeah, yeah . . . great"), seven days a week ("Yeah, I know . . ."), and that I had no money ("Waddaya mean, you have no money?!"). Well, I'd have very little money, but that everyone would get paid ("Oh, yeah. Fine, fine. No problem.").

The reason I've singled this story out is not only because you know him, but also because I've told it so many times through the years that I just wanted to have a chance to write it down. It speaks to me of Jung's acausal connecting principle of synchronicity and the mystery of why or how these things happen, seemingly coincidentally. This small film, incidentally, made not one iota of difference to his subsequent career and success. It's just that, as I say, chickie struck gold.

He reminded me of Scorsese. Danny DeVito.

∞

THAT WAS MARCH. Cast entirely with unknowns, principal photography for *Hurry Up, or I'll Be 30* began on June 26, 1971, on a forty-one-day shooting schedule, over an approximate seven-week period. The picture was photographed on locations in Brooklyn, Manhattan, the Bronx, and Fire Island. The original budget was $100,000. Nine months and $150,000 later, I had my second picture.

19

Joseph E. Levine Presents

IT WAS ANOTHER cold March night in New York. I'd rented the nine-hundred-seat Forum Theatre at the corner of Forty-seventh and Broadway, advertised to the trade, had gotten invitations printed, and everybody in the cast and crew had invited their friends and family, so the place was packed. The moment of truth was at hand, because until you've got an audience, and in this case, as sympathetic an audience as you're ever going to get, you really don't know what you've got. I was proud of this work. It had been a genuine labor of love, albeit one fraught with the problems of a little movie trying to put itself together, and a bunch of us making it happen through sheer enthusiasm, dedication, and force of will. Again, this put me as close to family as I had ever felt, and I believe not just me, but for others who'd worked on it, too.

The manager came up to me as I stood in back of the darkened theater ten or fifteen minutes into the film and whispered, "We just had a bomb threat." I just stared at him. "Somebody just called and said there's a bomb in the theater. What do you want to do?" It felt surreal; it took a moment for me to grasp it. "I think you have to call the cops," I said. He asked if I wanted to make some kind of announcement. "Give me five minutes," I said, "then turn off the film and bring up the house lights." But I wasn't gonna sing "Mammy."

In 1972, a bomb threat somehow didn't evoke what it would today. There was just enough room for disbelief. I defaulted into calm and logic. The film groaned to a halt as the screen went white and the house lights came up: "Ladies and gentlemen, we have a small problem. . . ." By now you could hear the sirens wailing outside, as the side doors of the theater clanged open and the sounds of the Broadway traffic and the cold night air came rushing in. People got up quietly and filed out in an orderly way, no more believing it than me, I suspect. The cops showed up with their canines and sniffed the place out. No bomb. Nothing. All clear. Twenty minutes later everybody got back in their seats and we started over. It had all been a big "Boo!" Everybody applauded at the end, too.

Next morning I had a call from Don Gillin, a producer's representative I'd kept in touch with even after he politely declined to represent me after my first film about three years earlier. I'd visit at his office occasionally for advice. He became a friend—and remained one.

"Joe, it's Don. How'd it go last night?"

"I think it went well, Don."

"I heard you had a bomb scare."

"Huh? How'd you hear that?"

"Joe Levine called me and said Walter Keenan was there last night, and that everybody froze their ass off for a half hour but they all came back in." Keenan worked for Avco Embassy Pictures, a film distributor, as operations liaison, generally responsible for technical and laboratory coordination. The entertainment business generally (and especially the movie business) is very informal and built on establishing relationships. Pictures get made without signed contracts, which are often signed later. It's all about trust. Jack Rollins, famed theatrical manager of the team of Rollins & Joffe (whose clients included Mike Nichols and Elaine May, Woody Allen, Robin Williams, Dick Cavett, Billy Crystal, Dave Letterman, Robert Klein, and maybe one you never heard of) once told me that he didn't have a shred of paper between himself and his clients. So I wasn't surprised to hear from Don with an opportunity in his hand. "Levine wants to see what you've got. Can you get a print over there?"

I couldn't make this up. It was too good to make up.

Joe Levine was either a real movie mogul, in which case he was genuinely the last of an old breed, or a good movie mogul facsimile, and I could never make up my mind which because I'd never met one before him. In a way, Levine was a walking anachronism, like Goldwyn, the perennial outsider looking for respect, even though he controlled major motion picture productions. To an outsider like me, "Joseph E. Levine Presents" was Hollywood.

The man himself was a lot less than the image that preceded him, and to that extent he was a master showman and a genius at self-promotion. There was just no way this man could be related to in any human terms. He was there to service his own needs, and you were there to service them with him. He respected talent, though, and I suspect he had a nose for it, although he had short memory of it, and little respect for it, if it betrayed him at the box office. I believe he genuinely loved the movies and most certainly the respect that accrued to him through the great ones; those he had shepherded.

Glory meant more to Levine than money; that, and winning, because winning was vindication: "You never thought the little Yid would make it, did ya!" were the words he uttered the day the Jesuits honored him in his own hometown of Boston, where he'd begun his career as a "film peddler" (salesman) and later, in New York City, as a distributor-exhibitor. He liked telling stories and he liked holding court. There had to have been more to him than I could ever fathom, though, because this hateful little man had produced or distributed Jean-Luc Godard's *Contempt*, Federico Fellini's *8½*, Vittorio DeSica's *Bicycle Thief* and *Two Women* (the latter with

Sophia Loren), Anthony Harvey's *The Lion in Winter* (with Katharine Hepburn and Peter O'Toole), Mel Brooks's *The Producers*, and Mike Nichols's *The Graduate* and *Carnal Knowledge*, just to name a few. Was it all dumb luck? I doubt it.

I would come to think of him as the Little King from the funny papers, a mean version. Levine was known to pop his head into an employee's office and ask "What have you done for me today?" His style was fear and intimidation, and his diminutive figure cast a tall shadow. This kind of overlord mentality could be palpably felt in the Halls of Levine, and I would marvel as I occasionally watched him limp down that long empty corridor, from his office to the elevators, with a cane that looked to be an umbrella, and wondered what kind of mysterious force this could be. His portly, pint-sized figure walked slowly and stiffly down that long, drawn-out corridor that led to his office, while he breathed fear into the faces of those unfortunate enough to catch his gaze, respecting them even less for it, although he respected no one who was in his employ or in his need. After getting an opinion that was not the same as his, he would proclaim, "What the fuck do you know?!" But he heard them out anyway, and whether he admitted to it or not, and he did not, he factored them in.

One day he reached for a script that seemed to be forever sitting on his desk. I couldn't see the title. "Dickie wants to do Gandhi. Whaddaya think?" I couldn't answer the question. All I knew of Gandhi was what I'd learned in school. I suspect it was my very lack of knowledge that he factored into his ongoing assessment. At some gut level, he was constantly sniffing. "Dickie" was Richard Attenborough (not yet Sir Richard Attenborough), and Levine had owned that script for more than a decade, but in all the years he'd owned it, he could not make up his mind. Years later he finally sold the script back to Attenborough, at an enormous profit, and in 1982 *Gandhi* won eight Academy Awards, including one for best picture. He had held it in the palm of his hand, and he had let it slip away. Of this I am certain: Levine would have given you half his portfolio to have gone out in a blaze of glory with the best-picture Oscar for *Gandhi*. God knows what he would have said in light of what he'd told the Jesuits, but it would have been fun to find out.

Avco Embassy Pictures had its offices in the JC Penney building in Manhattan, and when you stepped off the elevator you might just as well have stepped into the waiting room of a whorehouse: red velvet wallpaper, low lighting, ornate armchairs, and pixie bulbs surrounding the framed posters of his latest releases. Even the ceiling had its pointed stars, each with a movie title, and each varying in size depending on the relative success of the movie it represented; all designed, I was told, by Mrs. Rosalie Levine herself.

Levine had asked for the meeting after screening the picture with his sales manager and marketing people. A secretary came to the outer door: "He'll see you now." Don nudged me ahead and I followed her down the long corridor that led into her open office and a second door with an American eagle emblazoned above it, not unlike that of the president of the United States. She opened it slowly so as not to disturb him, just in case he wasn't expecting us. I entered the hallowed turf with Don directly behind me, and found myself looking at what appeared to be the windows of a large empty office. Suddenly I noticed off to the far left a huge desk and a squat sixtysomething man sitting quietly behind it, his hand at the ready to lift the telephone receiver encased in a gold plastic laminate. He was the very model of a modern major movie mogul, one that could well have inspired Gilbert and Sullivan. He liked catching you off-balance.

Apparently deciding not to place that call after all, he stood up, which wasn't a hell of a lot different from when he was sitting down, and Don, puffing on his pipe, greeted him. "Hello, Joe. This is Joe Jacoby." I think my exact words were "Hello, Mr. Levine." His first words to me were "I screened your fucking picture." He was trying to butter me up. "Where'd you find that kid? He out-Dustins Dustin." Dustin, of course, was Dustin Hoffman, and he was referring to my lead actor. Don and I took our seats in front of Levine's billiard table–sized desk. The man spoke from the gutter; that was his style. He didn't so much speak his words as squeeze them out of himself; each was coated in anger, resentful even of having to be called on at all. "What'd this picture cost you to make? [beat] *And don't you lie to me!*"

Don put his arm across my chest. "Joe, we want a gross deal." A "gross deal," unlike a "net deal," is defined generally as a fixed percentage of the distributor's gross receipts absent any distribution costs or expenses. "I'll give you a gross deal," he said. This would have tended to confirm Levine's enthusiasm for the picture because net deals aren't worth the paper they're written on, but it might also have signaled his unwillingness to advance any money for the picture so that if it didn't do business, his losses would have been minimal and we wouldn't have made any money.

"I don't mind answering the question," I said. "Three hundred thousand dollars." Levine's jaw drooped into his chest. He seemed genuinely nonplussed. "How the fuck do you kids do it?" He looked at Don. "It's like the Hercules pictures I picked up. Twenty-nine thousand dollars for the pair. A coupla herrings." Levine meandered. What he couldn't remember, such as some of the titles of his own pictures, he wrote inside matchbook covers. I discovered, however, that the things that mattered to him he remembered. "Who else has seen this picture?'

"No one," I said.

"You screened it the other night and they froze their fucking asses off but they all came back in." That impressed him. He looked to see if I had something else to offer; an Achilles heel, perhaps? The man had the killer instinct of a hawk. I smelled doubts, though. "Can you leave the print here?" he asked Don. "Bud's got the sales guys coming on Thursday. I want them to look at it." The meeting was over. Don let Levine know we'd talk on Thursday afternoon. In other words, we'd move on to the next store if there wasn't a firm offer.

We were standing now at the elevator. I didn't like the idea that Levine had gone from offering a gross deal to opening this up to a bunch of salesmen. All committees, just like audiences themselves, produce mixed reactions. "Don't worry about it, kid," Don assured me. "When Joe makes up his mind he wants something, that's it." That was fine and good, I thought, but I hadn't seen Joe make up his mind. All I'd seen was a man go from offering a gross deal in one sentence, to indecision in the next. Hamlet couldn't make up his mind, either, and look what happened to him. But I wasn't worried about Hamlet; I was worried about me. I had a lousy feeling. As we went down, Don asked me "What'd the picture cost you to make?"

"A hundred fifty thousand dollars."

"Uh-huh." He puffed his pipe.

∞

JACKIE MASON: "So what's happening with your picture?"

ME: "I showed it to Levine. But he can't make up his mind."

JACKIE: "What you should do is call Israel Katz."

ME: "Who's Israel Katz?"

JACKIE: "Katz is Levine's accountant. He listens to Katz."

ME: "What about your picture?"

JACKIE: "We're still editing. Maybe you should look at it."

ME: "How'd it work out with your director?"

JACKIE: "To tell you the truth, I don't know. He never spoke to me. Call Katz. He's in the book."

With that, Jackie Mason continued his walk up Central Park West, and I continued mine down. I'd met Jackie a few months earlier through his attorney, who, in turn, I'd met through a mutual friend. I had to see what Don had to say, but I figured Levine's accountant might know Levine better. Levine was in New York. I was in New York. Something about his name on top of those movies haunted me. I wanted that for myself. I'd not only bought into his transcendence; we had something else in common. Here was authority who despised authority, and here I was looking at authority, despising them along with him, *including* him. He was an outsider, paradoxically, perhaps the underdog, him against "them," and that I understood at once. And on that basis, and only on that basis, he and I commiserated. And where chickie smelled an outsider, I had faith. And I still believed he loved movies.

Just as I'd suspected, the screening had produced a mixed response. Levine's initial bout of enthusiasm had waned, and it would be a tough, if not impossible, battle now, to get him back to his initial instinct. Don was not a man to chase rainbows. His polished, soft-spoken, easygoing, pipe-smoking manner betrayed his belief in not trying to convince the unconvinced. He didn't need to do that. But I did. I called Israel Katz.

"So when you're in the neighborhood you'll drop by," he said in his ever-so-soft grandfatherly tones. "I should drop by when I'm in the neighborhood?" "Okay," he said, and hung up. "Okay?" Okay what? He's agreeing with *me*? I was asking *him*. Joe Levine's accountant was so unbusy that I could just drop by, just like that, any time I wanted? I thought that's what he meant, though, and therein lay the essence of Israel Katz. He put the suggestion to you, and you made of it what you would. He gave you just enough to surmise, infer, imagine, intimate, or assume anything without him ever making a direct commitment or offering any confirmation, except to acknowledge conclusions *you* might come to, which he invariably had led you to.

If you needed to believe in the good tooth fairy, for example, he by no means would have discouraged you, and might even have led you to her, smiling, swirling his cigar, swamilike, until finally, he would point it at you, as if to punctuate, at long last, your arrival. Best, you thought, to leave it up to him. Smiles all around. And here—have a cigar.

You could never make heads or tails of him. Groucho Marx sitting opposite Israel Katz would've topped anything George S. Kaufman had written. While he may not have known Groucho, Katz represented a luminous roster of theatrical clients whose names you surely know. How he got them, I do not know. What he did to them, I know something about.

In 1976 I made a picture released as *The Great Bank Hoax* (Warner Bros.), in which Burgess Meredith played Jack Stutz, a character based on Israel Katz. I'd written the script with Burgess in mind, in part because I felt he could assume Katz's physicality, but more importantly, I knew that Katz had earlier represented him, as well as Alan J. Lerner. I had heard the story that Burgess had sold his house and property to Lerner for one dollar and that Lerner, in turn, subsequently sold it to Katz for the same amount. When I asked Burgess if the story was true, he bowed his head sheepishly with a nod of having no more of an understanding of what had happened then than now. At that very moment, there was a shared simpatico, and I knew I had my actor.

In less than an hour, he agreed to play the part. "Ya know," he said, "you've got to be pretty brave to make this picture." "Why?" I asked. "Well," he mused, "in the first place, there are no car chases, nobody shoots anybody, nobody even yells at anybody, and nobody gets laid." Continuing, as if not allowing me to think *too* long, he said snappily, "*But*—if you want to make it," slapping the script to the table and jolting himself up for a new order of business now to get done, "I'll make it!" And with that, he jaunted his way down the long, narrow path that led to his Malibu beachfront, adjusting his blue knit *Rocky* stocking cap as he went.

I am fortunate to have had the opportunity to learn much from Burgess, a man of enormous vitality and curiosity, and of many more and varied interests in life than one might expect of the brilliant actor that he was, and to have been able to call him my friend long after the picture was finished.

Long before that, I stepped off the elevator and found myself standing in an open reception area that was jointly shared by two firms—one a law firm, the other the accounting firm of David W. Katz & Company (the firm was named after Israel Katz's deceased older brother, whom I never knew). I announced myself to the receptionist and she had me take a seat, advising Mr. Katz of my arrival. He had told me to drop by, after all, and that's exactly what I'd done. As I waited, I recognized the gentleman exiting the men's room, now, trying to get the cap back onto his pill bottle as he made his way toward Katz's office: Alan J. Lerner, looking thin and gaunt. *My Fair Lady* had been my first exposure to Broadway, and had ignited a wonder in me that I had never felt before. What the hell was I doing here? I didn't even have an appointment.

It could not have been more than ten minutes or so before Mr. Lerner returned and stood waiting at the elevator. I was advised by Sarah at the switchboard that Mr. Katz would see me now; go down the long hallway and make a left, first office at the end. The hallway, itself, had the feel of an art gallery rather than an accounting firm, with oil paintings hung every few feet along the way. In the corner office, Israel Katz stood in an open shirt, rolled-up sleeves, leaning casually against his desk, his paunch against it; his cigar hand cupped upward so as not to scorch himself. A solidly built man of average height, a full head of white curly hair, somewhere in his sixties, exuding a Buddha-like wisdom beyond age.

His office walls were covered with paintings, and framed canvases were stacked up against the back wall for lack of wall space. Not exactly a kingly setting, but one of disheveled opulence nonetheless, a dishevelment reflected in his personal dress as well. It felt like an office in flux, cluttered and unfinished, as if the paintings themselves had newly arrived and he just hadn't had time to sort them out. This perpetual state of "pendingness" and the promise of a completed tomorrow always a day in the distance was endemic to this man's indefatigable personality. For as long as I knew him it was the hope, or rope, that kept you dangling. It was the dangle that held you to him, and he played it masterfully.

He smiled impishly, motioning me to come in and sit down in one of the two iron-framed leather chairs in front of his desk. Imagine a beardless, cigar-toting Santa, talking barely above a whisper, punctuated by an orchestrating cigar that relieves itself of its accumulated ash at the conclusion of each improvised stanza; the cigar being nothing less than the baton of a maestro. "So, how'd it go with Joe?"

I was amazed that he remembered who I was or why I was here. It was as if we were picking up on a conversation briefly interrupted. He had an uncanny ability for instant intimacy, and as I would come to learn, recall, as well. I told him everything. We must have sat and schmoozed for another half hour. For a man as busy as he was, it was a long-time schmooze, but he loved holding court. Nor was he above dropping a name or two for color and response. I was the perfect audience, rapt in my attention. I had been listening to his stories, asking questions along the way, wanting to ingratiate myself, offering encouragement for more, which I could see he relished. Then he mentioned Paddy Chayefsky. "You represent Paddy Chayefsky?" I asked. He smiled impishly once more, slowly churning his cigar, cherubically suffusing satisfaction at what he undoubtedly saw now on my face. I fell silent. I had nothing left to say. "So listen," Katz concludes, "I'm meeting with Lenny on Monday. You'll come up with me and we'll, ya know, sort it out then."

"Who's Lenny?"

"Right." He was thinking of something else now.

"Do you want to see the picture first?"

Katz gave me a grandfatherly smile. "I see you. That's enough."

"Should I meet you here?"

"Right." Again he's agreeing with me. "And, ya know, we'll go over there together."

'What time?"

"Listen, call Sarah on Monday and we'll . . . sort it out."

I left the office knowing I was to call Sarah on Monday and sort out the time to meet Katz, to sort it out with "Lenny," and he didn't even have to see the picture because he'd already seen me. I could have asked for clarifications but I didn't want to risk it. I understood none of this. But it all seemed so promising. Throughout life, for reasons I don't fully understand, except for the seeking of acceptance, approval, and *inclusion*, I have always been upbeat, optimistic, full of energy, ready always to sell what had to be sold, to do whatever had to be done to realize the fulfillment of my passions, and to do so energetically and usually effectively. My energy was, and is, unbounded, and I was drawn to others with similar energies and positive outlooks. "Chickie" spotted them blocks away, and they were drawn to me as well.

Leonard "Lenny" Lightstone had been Joe Levine's right-hand man for more than twenty years. As executive vice president of Avco Embassy Pictures Corp., Lightstone had the authority to enter into distribution agreements. I met him only this once, as I sat patiently in his office while he and Katz discussed matters having nothing to do with me. I figured Katz would get to it. At the close of the meeting Katz stood up and said there was something else he wanted to talk to him about, pointing over at me now, and Lightstone nodded sheepishly, and then Katz nodded sheepishly back, a smile on both their faces, which is as Talmudic as it gets, and that was the end of it. I couldn't figure out what the hell had happened.

When we left Lightstone's office, Katz smiled and told me we had a deal. I was stunned. There had to have been some kind of code going on because I couldn't figure out why he'd had me there. "Listen," said Katz as we waited at the elevator, "we'll have a gross deal and it'll be a smash and, you know . . . Joe will get behind it." I didn't know. I didn't know anything. I didn't even know if Joe knew, although I was pretty sure he didn't, and I wasn't even sure it mattered anymore because the two times I'd come up here I came away with assurances my instincts told me were bogus. Don, once he smelled it, wouldn't chase it, but I did.

With his heavy brown leather satchel in tow, one he always carried but that I never saw him open, Katz was headed now over to "the Club" for a nosh, and asked if I'd like to join him. David W. Katz & Co. represented New York's famed "21" Club. Two of its owners, Sheldon Tannen and Jerry Berns (Peter Kriendler being the third), greeted him at the door with open arms. I realized, now, that this man represented the world. What the hell was I questioning? How lucky could you get? He'd even offered me a cigar. I'd never smoked a cigar. I must've had something to celebrate, though, and while I might not have known what it was yet, that seemed a minor technicality.

Once you'd accepted the world according to Katz, celebration was the order of the day. *He* knew, after all, and I *knew* he knew because everybody else around him knew he knew, too, and I could see that, and if it was good enough for them, it was certainly good enough for me. And so here I was, noshing at the "21" Club, smack in the middle of the world; now a made member. And Katz didn't even have to see the picture because he'd already seen me. But my greatest fear, really, was that he'd already forgotten there *was* a picture. Jerzy Kosinki's closing line in his screenplay for the film based on his novel *Being There* is "Life is a state of mind." So have a cigar. And thank you, I did.

Pretty soon I was venturing up to Katz's weekend estate in Rockland County, the very same property that had once belonged to Burgess Meredith and would later belong to Alan J. Lerner. Katz used the house as a honeypot, attracting interesting and successful people. This man was a party animal long before we called it that, but more than that, he was a collector, not of butterflies, but of people. Katz was a Felliniesque figure, albeit a dangerously draped and shadowed one, an allegorical clown dressed in top hat, red velvet jacket and boots; his microphoned cigar in one hand, that heavily laden satchel in the other, his girth distended heavenward. Commanding your attention now, and bathing in its glow, one might now have thought of this accountant as ringmaster. He fed upon the stimulus he accredited himself, the dependence he engendered in others, much the way the spider feeds upon the fly, absent satiation.

I had no doubt now, with the summer months upon us, that my picture had fallen from his scope. Katz suffused indifference the moment he sensed capture. I was as much under this man's spell as others had been before me. What drove him beyond the need for attention? If he had nothing to gain otherwise, what would have been his motive? How could this grandfatherly cherub be so benignly malevolent? My very inability to answer these questions for myself, unless I were ready to buy into the notion of this man's utter madness, was the very glue that bound me to the notion that a deal would be forthcoming, and given the time already spent, the dangling carrot was nearer than far.

In August, five months now from the time I had first entered Israel Katz's office, Lenny Lightstone suffered a debilitating stroke. With Lenny gone now, the string that had dangled me had run its course. And without the string, there was nothing to hold me, and with nothing to hold me, Katz sprang into action, lest his canary fly the coop. Within sixty days, a distribution deal was signed.

And on the seventh month, Katz rested. All that remained now was for the picture to open. The few changes I'd wanted to make in the picture I was now able to. Katz had apparently overlooked something, though: Levine had no interest in opening the picture, and worse, no requirement to do so.

What good was this if the picture wasn't going to open? Levine, meanwhile, was miserable, "dancing out" his contract with Avco Corp. He smelled the outsider in me, just as I had in him. I became a fixture in his office, dropping by two, three times a week. There were people who thought I was employed there. When Levine saw that I just wouldn't let go, couldn't let go, he saw something of himself. He decided to "test" the picture . . . in Boston. It would open at the Paris Cinema on Boylston Street, in March 1973, one year now since its completion.

test (n.) a procedure intended to establish the quality, performance, or reliability of something, esp. before it is taken into widespread use.

That's how I read it as well. Even without a dictionary.

Part Six

Disclosure

Mommy, Mommy, what did I do?

20

You Know These People

THAT WAS MARCH. Now it was June. The picture had run three weeks in Boston to generally good notices but inconclusive box office, best described in the trade as "soft" or in business parlance as "a wash"—nothing lost, nothing gained. If this had been a "test," I passed. The question was, by how much? If I was supposed to set the world on fire in Boston, it didn't happen. It had more the feel of treading water, but with good notices above the waterline, and with that, New York seemed tantalizingly close. Everything spins off New York. The national media are based in New York, and films gross more there than in any other city. But most importantly for me, or any young filmmaker, New York is a launch pad for a career, and this was a New York story; a kid from Brooklyn, after all, should qualify (my character, not me, but I'd hitch to his wagon), and while I may not have been fully aware of its autobiographical undertones, the work had been a genuine labor of love, a feeling shared by others. The simple fact was "if I can make it there, I'll make it anywhere," and that's always been true. They don't call it the Big Apple for nottin'.

By now I'd not only become the fly on Levine's wall, but also, like the wall itself, immovable, and just stealthy enough to stay invisible while remaining ever present; puppetry undoubtedly contributed to this feat. I would loiter in that hallway waiting for the man to appear and run into *me*. Given what I knew of his proactive, mercurial nature, it would have been unwise for me to confront him. Levine pulled the strings. He had no legal obligations to me, anyway, none at all. Katz had already seen to that. The timing would have to be Levine's, the initiative his, and he would have to be in the right frame of mind just to hear me out. Not good odds. But I never figured the odds. Odds sometimes offered options; risks you didn't have to take. I never knew from options, and all I knew about life was risk, and when you had a singular goal there was no choice, and achieving that goal was always in sight. As a kid I'd been told I was stubborn—"like a mule." That usually meant I wouldn't do things somebody else's way. As a kid I got in trouble for that, just another of my behavior deficits. But Joe Levine had a different take on it.

He walked slowly down that hall, an interminable walk it seemed, his slick black silver-tipped walking stick assisting, to the remarkable "coincidence" of me being here. Eighty percent is showing up.

"You won't take no for an answer, will you!"

What he's really saying is "You won't give up." It's respect: his tone, the way he looked at me, that beat or two before he spoke, all were recognition and reflection.

I'd intuited something about this man in our very first meeting. While I would be somewhat taken aback by Levine's instant, unprovoked combative style, which I suppose would've been my expectation of a movie mogul's persona, a fantasy persona, except that this one was real, albeit defensively so, I understood his anger; anger not directed at me so much as at the world at large, and I respected the fact that he had harnessed, mastered, and used it for purposes of his own. This little man, who was nothing to look at, was a force of nature unto himself.

Any conversation with him was no conversation at all, but rather a one-way diatribe, with you the listener, the "audience" for him holding court. He would occasionally pause for a comment you might have, which he would not engage except to refute, or benignly accept, without attribution to you. But his guttural street talk had more direct honesty and command to it than other people's polish. It intimidated some, certainly the people who worked for him—I doubt anyone ever worked *with* him—but I had immunity. What he lacked in polish he made up for with posture, and he postured precisely to preclude miscalculation, *your* miscalculation, just in case you thought you'd put one over. He wasn't so much getting tough with you as putting you on notice not to get tough with him—little dogs seem to do the same thing—as when he asked me that day, "What'd this picture cost you to make? *And don't you lie to me!*" Which I did, of course (producer's privilege). But he would've admired—nay, *expected*—even that, if I was any good at all. And besides, it was cheap enough at twice the price, which was four times the real price, which I suspect impressed him all the more.

His smarts were street smarts, the best smarts. Something propelled him, though, and that's what I respected. He both nurtured and fed upon myth, myth and perception being the coin of the entertainment business. The Wizard of Oz had nothin' on ole Joe. You could despise him for his callous indifference, crudeness, and meanness. "Say what you want," as he would say, disavowing any interest or concern. Yet there was something reserved in me toward him, even beyond my own self-serving interests, that kept me from despising him completely. I never quite understood *why* I understood, unless what I understood was that Levine had handed me no less than I deserved, and I suspect that was part of it.

This was a shrewd creature of instinct, a man more of his word and gut than contracts or convention. He went against convention; made his own, in fact, another admirable trait, one that would have landed him in Hawthorne at a different time and circumstance. And while I might not have known it then, and I *did* not know it, this also was a man who had come from misery, poverty, and hunger. The people who start from nothing make their own rules; survival requires self-invention. It's that simple.

They also tend to remember. I watched him chastise his lawyer one day, when he was trying to undermine the promise Joe had made to me when Don and I had sat in his office: "I promised him a gross deal" (even though the deal itself might not have been worth the paper it was written on). He was telling the guy, "I gave him my word," and I saw the anger on his face when that was being undermined, because his word was the code that had gotten him here, especially in a business that traded on one's word and was built on relationships. Though one he once likened it to "a bunch of Gypsies on a desert swapping rugs," it meant more to him than any goddamn contract or lawyer. This was the fabric of the man.

This is not to say that Levine couldn't wiggle, I *heard* him wiggle, this son of a bitch. In October 1973, about a month before my own picture was scheduled to open, I heard Levine arguing in his office with Carlo Ponti, the famed producer and husband of Sophia Loren. Levine and Ponti went back quite a way together, including *Two Women*, with its Academy Award for Sophia Loren. Now Ponti had produced Roman Polanski's *What?* which had not opened to good notices, and business was soft. Apparently, though, Levine was contractually committed to spend a million dollars in advertising, but was refusing to spend it all in light of the opening results. Ponti was insisting that his contract be honored. Levine pointed out to Ponti that while, yes, he had agreed to spend it, apparently the contract did not stipulate *when*. Friendship in these matters took a backseat to "wiggle room."

"Say what you want," as he would say, but the foundation from which he wiggled was his code of honor, and that foundation was the street itself. In spite of it all, Joe and me, we commiserated.

There is a scene in Albert and David Maysles's documentary that lingers:

It's 1962, the day after the "West Enders" have honored him up in his hometown of Boston. They're sitting around a table; bottles of scotch *clearly visible, Levine holding court with a few of his childhood chums who'd been up there the night before. They're fawning on him, throwing him lead lines; he's used to it. He doesn't particularly respect them for it, mind you, but Little King likes being Little King. Besides, this is his day. Now listen. He's got something to say:**

JOE LEVINE

"So. Listen to this! I'm fifty-six. This means when I was about eight or nine, *forty-eight years ago*, I used to leave the school and go and sell papers. I used to sell broken cake . . . and then I'd go steal some wood."

He catches himself on the word "steal." He's clearly uncomfortable with it, embarrassed even, but reluctantly admits:

"Steal. . . . yeah—*steal*. As long as I could lift anything, I'd steal it. 'Where do you go every day?' says Hilkie to me. The name stuck in my mind. I told him. He wants to go with me. He was a rich kid . . . *shoes*, ya know. . . . So he went with me: papers, cake, wood. . . . He starts crying. What're you crying about? 'Cold.' Never occurred to me to be cold before. Until Hilkie reminded me you're supposed to be cold. So *I* started to cry. . . . But it stuck in my mind for fifty years. This Hilkie. So I put this in my speech . . . and when I . . ."

He suddenly chokes up. His long-buried feelings now catch up with his words. In an effort to stem any display of emotion, he quickly rises and juts his arm outward, as if to deflect you from any trace of feeling you may have caught and he continues unabated. It is fleeting, barely a moment on film, but it's there, and time enough to see this man's vulnerability.

---

* From the documentary film *Showman*, by Albert and David Maysles. Used by permission, courtesy of Albert Maysles and Maysles Films, Inc. *Showman* (1963) was never made available for public exhibition because Levine "had complicated feelings about the film because Hollywood friends thought the film to be anti-Semitic," according to Albert Maysles. I viewed the film in October 2003, when Albert Maysles generously loaned me a print. I never felt any anti-Semitism in the movie, nor did Albert, who (being Jewish himself) never intended it.

∞

HAVING REACHED ME now in the hallway, he looks me in the eye, searching. Perhaps he sees Marley's Ghost; I can't be sure what he sees, but perhaps he sees something of himself. "You won't take no for an answer, will you!"

Never occurred to me I'd heard no. I nod, nothing more.

"Has Judith Crist seen this picture?"

"No critic in New York has seen it."

"I want Crist to see this picture. I respect that woman's opinion. She loves pictures. Tell Spiegel I said to set it up."

It was over. More than a year had gone by in less than thirty seconds. And with that he continued his slow-gaited, straight-caned walk like nothing had happened. Don had said, "When Joe makes up his mind he wants something, that's it." Joe had finally made up his mind.

I wondered, though. It had been almost three years. Would she remember?

"Joe, it's Ted Spiegel. I screened your picture for Judy Crist and she loves it. She said she'd be happy to speak with you if you'd like to call her."

I dialed the first six digits a half dozen times and hung up. I hadn't done this since the times I tried calling the girl in high school but always hung up because I couldn't bear the rejection. This was different, of course. I knew what Ted had said and I just didn't want to say something dumb because I knew what Levine had said and I knew what this call meant.

I hadn't disappointed her, she said, and asked if there was some way she could help. I told Ms. Crist of Levine's respect for her opinion and that I sensed it would make the difference of whether he'd open the picture. She asked if I would like her to call him.

Twenty minutes later. "I'm opening your fucking picture. Judith Crist loves your picture and we're going to have a fucking disaster."[beat] "I'm only going to be here for the next twenty minutes."

"I'll be there in twenty minutes."

"I'm pressed." And with those exact words, he slammed down the phone. I was out of the gate.

∞

ON NOVEMBER 13, 1973, Joseph E. Levine presented my fucking picture.

A few days after reviews began appearing, I got a call from a theatrical manager whom I just happened to have met through the Katz office and who just happened to be a friend of someone whose work I had deeply respected as far back as my teenage years. Paddy Chayefsky had requested a screening.

As the lights came up, I walked cautiously into the room, curious to see if there was any resemblance between Paddy Chayefsky and Marty. Chayefsky was a burly man, or as Marty would have put it, "I'm the stocky one, the heavyset fella," of average height. Of course, *Marty* had been eighteen years earlier. My impression now was of an intense, no-nonsense man whose cutting-edge satiric work, up to that time, included *The Hospital* with George C. Scott, which won the Academy Award in 1971 both for best story and for best screenplay. This was the Chayefsky I was meeting now, not some sentimentalized version I'd imagined.

I held my own sentimentality in check as well; something about growing up did that. He was open, though, in a quiet, supportive way, and clearly appreciative of what I'd attempted. He glanced at me intermittently, but his thoughts were elsewhere. He wouldn't have told me if he didn't like it, anyway; I knew that, and I would soon come to know that he was especially supportive of young writers. And to young people who otherwise wanted to be in show business, he would counsel, "Write!"

I'd essentially paid homage, and with consciousness of thought, no doubt, although never that I was trying *to do* Marty, it's just that I kept running into him, and I suspect that's how Paddy took it as well. It was really nothing more than that; a brief hello, a few moments, and it was over. I wasn't sure I'd see him again, but I felt now like I knew him, and was grateful for having had the chance to meet him.

It couldn't have been more than a week or so later, as I was walking down Seventh Avenue in Manhattan right before the Carnegie Deli at Fifty-fifth Street, that I heard a voice yelling, "Joe! JOE!" Paddy Chayefsky, looking out the window of a taxi, had recognized me. "Wait! Wait a minute. Where're you going?" I don't remember where I was going, but wherever I was going, I wasn't going there anymore. "Let's grab a sandwich." The Carnegie Deli was Paddy's lunch haunt (his office was right next door, at 850 Seventh Avenue, as was that of Bob Fosse, his best friend), and Paddy even had his own table. Herbie, the fellow in the brown pants and cream-colored shirt who stood guard with the menus near the door, sat us. Herbie (known as a "floorwalker" in the trade) not only seated you, he also *evaluated*. Seating people for pastrami sandwiches at the Carnegie ("World's Best") was no less an art form than the sandwiches themselves—you sit here, there's a deuce back there somewhere, come follow me—and he'd slap the menu on the table, waiter to follow. Lunchtime was choreographed mayhem, ebb and flow, and then you had the tourists. The regulars knew who they were, though, and Herbie did, too, and no one was more a regular than a Chayefsky or a Fosse. From the moment he saw me with Paddy, he evaluated, because the *next* time I came in, he needed to know (sotto voce) ". . . so how do you know Paddy?" which is another way of asking, "Who are you?" You could be nobody, of course, but if Herbie saw you with somebody, then you must be somebody, too. The whole world's a Herbie.

Paddy asked what I was working on. I wasn't working on anything except getting Levine to seize the New York momentum and open my picture nationwide (which he never did). It had all been energy absent reverse throttle. The rotten thing about living with a picture so long, though, is that you don't know when to get off, bum deal or no bum deal, and I think that's especially true with youthful beginnings, most especially when you're impassioned, and passion's what got you here. But as Ralph Rosenblum would later sum up, "You were fucked, Joe." And like any great editor, Ralph had that rare gift of synthesis.

We ordered sandwiches, Paddy and I, and then he said, "Give me an idea, I need an idea." Who would've thought Chayefsky would be asking me for an idea? Generous, I thought, for him to have asked. I took comfort in his revelation of need and his openness. He had taken me into his confidence, and in so doing, he had welcomed me into his club. But with this affirmation came the discomfiture of sitting here with a giant, the gravity on our respective sides of the table being somewhat askew.

His wife was producing a pilot. "Susan's got a deal with NBC. They're looking for a writer, and I told her you're her guy. *You know these people.*" That last sentence was supportive but not right. He was talking about my characters and even my depiction of family life. The problem was I didn't really know any of this; not the way he thought I did; not the way he meant it; not the way he knew his Marty or Marty's friends or Marty's mother or even the neighborhood of Marty's Bronx, where Chayefsky grew up.

I knew Brooklyn, but only as fractured geography; what I knew of life I knew through observation, not from what I'd lived, and I think there's a distinction; one is interaction, the other the embodiment of a loner. With the sole exception of Flatbush, my feelings for neighborhoods had to do with scattered impressions of places; places walked in but not lived, scant memories, including memories of loss and departure. Cut goods. So many pieces still to pick up.

"She has one son. For the last few years she has been supporting herself and her child. Recently she had great difficulty of providing the necessary money and was finally evicted by her landlord. This precipitated a complete breakdown. Patient became very agitated and depressed and was found wandering around the streets with her child . . . she was picked up wandering with the boy in the streets by a neighbor and placed in a hotel room for the night." {Brooklyn State Hospital clinical summary}

What I knew of family I'd observed from across the fence, and I don't ever remember being in any friend's home prior to college, with the exceptions of Jimmy Blumstein's and of Bob's that one time, and I suspect he was less a friend to me than I was to him, as he would later, with kindness, acknowledge. How could I know these people? I could work from sentiment and loss, I could imagine and observe. I could intuit and infer. I could even recognize it on the street and ask it in, and maybe borrow the rest. Actors give you that, you know, and some give you a lot of that. I could tell a story and structure a narrative as I had always structured life itself, from within, but how could I know these people without life itself to draw upon? I don't know how.

> "Somehow she landed at the Kings County Hospital mental ward. I then was apprised of the situation and called upon her. . . . She was very disturbed about herself but mainly about her son. I am of the opinion that good medical care and home surroundings would quickly restore her. Such care I am not prepared financially to supply her. I read the statement of the doctor who cared for her at Kings County Hospital and am not surprised under the circumstances. Not being a medical man, I still feel that she can be restored, given proper care. I bespeak for her that a short time under favorable conditions can restore her to normal condition. The patient informs me that she has personal property now in your custody which she values at $1,000, consisting of rings and a bond in the value of $75, which she wants me to get permission to apply toward helping to place the son where he would get better care than at an Orphan Home. This is a matter that I cannot do anything about until she regains her mental equilibrium." {Max Gluck, my mother's uncle by marriage}

"Do you want to do it?" Paddy asked. "Sure." After all this, I could not let him down.

I can remember our apartment, though, an apartment, not a life, and even have vague glimmerings of an apartment before that, during infancy—even the high chair, the baby food bottles, the colors I liked and didn't like, throwing those I didn't like to the floor, the frustration of a wooden walker that would jam itself in the cracks on the sidewalk, even the crib; but continuity was something I otherwise invented.

"Patient's thoughts are preoccupied with her sickness and her relationship to her dead mother. She is greatly concerned about the fate of her son and will cry bitterly whenever he is mentioned. Diagnosis offered: involutional* Psychosis: Paranoid type." {Brooklyn State Hospital clinical summary}

My early continuity in life was television; its live intimacy and sustaining personalities and characters, some real, some puppets, some puppets that were imagined real, too, that provided the semblance of a continuum no matter where I was; a life lived through observation and fantasy, with an awareness, however, of the camera as a tool for transcendence, and in my own hands, one of authorial control.

"When patient was twenty-five she married, at her mother's insistence apparently, a dentist twenty years her senior. Marriage was not a happy one; they were incompatible and separated after about fifteen years . . . she has tried to be self-supporting after the separation, operating a dry goods store. . . . she believes patient's worries about caring for self and son brought on the illness and that her being dispossessed was the "last straw." She had never demonstrated any signs of mental illness. There is a boy who the dentist says . . ." {Brooklyn State Hospital clinical summary interview}

I had stood outside the window that night, alone with my mother in front of the radio store on Franklin Avenue in Brooklyn, looking in at that naked

---

* Involutional: "A kind of opposite of evolutional, indicating a physiological decline or degradation, often associated with menopause, *sometimes with childbirth*," Dr. Roger Christenfeld told me. Stress has a major role in symptoms. With regard to my mother, Dr. Regan offered the opinion of bipolar, which would today be treatable. Hospitalization would be for a short period, not life. The main drug would be lithium or other medications.

metallic chassis cradling a large picture tube, vacuum tubes sur-rounding it at its base, alit; the likes of which I had never seen before. With my nose pressed against the store window, it was a looking glass within a looking glass, an alternate reality, the finest I'd ever seen. The kid outsider looking in, marionettes dancing on roller skates, a boy and a girl, and somehow, in ways both incomprehensible and unimaginable to me, at that very moment, a die was cast, even to the extent of the observer . . . and the dancer, too. I've been enthralled by movement, always; dance movement, cinematic movement; puppetry. But I won't dance; don't ask me.

"... *isn't his.*"

21

Denial in the Pursuit of Passion

27 March 2002

James Regan, Ph.D.
Chief Executive Officer
Hudson River Psychiatric Center
10 Ross Circle
Poughkeepsie, NY 12601

Dear Dr. Regan:

Further to our conversation earlier today, I am the son of the late Frances Richman, whom I believe was under the care of your institution through her death in 1985. I am a motion picture writer-director-producer and am completing a memoir. . . . The final portion of my book will deal with questions for which I require certain answers that may reveal themselves in my mother's records. I am requesting access to these records.

WHENEVER I'D THOUGHT about Poughkeepsie, such as when my friend Bill Henry once asked, "Do you know where your mother is?" I would avoid any kind of direct answer, in part because I really didn't have the full answer, having kept myself in the dark. Though I thought I knew where she was, which it turns out I did, I would be too embarrassed to acknowledge that I was not even certain if she was alive, and if she were, why I hadn't seen her, and Bill (a Pulitzer Prize–winning investigative journalist, but one of extraordinary compassion and sensitivity) would respectfully, though painfully, disengage. Just as during my entire childhood I'd deflected those who'd threatened to come too close, a deflection not unlike that of a magician's misdirection, except that the magician usually doesn't lose himself in his own disappearing act, which I believe is part of what happens when you're reinventing yourself from scratch.

The train from Grand Central Station to Poughkeepsie is a ninety-five-minute ride, though I'd always imagined Poughkeepsie as some faraway place, with smokestacks. I don't know where the smokestacks came from, but I discovered that Poughkeepsie is a rather beautiful part of New York State, including historic attractions such as the home of Franklin D. Roosevelt (which is actually $3\frac{1}{2}$ miles north in Hyde Park, but close enough). Vassar College is in Poughkeepsie. The smokestacks, then, were the smokestacks of my mind, smokestacks that evoked a sense of barrenness and haze, gray skies that were sootily overcast and clouded. I didn't think of a mental institution as being someplace sunny, anyway. I'd never thought of my own childhood in that light, either. And so the distance of dead-end gloom and the unknown, including the feared unknown, was infinitely farther, and protectively farther, than ninety-five minutes from me.

"Are you sure you're ready for this?" Dr. Jim Regan had asked in our very first phone conversation, one in which, incidentally, he had initially thought I was someone else calling, but someone else in the same line of work as I and the same first name, who had apparently wanted to shoot a film scene in one of his hospital's buildings. Given this fortuitous synchronicity, and my having identified myself as a writer-director in the message I'd left, he had returned my call without a clue as to why I was calling. Now he was more careful. "Are you sure you're ready for this?" was a head's up; a suspicion that the stuff I might find in Poughkeepsie might not be so sunny at all.

"If I'm not ready for this now," I responded, "when would I be ready?" with a tone of clarity and certainty that there would be nothing in "this" to upend me. To the contrary, my concern now was that I might not get at the truth, just as I hadn't gotten at the truths I'd so often sought as a child, and even later, as an adult.

I've learned that there are some things in life you do need to be ready for, and for whatever the reasons, *you* know when you are, and this is knowable at all ages, and not just because *they* "allow you" or tell you if you're "ready" or "grown up" enough, which is someone else's alibi for your embargoed truth, and I had gotten here not a moment too soon. I had set out on this journey of my own volition; with the timing and methods entirely mine. I was under no contract, no obligation, with no schedule except my own.

Speaking primarily, though not solely, from a child's perspective, the authorities have made themselves an industry in protecting you from you; withholding information that is rightfully yours, but that they deem you should not have, and in doing this, *and of this I am certain,* they succeed in confirming a child's worst imaginings. From a child's vantage point, why should there be secrets otherwise? Just like the way my mother spoke Yiddish when she did not want me to understand something that I, in turn, assumed had to do in some terrible way with me. Unaware, she had left me to my own imaginings, imaginings that confirmed for me the certainty of my own worst fears, given my sense of guilt and my expectation of certain punishment.

What a child has no way of knowing, though, is that authority's instincts are, first and foremost, to protect itself within the status quo, and it does this through control, with which I was bridled and which I abhorred with every fiber of my being. The harboring of secrets, specifically, knowledge that is rightfully yours, not theirs, enforces further dependence on the keeper of the secrets, and maintains a non-negotiable hierarchical relationship that is in no way equal or morally defensible. They hold all the cards. Its insidiousness lies both in the fact of its own self-interest at the expense of the child, and the disingenuous guise of being primarily interested in the child's welfare, which, in turn, reinforce the myth that secrets are being kept for the child's own good. This is duplicitous and a fundamental conflict of interest. So endemic to the way of doing business has this become, though, that I believe it attracts practitioners who, with rare exceptions, seek power, refuge, and the personal security that accrues from each in deniability and the protection from accountability that comes with bureaucratic insulation. The evidence for this is on the evening news. There is a solution, and it needs to be legally mandated: no secrets. Children will find their own equilibrium under openness. And let authority fend for itself, including the sorting of its wheat from its chaff.

"When would you like to come up?" Jim asked. He had offered no resistance whatever. Two weeks from the day we'd first spoken, he picked me up at the station.

He was standing beside his car as I got off the train. "Jim?" I inquired as I extended my hand and introduced myself, "I appreciate your meeting me." I sensed just a tad of diffidence, an observational stance. Dr. Regan wasn't exactly some long-lost friend. He was taking measure. We'd spoken now only a few times prior, and he had no certain way of knowing me, really, or how I might respond to the material. I was, after all, my mother's son. The way he was looking at me now, though, told me something more: he'd seen her picture.

I wanted to put Dr. Regan as much at ease as possible, lest he withhold information I'd come so close now to obtaining, although I had no reason to believe that he would do so. I had some practice at this, too, after all; even making movies is about getting people on board. During the fifteen-minute ride from the train to his office I asked, "Did you happen to find any pictures?"

"Yeah, I think there may be one in there."

"Uh-huh. Only one?"

"I think so," he said, and I wondered if it was the picture I had now in my mind's eye; the one they'd sent me when I was about thirteen at Hawthorne, and that I'd torn up because I knew she didn't want to see me anymore and they were protecting me by not telling me that and the picture somehow was the next best thing they could do, but it wasn't the same. It had never been an act of anger, only one of contrition and closure.

I went on to describe the picture, her blondish hair, her smile, high cheekbones, middle-aged at the time, and so on. He wasn't sure. I sensed he'd seen a different picture. "Are there any negatives?" I asked.

"See that building over there?" He was pointing now as he drove. It was an enormous gothic-looking brick building on top of a hill. "All that stuff would be stored in there." "By name?" I asked. "I doubt it; it's all just been put together," he replied. "You have to remember, at one time we had six thousand patients up here. Your mom lived in one of these buildings, until she was transferred over to the building we're going to now." I was looking at that building, deeply recessed from the road and incongruously surrounded by greenery. It was so massive and overpowering a structure, and so frighteningly gothic, that all I could think of was a huge human warehouse. The austerity and bizarre majesty of this edifice struck me as something straight out of Frankenstein or Dracula. It was as if an architect had been told, "Hey, we're gonna have crazy people here. Design something," and had gotten it into his head to design crazy, scary buildings. More than a hundred of them.* A hundred million nightmares, with

* "The declining patient population is due to many reasons and psychotropic medications are but one. Other factors include more community housing, more sophisticated psychotherapy, better community mental health systems (aiding quicker intervention), fiscal incentives for general hospitals and nursing homes to accept those with severe mental illness, and better community acceptance," Jim Regan said. In my opinion, a cutback in state funding is a contributing factor as well, with many of these people now among the unaccounted homeless. Whether they are better off "homeless" is, in my opinion, a matter of serious debate. At the time I visited the Hudson River Psychiatric Center in 2002, it housed 140 patients. Given the option, I'd just as soon go homeless.

the state's bureaucrats signing off on buildings that looked like what they were meant to be. I would have to get a picture of that, I thought.

Jim explained to me that several hundred patients, and staff members, had lived in each of these buildings; none as large as the main gothic building, however, with the one I was looking at actually being one of the last remaining, though many had survived into the 1960s and early '70s, on what was then more than one thousand acres of land. But regardless of the greenery and sunshine, I could not get past the thought of the shadows these buildings must have cast at sundown, like the restless shadows of the mind. It's a good thing, I thought, that these buildings are gone now. It's a good thing, too, that one remains, to remember.

As we got out of the car and headed toward the more contemporary five-story building that housed both patients and administrative offices, with him walking briskly ahead and me following, Jim suddenly turned and asked, "Do you know where your mom is buried?" I heard, but I couldn't connect. "Mom" rang with a familiarity I couldn't recall. He'd spoken of her now as if he thought I knew her. An awareness came over me now that there were feelings here I needed to find, and of the distance traveled that had long ago dimmed the love I'd felt as a child.

"No," I admitted, "I really don't."

"Yes, you do!" he snapped back, pulling a sheet of paper from his pocket and swiftly passing it to me, as if it were a hot potato to be handed off. There was nervous energy here; not mine.

I just froze in my tracks, standing there on the tarmac looking at the paper, disbelieving what I was seeing but trying to make sense of it. There seemed to be some mistake, I thought. How did my birthday get in here? "Are you okay?" Jim asked. "She died on my birthday," I said, in a tone that searched for an answer I knew couldn't be. He nodded as much, and I followed him in, knowing, of course, she would wait.

We entered his office, and sitting there on a round table were four or five stacks of paper, some with rubber bands separating smaller sections within the stacks, and each with a sticky note on top identifying the categories: correspondence, treatment plans, medications, physical examinations, etc. The sheer volume of material stunned me. "How many pages is this?" I asked.

"Around seventeen hundred," Dr. Regan replied, which his secretary confirmed by presenting me with the copying bill. Seventeen hundred pages of printed microfiche, a story spanning thirty-seven years of my mother's life, of which fewer than a hundred pages would essentially tell the tale: a "History of Patient" and a "Clinical Summary" of all her years from the day of her admission to her final day of life. Looking at these stacks, I felt I'd come upon a long-lost hidden piece of me. Amazing, I felt, after all these years, that this still exists. A connection I'd never imagined was suddenly sitting here for me, like a gift, of sorts, and a sense of completion. What the social workers never told me about me, I might now discover through her; things I never knew, I felt certain would be here; what these things were, I had no inkling. I was eager to begin. We sat down now at the table. "There's a lot of stuff here," Jim said as he shuffled through papers I knew he'd looked at earlier, "most of it's just a lot of clinical day-to-day stuff, treatment plans, medications. What you're going to want, I think, is pretty much in the summary."

"Can I see that picture?" I asked.

He was going to do this his way. "Did you bring your birth certificate?" I reached into my canvas tote. He looked at it, not so much to be sure that I was who I said I was (he already had evidence of that), but for another reason. He looked, now, at another sheet. My sense was that he was trying to piece something together here, like a puzzle. All my birth certificate could give him, though, in addition to confirmation of something he already knew, would be my date and place of birth, my mother's maiden name, my father's name (Benjamin Jacoby), their ages, country of birth (mother: United States, father: Russia), "number of children born alive to this mother previous to this pregnancy" (0), occupations, residence of mother (interestingly, the certificate does not ask for residence of father). Right at the top, where the line is for "first name"—my first name—the space is left blank. Only my last name is typed in: "Jacoby." I have no first name.

"Does the name 'Gluck' mean anything to you?" he asked. What a horrible name, I thought. That name would *have* to be a Brooklyn Jewish name. I just don't know where else you could find such a name, but with my luck Gluck probably had something to do with me.

"No, not really," I said, disowning any reference to me. "I'm sure it's one of those names I've heard before but I can't say it means anything."

"He was your mother's uncle by marriage." My mother's uncle by marriage, I thought. I never could figure out family relationships, anyway; I'd never had a family to figure.

"Can I see that picture?"

"Max Gluck," he went on, "was a clerk on the Municipal Court."

"To: Clarence H. Bellinger, Esq., Director, Brooklyn State Hospital

Dear Sir:

Complying with your request RE: Frances Richman:
{She was} Married . . . {they} lived apart for many years, no divorce, some settlement not known to me. There is a boy now at a Hebrew Orphan Home. Schooling through high school. . . . In business somewhere in Coney Island with her mother who has died of old age. So far as I am informed, the patient supported herself with the boy for some time until the recent breakdown. I am informed she was evicted for non-payment of four months rent from 848 Franklin Avenue, Brooklyn. Though I am an uncle on my wife's side and connected with the courts for many years, either through false pride or mental {sic}, she was picked up wandering with the boy in the streets by a neighbor and placed in a hotel room for the night . . . with still no information from her as to her kin, the police were notified and somehow she landed at the Kings County Hospital mental ward. I then was apprised. . . ."

"And his wife," Dr. Regan continued, "knew your mom from childhood."

"Patient was an only child, born in New York. She was described as a normal healthy active child, suffering no illnesses other than the usual childhood diseases, which weren't severe. She was considered to be very bright, as a child and an adult; was believed to have gone through high school.

"Personality: Patient described as an energetic, capable, 'brilliant,' sociable person who didn't drink, take drugs, or bother much about religion."

{Brooklyn State Hospital report. Source: Mrs. Millie Gluck}

As he continued sorting through the stacks, I couldn't help but notice his knee movement under the table, the same nervous energy I'd felt outside when he'd handed off to me my mother's burial information. He was trying to piece something together here, ascribing coherence to something that inherently lacked any, just as I, perhaps, had ascribed coherence to myself, but remained a mystery to those few who had known me. These very contradictions had, in part, propelled me here. I was in on my own discovery. But how one cobbled this together in a way that was meaningful may have been what Dr. Regan was grappling with. And with a grown man, now, her son, sitting opposite him, he had all the more cause for his uncertainty. But no matter how you shuffled these cards, whatever was or wasn't in the deck, that was the hand you played, and Dr. Regan held a limited hand. To tell you the truth, I forgot about the picture. I wanted him to get through this.

He came across something he'd seen earlier. Almost parenthetically, sliding it across to me, he asked, "Do you remember this?" It was the letter I'd written in 1963 to my mother's doctor, the one I'd written at the encouragement of Dr. Levy. I, in fact, recall having had resistance to the idea, but how could I not have wanted to know how my mother was? Seeing this letter nearly forty years later, out of context, and with no time to reflect on the impulse that had led me to write it, I was puzzled: "Why didn't I follow up on this?" I asked myself out loud, but for him to hear as well. It was the right thing to say, after all; exculpatory, perhaps, in its underlying intent. I would later refresh my recollection as to context; of the two letters that had preceded mine, including the one in which my mother speaks of having two children, and the letter written to me by her doctor after receiving mine. At the moment, though, all I could think was, "It's not like me not to follow through." But I suspect my real question was not "Why didn't I follow up on this?" so much as "Why did I write this letter in the first place?" The answer to that, I believe, is that I wrote it because I believed Dr. Levy thought it would be a good idea, and perhaps, too, to please him.

"Seen with regards to a letter from her son dated 6/10/63 . . . she replied that she doesn't feel like a mother. . . . When asked whether she would like her son to visit with her, she was hesitating and then said she didn't mind, but she wouldn't talk to him—Why?—'Because I wouldn't tell him the truth'—What truth?—'How I feel.' When asked for the last name of her son, she didn't know. When asked for her own name, she said, 'Frances Richman.' She didn't know whether this was her maiden or married name."* {Hudson River State Hospital, June 13, 1963}

In truth, I had no longer felt like a son.

Throughout my reading of my mother's records, my sense is that her responses have an underlying honesty to them, despite her defensive, occasionally hallucinatory, and often contradictory statements. Even her outright avoidances are open-faced; I believe they have to do with her need to cover guilt and shame, a guilt having not only to do with me, but with her relationship to her own mother as well, all of which I believe were contributing cumulative factors in her lifelong illness.

"Patient's thoughts are preoccupied with her sickness and her relationship to her dead mother. She is greatly concerned about the fate of her son and will cry bitterly whenever he is mentioned. . . . 'My mother let

---

* It is my mother's maiden name.

me do things I shouldn't do. I asked her where do you have these things from? I don't need them.' (What things?) 'Oh, maybe she stole them; I would have given everything to her. I have great feelings of guilt since she died.' (What are you talking about?) 'Never mind. She took things. Maybe she shouldn't have done it. I have feelings of guilt. Why did she give everything to me.' "

"When talking about her mother she will ramble a great deal without giving any explanation." {Brooklyn State Hospital admittance report, May 1948}

"Patient is oriented, has some insight. She felt the whole world was after her, due to the death of her mother." {Hudson River State Hospital, June 1968}

I remember standing outside the butcher shop on Franklin Avenue in Brooklyn, near where we live, the one with all the sawdust on the floor, as my mother places a phone call on the black pay phone hanging up against the wall in the shop. She is worried and I am watching carefully. She is calling Kings County Hospital, where my grandmother has been admitted; inquiring into her condition. It will not be a long call. She suddenly drops the phone and screams in Yiddish, clapping her hands at the news. I know the words. I understand. My grandmother's death certificate gives her death at age seventy-six due to "natural causes." The certificate indicates her length of stay at the hospital as having been "one day."

Her date of death is September 22. The same as my mother's. My birthday.

"She believes patient's worries about caring for self and son brought on the illness and that her being dispossessed was the 'last straw.' She had never before demonstrated any signs of mental illness to aunt's knowledge." {Brooklyn State Hospital. Source: Mrs. Millie Gluck}

Seven months following her mother's death, my mother was certified mentally ill and institutionalized.

Her shame and feelings of guilt that were undoubtedly reflected in my shame as a child, a burden I shared through unavoidable association, the guilt I felt for having been there, for making life so hard for her. We were reflecting pools of one another's deeds, with me having entered unannounced, conceivably unwelcome, and with nowhere to hide. Enter the camera, the puppet; even Jolson could hide behind blackface. She had loved me as much as I'd loved her, but we were mirrors of each other's unavoidable circumstances. I was here, after all, and while she had attempted to make it otherwise, only momentarily, in a sleep-walking state of short duration, I could not disappear. By 1963, though, I knew not to appear, protecting myself, undoubtedly, and a future still tenuous, but one for which I held a passion. Even if not quite risking an awakening of the guilt I'd felt as a child, risking what was unknow-able and perhaps fearful, including my concern for some obligation that might become mine, and the unknown consequences of that, conse-quences otherwise avoidable, was a risk I could not take.

"What about the name 'Backal'?" Jim asked.

I hit the ceiling! "I know that name! Now, wait a minute—don't tell me anything. Let me tell you: what a horrible name. I was maybe five or six. Living with my mother in a tenement on Franklin Avenue in Brooklyn, and in the entranceway there are these mailboxes, you know, brass mailboxes, in the narrow entranceway, maybe eight or ten of them and one of them, ours, has a piece of brown shopping bag paper in the slot with the name 'Backal' printed in, in pencil. I'm trying to get it out of that slot because I know that's not my name and it doesn't belong on our box but I can't reach it to scratch it out and the kids are teasing me 'Backal! Backal!' It scares the shit of out of me—I hate that name. I know it's not my name, I don't know how I know except that maybe my mother has told me something, and I don't understand where this name comes from or why it's on our mailbox."

"Israel Backal was your mother's husband."

"Marriage was not a happy one, they were incompatible and separated after about fifteen years." {Brooklyn State Hospital. Source: Mrs. Millie Gluck}

It was a psychic adjustment that must've taken me a moment or two, then left a calm understanding, the calmness that comes with revelation. Suddenly it all made sense. I had never before understood why I couldn't find their marriage license, Jacoby and my mother. I had come this far in life believing my birth certificate implied my parents' marriage. That my father, Benjamin Jacoby, had either left or died. I never knew which, of course, but suspected the latter, which in my child's imaginings was why they never told me, probably because I was in for the same unspeakable fate. They were "protecting" me, after all. Why else would my mother have tried what she had tried? I had me coming and going, with the keepers of the secrets protecting me in tow. I can make the case for her, but I still can't make it for them.

And yet she had chosen not to put her legally married name on my birth certificate. Except for the authorities who had kept hidden from me the answers I'd sought through the years, and my imaginings, *the imaginings of a child,* hers remained the only truth out there.

"When her son's name, Joseph Jacoby, was mentioned to her, she smiled wittingly and said, 'He was illegitimate.' Then she contradicted herself and said that she did not have such a son. She is fairly well oriented." {Hudson River State Hospital, June 1963}

"Why does your husband want a divorce? 'I have a little boy and he is not his.'" {Kings County Hospital, Brooklyn, admittance report}

Swiftly, Dr. Regan reached from across the table and slapped her picture down in front of me. I had held an image in my mind's eye of a smiling, bright, blondish, middle-aged woman. But the woman I was looking at now, age seventy but looking far older, I could not recognize. I could see her eyes, though; I had her eyes. Suddenly, from this small black-and-white microfiche printout of a photograph, as I strained for recognition, I recognized the dress; the floral dress I'd remembered from childhood. How a dress could have survived all those years I don't know. And I wondered, too, how she could have. And though distant I felt still, I could not help but feel that to have lived just three months shy of eighty-six years could not have been a blessing.

"When asked as to her plans for the future she said: 'Flowers, perhaps, for my funeral, you know.' " {*Hudson River State Hospital, June 29,1965*}

My mother passed away September 22, 1985.*

It felt like it had come to a soft, anticlimactic, finish. I'd grasped the broad strokes; I would get to the details, alone, in my reading. I checked my watch. The 3:33 out of Poughkeepsie would get me into Grand Central at 5:15. "Well . . ." I said, with nothing really to say. "Wait a minute—" Jim interrupted, more at ease now and wanting to somehow move this into the moment. "Let me just see something." He pushed back in his chair and went over to the computer. There was an address for "Gluck" in Coney Island in the microfiche and he wanted to see if there might be a listing.

"Jim, what you're doing—it's forty years ago. They're dead." I like to make everybody dead. It keeps it clean that way; everything's resolved. He checked anyway. No listing. It is eerie, though, how you can get caught right up with the intensity of the past; having thrown yourself back there, psychically, and come out of it still partially stuck

---

* My mother's physical illness was not lengthy. She was admitted conscious but confused with a bronchial condition, which worsened. Infection set in. On the third day of her admission she developed chest pain. An EKG showed myocardial infarct changes. She was placed on the critical list. "After a week, she suddenly expired." (Release/termination summary, Hudson River Psychiatric Center)

there, something about the elasticity of time makes you think; like coming out of a dream and having that moment of confusion as to where you are and what's real. My having come this far, though, was far enough.

It was amazing, still, I thought, that a trail that had long ago gone cold could be sitting here waiting, just in case I'd show up, just as I had. This link toward a completion, even if only seventeen hundred pieces of paper, felt possessory. "Have you got a box I can put this in?" I asked in an almost tentative way. Even now I felt maybe somebody might say "No, you can't take this with you. It belongs to you, sure, but you can't have it." Nobody said it.

"You know," Jim said as we drove back down to the station, his eyes straight ahead, speaking to me unguardedly and with blunt candor, "had you come up here it would have ruined your life." I looked over at him, now, somewhat surprised by the statement, but one that I could see was from experience and considered. I wondered if he was concerned about something else, though. My comments about my own letter that may have been, in part, exculpatory.

"Why do you say that?" I asked. "I just think it would have," he replied. "You might even have moved up here." I found that inconceivable, but he didn't. Whatever instincts had kept me away, I doubt the fear of moving to Poughkeepsie would have been one of them, but how could I really know what I didn't know, or what might have been? It was the unknowable, in fact, that had kept me from coming, and, like my mother, the distance I'd felt with the passage of time.*

As I reached in for the box and thanked Jim for the lift and all his help, he cautioned, "You know, you might have a delayed reaction to this." I didn't believe that, frankly, not for a moment. "Just to give you a heads up," he added.

When we spoke a week later, Jim asked, "How're you feeling?" I told him I was feeling fine, wondering if perhaps I shouldn't be or, at least, not

---

* "We have no hard data but family visitors in the fifties and sixties were rare," Dr. Roger Christenfeld told me. "For one thing, they felt psychiatrists blamed them. That's certainly not the whole reason families shied away—stigma, insalubrious environment, and all—but it played a part."

admitting to it so openly. Why is it exactly that when you're not feeling whatever it is someone suspects you might be feeling—even when they don't want you to—you don't want to disappoint their concerns? Then I asked, "Jim, do you recall what you said to me in the car last week; that had I come up to visit my mother it would've ruined my life?"

"Sure."

"Let me ask you something," I continued, truly wanting to understand something I just didn't believe. "Are you concerned I might be feeling some sense of guilt for my not having come up?"

"Joe," he responded firmly, "I'm not your shrink. I said what I said because I believe it. It just would have screwed up your whole life," and he repeated that I might've moved up there. He said it with a sincerity and certainty I had no reason to doubt. I found it both affirming and mysterious, because it told me something about a life's choice I had made, albeit intuitively, one for which there must have been a myriad of sensors, although I still didn't believe I would ever have moved up there. I just had too much of a will to succeed.

"Well," I said, giving lip service to the only remaining possibility I could reasonably think of and wanting to accommodate his concern, "maybe I'm into denial." "Maybe you are," Jim echoed. I may have stumbled onto something.

You can live a life with denial and get away with it, too. Not a bad way to go, under certain circumstances, or at least in my case, where "you should either be dead, on drugs, or in jail." It was the only way my child-psychologist friend could figure it or, more aptly, not figure it. Nobody could, really. I never tried. I just made it up as I went along, and as long as I kept on swimming and could see the shoreline ahead, I never gave it a second thought. And I never looked back. I even saw stuff I didn't really see, to be honest, just taking it on faith. Not faking it, mind you; deeply knowing it, though. Like in the fifties when I went out looking for a television studio, not knowing where one was, but taking the subway into the city, knowing I'd find it. *And getting in.* Just *needing* it was enabling, prophetically fulfilling in ways I don't understand now and knew I didn't have to then. Pigeons find their way home all the time. I never really knew where home was, not even in my dreams, but I never felt homeless. The hand you're dealt is the hand you play, and a child knows only one hand. And even when you're walking the streets of Brooklyn without a real home, the passions of one's imaginings become far more enriching and secure than life's uncertain certainties, made all the more sustaining by having them within. If it was ever a question of entitlements, though, I took mine on the sly. A presence, too, often by observation, participation through presence, yet once removed. Awkward at times, the best I could do. A denial of need, sure.

Some things in life you just can't figure, and I figure that's a good thing, too, 'cause I can't figure how any of this would have happened if it had to make sense.

"Never face the facts," Ruth Gordon clarioned. And dreams, in the light of facts, never process anyway, any more than film gets processed in daylight. Dreams are hatched in spirit, a sequestered daylight, an unquenchable optimism, yet one that is fragile, best kept from naysayers and noisemakers, those that discourage and distract. I'd kept mine hidden. Given the options—door one, two, or three—who could quibble? But I never knew from options.

All I knew were goose bumps; the shiver that comes over you when passion flares; the television chassis in a storefront window. The puppet dancing on a string. The camera. Jolson up there on the screen, singing his heart out in blackface, with me sitting next to my mother, wanting to do that, too, to tell her I loved her, hidden in blackface, just in case.

I don't know where passion comes from, or what might have been if what had been hadn't, but I am certain there is upside in having nothing, especially at the start, because nothing leaves you needing, and everything's affordable within the realm of dreams. How else could this make sense? Denial?

Whatever works.

∞

I HAD SOME unfinished business to tend to. Two items, to be exact, except that there'd be a third I hadn't thought of. In January 2004 I needed that picture of that gothic building up on the hill, and I wanted to visit my mother's grave site. Which one I needed or wanted more, I don't know, but the place I came to first was the hospital's administrative office, where I had visited with Dr. Regan almost two years earlier, and my first order of business was to get that picture.

I discovered that Dr. Regan had moved onto a full-time teaching assignment at Marist College, also in Poughkeepsie. The hospital's new CEO, Ms. Jean Wolfersteig, put me in touch with Dr. Roger Christenfeld, the hospital's research director, who had a long history with the hospital and who she felt might better be able to answer any historical or other questions I might have.

It was a frigid January morning. A friend had offered to drive me up, given my planned trip to the cemetery, which was some distance from the hospital, and the fact that I didn't own a car. She also felt I might need some moral support, which would never have occurred to me, although I could understand why others might think it. I assured her that while grateful for her concern and happy for her company, I was just too distant from this now to feel any emotion, just as I'd not connected with Dr. Regan's use of the word "mom."

It was a pleasant ride up there, with a pause only once for coffee and, for me, a one-dollar blueberry muffin without blueberries, the kind of thing that upends me, in case you're wondering what it takes. I was glad she came.

Upon meeting both Ms. Wolfersteig and Dr. Christenfeld in Dr. Regan's former office, we quickly got into an informal but animated conversation about my book and my mother's illness and what I'd learned from the microfiche. I inquired into Dr. Christenfeld's opinion of her diagnoses, having felt always that there was still something missing. I'd told him of when she'd choked me and the guilt I'd felt as a child and beyond, and he suddenly blurted out, with no visible reflection but rather with a certainty born of experience suggesting I'd fallen into some archetypal box: "Your crime was that you were born."

Just as I'd fallen silent in acknowledgment and recognition when Jim Regan had said to me two years earlier "Israel Backal was your mother's husband," I knew now what this meant. And I couldn't help but wonder why I hadn't known it sooner. My friend looked as dumbfounded as I must have looked to her.

He continued, but I barely heard. "Along with the involutional paranoia there may have been some postpartum depression. The tendency of all small children is to blame themselves. Whatever is happening to their parents, they think it's their fault. Of course your being born, your being here is what caused your mother such pain," Dr. Christenfeld stated expressing a child's perception.

Today you hear about the young mother who goes off the deep end and drives her kids into the river. There were obviously so many other factors in my mother's case, not just my birth, but I find it fascinating that *my* perception as a child, *my* guilt, was premised on something very real, with choking me as added corroboration, and the simple fact, unbeknownst to me, that there was nothing I could do about it. And so the answer to "Mommy, Mommy, what did I do?" is suddenly clear.

The cemetery was the tiniest I'd ever seen, with homes across the street and another cemetery adjacent. It was a bitterly cold day, and the snow was frozen over the land. The woman who was the keeper of the records could not find any reference to my mother's grave site, though I have the records of the service, the rabbi who performed it, and the fact of her burial at this Jewish cemetery. But there was no money for a marker. I was not surprised.

When we got there my friend and I both looked for one, but I have to say she was more aggressive about it than I was. I just knew it wasn't there, but I also knew my mother was. I had virtually no emotional response, even though my friend kept a distance from me, thinking I might want to be alone. More than fifty years had passed. I had always suspected I wouldn't find her, just as I imagined the smokestacks in my mind. But if you look very carefully at the picture of that gothic building, now a landmark, there are smokestacks, and in one picture, shown to me by the hospital, you can even see the smoke.

∞

I WAS PASSING a Blockbuster video store in the early nineties and decided to peek in. I went to the family/children's section just to see what they had and rented half a dozen tapes. Retreads of *Sesame Street* were everywhere, but I already knew the quality of that show and would soon discover it was in a league of its own on those shelves. Nothing I saw came close.

But *I* could come close, I thought, and in a way that hadn't been done before. I hadn't felt this way since my first feature—"déjà vu all over again," as Yogi would say. I would combine those things I'd practiced professionally—filmmaking and puppetry—and had come to understand all the way from childhood. The name for the company flew into my head from nowhere: "Children's Video Theater." It expressed perfectly what I had in mind.

I called on someone I may have spoken a few words to in the sixties, but otherwise had not known, although I remembered him and he remembered me, too, because I was a Bil Baird puppeteer in the sixties and he was Bil's son, Peter.* A brilliantly gifted puppeteer/performer in his own right, Peter had ownership of the primary Baird marionettes, and we entered into a business agreement. Our first filmed musical was to be *Davy Jones' Locker*, which began principal photography in 1995.

I asked my good friend Betty, a wonderful graphic artist, if she would design a logo for my company based on a sketch I provided her, keeping in mind that I cannot draw a straight line, as evidenced here. But I knew

---

* Peter B. Baird died on July 16, 2004, from esophageal cancer. He was fifty-two.

the concept. Here is the sketch on a simple Post-it note I gave Betty, and for some strange reason, kept, and the final logo, as rendered:

It never occurred to me until now that the sketch I had given her was almost identical, both visually and conceptually, to the experience I'd had that night, long ago, standing there with my mother, my face pressed against the storefront window of a radio store on Franklin Avenue in Brooklyn. And there sitting amid the radios, regaling in their finest cabinetry, but for this lone picture tube, naked, lit vacuum tubes adorning it; were two marionettes, a boy and a girl, dancing. Goose bumps. And I knew then, at that very instant, I wanted this.

I came back. And I don't know how.

Epilogue

November 2004

"WHAT'RE THE ODDS?" I asked my editor.

"Sixty–forty," Walt said. "For or against?" "Against," he responded. I was looking for a reason not to go.

"You really think it's that close, though?"

"Yeah, I do," he said matter-of-factly. It would probably be a wild-goose chase, I thought, but sixty–forty was no reason not to go. I couldn't justify leaving something like this unturned anyway, regardless of what I believed or didn't believe. You could have told me it was ninety–ten that this Benjamin Jacoby *was* my father and I wouldn't have believed it. I don't know why. Too simple, maybe. Too easy. Nothing was simple. Nothing came easy. Or maybe I knew something I didn't know I knew, in which case I wouldn't have been able to explain it anyway. Maybe I didn't want to know. That's possible. You could drive yourself nuts trying to figure these things out; it was easier to just go and find out! I was this guy who turned over every stone, *every stone*, and suddenly here's this one stone, a stone's throw from me, and I'm looking for reasons not to.

Laura Jacoby wasn't making life any easier, but I wasn't going to get beaten down by a ninety-year-old. "Go visit her!" my neighbor Betty had said. "Bring her flowers."

Betty might've sensed something, though, just like when she'd said to me, "Your mother must have really loved him. She wouldn't have put his name on your birth certificate otherwise." I'd wondered about that. My mother was legally married to the dentist even though they were separated. She could've put his name down. The kids taunted me with it: "Backal! Backal!" and they scared me and I ran.

Who was this Backal? "What is *my* name?" I asked her. "Where is my father?" "He's in California." By putting my rightful name down, right there on my birth certificate, my mother might have been expiating some guilt. No first name, though; she'd left that open. Maybe she'd planned to share that decision. Ben might have had something to say about his son's name, after all. The surname, though, was non-negotiable.

Perhaps I was her gift to him, one he never picked up. She could have wished it otherwise. I was the physical embodiment of a union that might have been, the fulfillment of that wish, perhaps, for him as much as for her; but one she could take only as far as she could. Maybe she was angry with him. Maybe that's why she choked me. She seemed almost always to tell the truth, though, and when she didn't, I think it's because she couldn't.

"When her son's name, Joseph Jacoby, was mentioned to her, she smiled wittingly and said, 'He was illegitimate.' Then she contradicted herself and said that she did not have such a son. She is fairly well oriented." {Hudson River State Hospital, June 1963}

In April 2002, out of a requirement for "stone turning" more than any genuine expectation, I'd gone to the Social Security Death Index (which records the death of anyone who contributed to Social Security) on the Internet and typed in "Benjamin Jacoby." Thirteen possibilities appeared. I narrowed the thirteen down to five candidates, mainly through date of birth and death (my father is listed as forty years old on my birth certificate), but I allowed some margin for error. The Internet site gave me Social Security numbers (dead people's Social Security numbers are a matter of public record) and addresses at the date of death. I wrote the Social Security Administration under the Freedom of Information Act, and got copies of the original "application for account number" by these five people. This application sets forth the name, place of birth, address, business name of present employer, age, father's full name, mother's maiden name, gender, eye color, ethnicity, and a dated signature. None of them quite fit.

Social Security had sent me a couple of wrong names, including a Benjamin Jacobs. How he got in there I had no idea. This Jacobs was born in Romania, not Russia (as stated on my birth certificate), lived in the Bronx, not Brooklyn (as I was expecting), and was six years younger than he should have been. There was no mention of him working for a "dress company" or being a "salesman," as my birth certificate states.

With nothing matching, coupled with my own low expectations, I let it drop. Social Security was enacted in 1935, when my father would have already been in the workplace, so he might not have filed. This might also account for why I was never able to find a file on my mother's husband, except for confirmation from Albany that he had been a licensed dentist.

Sometime in 2003 I looked again. Thinking that he might have had an extraordinarily long life, I searched for any date of death between 2001 and 2003. This time only one record appeared, for a Benjamin Jacoby who had died in October 2001 at age ninety-five in Forest Hills, Queens. I wondered why this hadn't come up earlier (it had, but as I'll explain, it would take me yet another year to realize why I hadn't connected the dots). This time I checked the Queens telephone directory online and found a number. Even though I expected that the phone would be disconnected by now, I dialed the number anyway.

"Hello?" An elderly woman with a gentle, frail voice and what I supposed was an Eastern European accent answered. I knew at once that I was speaking with an Orthodox Jew.

"Hello. Is this Mrs. Jacoby?"

"Yes, this is Laura Jacoby. Who's this?"

"Mrs. Jacoby, my name is also Jacoby. Joseph Jacoby." Nobody calls me Joseph, not even me, but that's how I introduced myself. The only person I can remember ever calling me that with regularity was my mother. Perhaps I was appealing to her maternal instinct.

"Hello, Joseph. How are you?"

"I'm fine, thanks," I said.

"How can I help you?" she asked.

"Well, I just want to make sure I have the right party. I'm looking for Mrs. Benjamin Jacoby."

"Yes, dear, but Ben died a few years ago, my darling." I told her I was sorry. "We had forty-seven wonderful years together," and she thanked Hashem (God's name in Hebrew). She talked to me with striking openness, and there was nothing "elderly" about this ninety-year-old's mental acumen.

"You know, Laura, my father's name was also Benjamin, but I never knew him."

"Well," she said, with the wisdom of a woman who had discovered long ago that anything was possible in this world, "so you think maybe Ben was your father?"

In the guise of protecting this revelation from *her* (certainly not *me*!), I used a magician's misdirection. "I don't know about father, but maybe a relative. Or an uncle, even."

"Well, maybe. Who knows?" she proffered. "To tell you the truth, darling, Ben never talked about the past. When I met him I was thirty-nine and he was already forty-seven, forty-eight."

Could I ask her a few questions? "Sure." When I asked what year she had met Ben, she hesitated only a split second. "Nineteen fifty-four."

What kind of work did he do? "A tailor." A tailor? "Yes. But Ben did a lot of things before I met him. He didn't talk about the past." Of women's clothes? "No, no. Men's. Never women's." I asked if she was sure. "Yes." Where was he born? "Romania," she replied. Not Russia? "No. Romania. Are we getting close?" she queried, as if we were putting together a giant jigsaw puzzle—which, in a sense, we were. I asked where he'd lived when she met him. "In Forest Hills," she replied.

She went on to explain that she had been previously married for twelve years. As a young girl in Czechoslovakia, she had worked for the passport office and had immigrated to Cuba when she was twenty-four. Her son would later tell me that after Chamberlain had signed the Munich agreement ceding the Sudetenland to Hitler, she was told by one of the diplomats in her office that she had better get her family out. She had not only gotten herself and her sister out, but also had managed to get more than fifty other people out by making "arrangements" with the various travel agents and doing what had to be done to be certain their documents were in order. She could not, however, save her own parents, who didn't believe it was anything more than a passing political phenomenon. They had their own shop, and business was just too good to leave. They would later perish.

In Havana she met her German-born husband, an automotive expert who had worked for Mercedes in Germany, and they went on to Youngstown, Ohio, and he'd gotten a job working for GM in Warren, Ohio. After saving some money he opened his own Amoco service station, which was quite successful. It was there that he was shot and killed on New Year's Eve, leaving her with their three small children.

Soon after, she sold her home ("a beautiful house . . . I didn't know what I was doing"). She drove to New York with her children to be near her sister, who lived in White Plains, but ended up in Forest Hills where, by sheer chance ("Hashem guided me"), she met Ben.

"So what do you think?" she said. "Maybe we should meet?"

In spite of my having taken the initiative to call her, I found myself wanting to defer meeting her; if only I had heard something about a "salesman" or "women's clothes." I was writing about my mother's life in Poughkeepsie and I was probably on overload. The possibility of having to unearth yet another life felt overwhelmingly tiring. But I was only deferring. I'd been writing my story chronologically and was doing the "advance work" in calling her. I knew now where to find her and I also knew she would be coming up shortly, but still, nothing had matched, and there was nothing she had said that had lead me to suspect I had the right person. "Well, I tell you, Laura; I'm just in the middle of one of the final chapters in my book. Could I call you in a few weeks?"

"Of course, darling. Call me anytime." And she blessed me.

For me to say that I wasn't hesitant, reticent, and perhaps unknowingly unnerved by my own persistence would be untrue. Throughout this journey I have grappled with the countervailing forces within myself, including deep emotional resistance, that I would often feel tugging against my conscious attempt at self-revelation and that would, at times, bring me to the point of mental and physical exhaustion. A lifetime of walls had to be scaled—indeed, broken down—for my own conscious will to prevail.

Windows of extraordinary opportunity in life often appear only once. And more often than not, gently and without fanfare. I have usually been pretty good at spotting and opening these windows as I came upon them, but I felt I could buy some time here. I had no way of knowing that the second time around, even though only a few weeks later, this window would jam and stay jammed. Best to seize the day.

"Hello, Laura, this is Joseph. Do you remember we spoke a few weeks ago?"

"Listen, Joseph, darling, I can't talk to you right now. I'm going to the doctor. Call me Wednesday."

"I just wanted to set up a time for us to meet."

"Yes, I want to meet you, darling. But call me Wednesday. Before noon is best." And with that she hung up. No matter how many times I called after that, over a period of months, I got the same line: "Joseph,

I can't see you today, sweetheart. I've got to go to the doctor. Call me Sunday." On Sunday it was "Call me Tuesday." On Tuesday it was "Better to call me Thursday." I played along with this for months, thinking she'd eventually tire of putting me off. The opposite happened.

I stopped calling. I imagined she must have spoken to her son and told him I'd been calling and he must've said something to her like "Ma, what do you need this for? You don't even know who this man is. You don't know what he wants. Maybe he wants money." In my mind, her son was poisoning her against meeting me. "Just go over there," Betty said. "Bring her flowers." I couldn't do it. I couldn't force myself on this ninety-year-old woman, especially when I didn't believe there was really anything there. My book was finished now anyway. And the odds were remote.

And then one day, completely out of the blue, I panicked. I wasn't done. There was one more stone.

What're the odds? "Sixty–forty," Walt said.

⚭

I WENT TO see the rabbi. She had given me the name of a synagogue she had attended with Ben for more than forty years. With no appointment, I took the subway and waited for the rabbi to show up. After a few hours, the door sprang open and the rabbi whooshed in from the brisk fall air. I guessed him to be close to ninety if not more. I respectfully stood up and introduced myself, saying I was working on a film and finishing a book, and might he have a moment? "Film," he quietly intoned, as if to inform himself. Even standing still the rabbi was in motion. "Yes, film," he said, taking off his large-brimmed black hat and long black coat, and continuing to his office. "Come in." Works like a charm.

Even with the rabbi I hedged. I threw out three or four names, asking if any of them rang a bell as being members of his congregation. Ben Jacoby was among them. He knew the name at once and told me the man had died but his widow, Laura, still attended services. He wasn't at liberty to give me her number. I told him I believed I already had it. I asked him if I looked like Ben. He looked at me more carefully now. "No," he said, "but my memory isn't what it used to be." To say he was being modest in his self-assessment is an understatement. The man exuded energy and his repartee was lightning fast. Not being religious myself, I began thinking it might be the water in Forest Hills, but more seriously, on reflection, it spoke to me of the importance of staying tuned to life. Laura had told me that she still helped people less fortunate than herself, apparently through the phone by putting people together with other people who could help, even though she herself was a woman of very modest means, from everything I could tell.

I never came right out and told the rabbi I was looking for my father, but I don't think I had to. He offered to speak with Laura and suggested that perhaps the three of us could get together, either in his office or at her home, which was just a few blocks away. He said I should have her call him, so that he could assure her he'd met with me and that it would be safe for her to do so as well. I thanked him, knowing now that I had an ally and, most importantly, that he might encourage her to meet me. It had been at least six months since I'd spoken to her, and I wondered if she'd even remember me. If not, so much the better.

"Laura? I called you a number of months ago, you may recall. My name is Joseph. And when we spoke I told you I was working on a book and you had told me you had worked for Human Resources during the Lindsay Administration, and I wanted to come and speak with you, and the rabbi suggested you might be a good source." This was my line.

"I don't understand," she said. "What's the rabbi got to do with this?"

"Well, you had given me his name and he thought it was a good idea that perhaps the three of us should meet."

"Well, okay, but I don't know what information I have that would be useful to you. It's been many years, my dear, since I worked for the city."

"I'm sure you would know things that will prove helpful." She asked why we couldn't do this by phone. I said I thought it would be better face-to-face and that the rabbi had agreed, and that we would come to her. She finally accepted, and we made a date for Wednesday. I told her I would let the rabbi know, and it was set.

Early next morning my phone rang. I hadn't given her my number, and I had called her on an unlisted line, but she probably had it from months earlier and, besides, I was in the phone book. "Joseph, this is Laura." "Yes, Laura." "Joseph, why did you call me yesterday about wanting to see me with the rabbi?"

"Because I do."

"But you thought Ben was your father?" My uncle, I said. "Oh, I thought you said your father." No, no. "But listen, Joseph, I can't make it on Thursday." Wednesday! I yelped. "Whatever, I mean Wednesday." "But," I pleaded, "that's the only day the rabbi has available." "No, listen, Joseph, call me Sunday and we'll make an appointment."

"No! Wait, Laura! The rabbi is expecting that we're meeting."

"I spoke to the rabbi," she said.

"Look, Laura, I don't have to meet you. Do you have any pictures of Ben?"

"Of course, I've got hundreds of pictures."

"Can I see just a few of them?"

"Of course, darling, you can see whatever you want. I'll send you some pictures." I said I'd send my messenger to pick them up. Would tomorrow be all right? She thought a moment: "Well, I'm thinking how old you want he should be." I said I didn't think it mattered—forties, fifties. She was actually considering which ones she felt would be most helpful. Her son Gary, then in his fifties, had some pictures, too. "Okay. Thursday I'll have pictures for you." I asked her what time I should have them picked up. "Anytime after twelve," she said. She promised she wouldn't forget. I thought I had a chance that this time she would not disappoint me.

Thursday morning, November 18, 2004. "Good morning, Laura, it's Joseph."

"Good morning, my darling. Listen, I have Gary's bar mitzvah album for you." I said that was wonderful. "Because I thought Ben's age and your age would now be about the same—you understand?" I did, I said (a very sharp woman, I thought). "So it's ready for you, darling, anytime. You know, my son Gary says to me, 'Mother, why don't you meet the man?'" Well, I said to her, he's right! She laughed. "He suggested maybe we should all get together and have lunch—you be our guest, and we have a very nice Chinese/Japanese restaurant nearby." I said I would love to meet her and that she'd be my guest. "And Gary," she said.

About two hours later Gary's black leather bar mitzvah album was delivered to me in a plastic shopping bag. Gary Jacoby's name was inscribed on the album cover along with the date. I removed the thin sheet of tissue covering it and opened it on my dining room table. I saw a thirteen-year-old boy and his father, then fifty-eight, posed for the picture. I couldn't have looked at it for more than a second or two before closing the book. I wasn't sure what I had seen. It had gotten kind of fuzzy and I needed to adjust before opening it again.

I don't know what I expected. I had been investigating and exploring my past for several years, with some long pauses, but now here was the simple fact of Gary's bar mitzvah album. I am pretty sure, though, that I did not see, on first glance, what I was looking at. It may have been that the instant recognition of something tripped a circuit breaker, and I needed to step back. I expected to see someone who looked different from what I had glanced at. I had seen something more than I realized I'd seen, probably.

I found myself hesitantly returning to the album and began to slowly turn the pages. As I strained for recognition, the pictures frozen behind their plastic protectors gradually became clear. What may have been a natural psychic veil—disbelief, disavowal, and protective denial—slowly lifted, and the more I looked, the more familiar, somehow, he became, though I have no conscious memory of him. One photograph showed Gary standing in front of him, partially covering his father's face while lighting a candle, his father looking on from behind in which all I could see below his yarmulke was his right cheek, white hairline, high forehead, dark eyebrows, and the downcast glance of his watchful eyes—and I knew.

The phone rang.

"Jo-o-oseph," she was singing my name, "It's La-a-aura. Did you get it?"

"Yes, it just came a few minutes ago."

"So . . . what do you think?"

I hesitated just a beat. "I think Ben was my father."

"Well, could be. It would be nice to have a piece of Ben."

IN AN ARMED Forces Selective Service questionnaire dated March 15, 1941, just shortly after my birth but prior to his induction into the army, one Benjamin *Jacobs* states his marital status as "Married, separated." He uses his older brother's address at 175 Riverside Drive in Manhattan. He states his older brother's name is Jacob *Jacoby*. According to Laura and Gary, Jacob Jacoby was a famous cantor of the time.

Ben is almost thirty-six at the time of his induction into the U.S. Army on August 15, 1942. (He will serve through June 14, 1944.) He lists his occupation as "Fitter and tailor of men's clothing. Fitting of garments and making the alterations." Notwithstanding his marital separation, he designates his wife and daughter, both living on Unionport Road in the Bronx, as beneficiaries, and offers Jacob *Jacoby*, his older brother, as the nearest relative to be contacted in case of emergency, with his young daughter next in line. She is twelve years old. There is no mention of his wife in this regard.

Both wife and daughter go by the name *Jacobs*. Ben was married in about 1929 but divorced approximately ten years later, and he had his own apartment for several years prior to the divorce. His daughter remembers he had a girlfriend then, too, because she found her slippers under his bed once and even went home and told her mother. Well, little girls do that. She also remembers that the three of them went on outings together, once to Coney Island. She has no recollection of his girlfriend's name, or anything else about her, except that she was nice.

Ben loved photography, as I did, had his own darkroom, as I did, and always carried a camera. Both Laura and Gary had told me how much Ben loved taking pictures and that there had been lots of pictures of him. Laura had thrown most of hers away after Ben's death. Many of them included other women, mostly Hungarian women, and while she had no reason to doubt his fidelity, she didn't want the memories and I understood. His daughter, however, had boxes filled with pictures that she's promised to send me. She said she thought there might be some women in those pictures. Who knows who I might find? I'd just found a half sister. Besides, I'd know her in an instant.

Throughout his military record, which includes a document dated more than three years after his honorable discharge from the army, when he is living at 17 West 87th Street in Manhattan, he remains "Benjamin Jacobs." In a letter dated December 6, 1950, he wrote his daughter that he has changed his name to Jacoby.

When Laura met and married him in 1954 he was Benjamin Jacoby. Why he went from Jacobs (he married his first wife under the name of Jacobs) to Jacoby (as he appeared on my birth certificate) and back to Jacobs during his military service and beyond, and then back to Jacoby so many years later, while all the while his older brother is Jacob Jacoby, remains a mystery about which one can only speculate. However, when my mother was institutionalized in 1947, if someone were looking for the Benjamin Jacoby on my birth certificate, I doubt they'd have found my father. Even if they did, he wouldn't have been a salesman for a dress company, nor would he be Russian-born—none of the things that are stated on my birth certificate. He was even six years younger than he was supposed to be. My mother was a stenographer, at a time when there were no such things as tape recorders, and dictation machines were not yet widely in use. Being a good and accurate listener was, quite literally, her stock in trade, and I doubt she would have intentionally recorded these facts incorrectly.

The final, single-page, document in Benjamin Jacoby's military file, "Notice of Death Message," dated October 23, 2001, has his name as "Jacoby, Benjamin." With the sole exception of a telephone slip dated

August 4, 1999, it is the only time this name appears in his file. The Benjamin Jacobs I'd missed the first time around was the Benjamin Jacoby I'd been looking for.

On his induction affidavit he states that he was born in Nagy Somkut, Satmar, Hungary, on October 8, 1906 (his Social Security application states Somcuta Mare, Romania). He was actually thirty-four, not forty, when I was born. In addition to his daughter from his first marriage, he had a son who died at age three from polio. My half sister has lived in California since her parents divorced and her mother remarried, in about 1940. Ben had no children with his second wife, Laura, but he raised her three children, two daughters and a son, as his own. He was not an Orthodox Jew, as Laura was when they met, though he had been when he had met his first wife many years before. He returned to it, however, well before his passing at age ninety-five and a day, following complications from a broken hip.

There was one more stone I could turn, and I knew I had to: DNA testing. Laura and Gary were able to find an old hairbrush, a comb, eyeglases, tefillin (phylacteries), and an old electric razor Gary told me only Ben used. I sent them to a laboratory for analysis. The results were disappointing; the DNA was degraded; the laboratory could not determine whether Ben was or was not my father to any standard that would hold up in a court of law. But they inclined to the negative.

∞

ON MARCH 20, 2005 I met Laura at her apartment in Forest Hills, Queens. She had finally agreed to meet me after I had visited the rabbi, which impressed her. I asked her if I could invite my friend Albert Maysles, the film documentarian, to tape our get together. She instantly agreed. My thought was that since I had no way of knowing what the emotional response might be, mine or hers, I wanted to memorialize that, thinking, too, that there might be things said, body language and other non-verbal reactions, that I would like to be able to look back on. During the two hours that we spent together, she said: "If I didn't know why you were here I would ask myself 'why do I know this man?' " She then went on to comment on my features, and at one point I smiled, and then she said: "You even have his smile."

⌒

I'VE HAD A fantasy in recent days, a warm feeling that's bittersweet and sad, too. I get on the subway and go to the shul that he attended on the Sabbath. I wander into the congregation, look around, and spot him, just as I spotted him in the photographs. He would be in his nineties now, but I've seen pictures of him at ninety or so, and I think I would know him. I lean over to the person next to me and whisper, pointing, "You see that gentleman over there? What's his name?" Later I find a way to get next to him and Laura. Me being me, I'm able to strike up a casual conversation, probably with Laura first. Laura being Laura, she keeps the ball rolling. She even says, at some point, "Ben—he looks a little like you" (this is my fantasy, remember). At this point I look him in the eye and say with a smile, "You know, in some ways, I do." He asks who I am, since he's never seen me here before, and I say something about visiting a friend in the neighborhood. From what Gary has told me, he was a very charming, sociable fellow anyway (although I imagine him as being reticent at first, probably because I am), which is why going to synagogue appealed to him. Performance, in a way (maybe that's where I got it from).

One thing leads to another, of course, and since they live only a few blocks away, I walk them home. I don't know that I say anything this night (probably not, because I want this to last), but I come back next Friday night, and the next, and maybe even the next, until, at whatever time is right, I say something like "Ben, I've always wanted to meet you, and I'm very happy that I have. I don't know if you ever knew about me. You may recall my mother. She went by Fay. Her real name was Francis, but that's the name she used on my birth certificate. My real name is Joseph. Joseph Jacoby. Your daughter told me that you lost a son to polio before I was born. I'm your son, too, Ben, and everything worked out fine. I just wanted you to know. It's okay." And I'd kiss him on the cheek. He'd probably look at me in recognition now, and I'm sure his eyes would well up because mine would, and we'd hug each other.

∞

THAT'S THE FANTASY. I'm not saying it would have happened exactly that way, but I bet it would have come close. I would have loved to have done that. That would have been the best. I'll keep playing it, though.

Film Notes

Animal Crackers (1930). Directed by Victor Heerman. Screenplay by Morrie Ryskind from the play by George S. Kaufman and Morrie Ryskind. Starring Groucho, Harpo, Chico, and Zeppo Marx and Margaret Dumont. Paramount Pictures.

Aroused (1966). Directed by Anton Holden. Distributed by Cambist Films.

Arsenic and Old Lace (1944). Directed by Frank Capra. Screenplay by Julius J. Epstein and Philip G. Epstein from the play by Joseph Kesselring. Starring Cary Grant, Raymond Massey, Peter Lorre, Josephine Hull, Jean Adair. Warner Brothers.

Davy Jones' Locker (1995). Written and directed by Joseph Jacoby. Cowritten by Peter Baird. Music by Philip Marshall. Starring the Bil and Cora Baird Marionettes. A Children's Video Theater Production. Seen on the PBS stations in the United States and NHK in Japan and home video.

Duck Soup (1933). Directed by Leo McCarey. Screenplay by Bert Kalmar and Harry Ruby. Starring Groucho, Harpo, Chico, and Zeppo Marx and Margaret Dumont. Paramount Pictures.

The 400 Blows (1959). Directed by François Truffaut. Screenply by François Truffaut and Marcel Moussy. Starring Jean-Pierre Leaud. Produced by Les Films du Carosse. Distributed in the United States by Zenith International Films.

The Great Bank Hoax (1979). Directed by Joseph Jacoby. Screenplay by Joseph Jacoby. Starring Richard Basehart, Ned Beatty, Charlene Dallas, Constance Forslund, Burgess Meredith, Michael Murphy, Paul Sand.

The Hospital (1971). Directed by Arthur Hiller. Screenplay by Paddy Chayefsky. Starring George C. Scott, Diana Rigg, Bernard Hughes. A Howard Gottfried–Paddy Chayefsky Production in association with Arthur Hiller. Academy Award for best writing based on original material. Distributed by United Artists.

Hurry Up, or I'll Be 30 (1973). Directed by Joseph Jacoby. Written by David Wiltse and Joseph Jacoby. Story by Joseph Jacoby. Starring Danny DeVito. Avco Embassy Pictures.

I, A Woman (1965). Directed by Mac Ahlberg. Screenplay by Peer Guldbransen. Starring Essy Persson. Produced by Europa Films. Distributed in the United States by Audubon Films.

The Jolson Story (1946). Directed by Alfred C. Green. Written by Stephen Longstreet. Adaptation by Harry Chandless and Andrew Solt. Starring Larry Parks and Evelyn Keyes. Music by Saul Chaplin and M. W. Stoloff. Academy Awards for best music and best sound recording. Columbia Pictures.

Make Mine Music (1946). Directed by Bob Cormack, Clyde Geronimi, and others. Screenplay by James Bodrero, Homer Brightman, and others. Original music by Al Cameron, Ted Weems, Alec Wilder, and others. Starring Nelson Eddy, the Andrews Sisters, Benny Goodman, Jerry Colonna, Sterling Holloway, and others. RKO Radio Pictures.

Marty (1953). Directed by Delbert Mann. Original screenplay and story by Paddy Chayefsky. Starring Ernest Borgnine. Acadmey Awards: best picture; Delbert Mann for best director; Ernest Borgnine for best actor; Paddy Chayefsky for best screenplay. Produced by Harold Hecht and Burt Lancaster. Distributed by United Artists.

Moulin Rouge (1952). Directed by John Huston. Screenplay by John Huston. Starring José Ferrer and Zsa Zsa Gabor. Academy Awards for best art direction and best costume design. Produced by Moulin Productions. Distributed by United Artists.

Quiz Show (1994). Directed by Robert Redford. Screenplay by Paul Attanasio based on the book by Richard N. Goodwin. Starring John Turturro, Ralph Fiennes, Paul Scofield, David Paymer, Rob Morrow, Johann Carlo, Mira Sorvino, Christopher McDonald, Allan Rich, Martin Scorsese. Hollywood Pictures.

Shame, Shame . . . Everybody Knows Her Name (1968). Directed by Joseph Jacoby. Screenplay by William Dorsey Blake. Starring Getti Miller, Augustus Sultatos. Jer Pictures Inc.

Rock Around the Clock (1956). Directed by Fred F. Sears. Screenplay by James B. Gordon and Robert E. Kent. Starring Bill Haley and the Comets. Original music by Max Freedman, Bill Haley, Freddie Bell, and others. Columbia Pictures.

Showman (1963). Written and directed by Albert and David Maysles. Never made available for public exhibition because Levine "had complicated feelings about the film because Hollywood friends thought the film to be anti-Semitic," according to Albert Maysles. I viewed the film in October 2003, when Albert Maysles generously loaned me a print. I never felt any anti-Semitism in the movie, nor did Albert, who (being Jewish himself) never intended it.

The Sound of Music (1965). Directed by Robert Wise. Screenplay by Howard Lindsey and Russell Crouse. Music by Richard Rodgers. Starring Julie Andrews and Christopher Plummer and featuring the Bil and Cora Baird Marionettes. Twentieth Century–Fox.

Acknowledgments

Dr. Warren and Sona Becker. For your friendship, fidelity, and trust.

Mrs. Williams at Hawthorne for planting the idea even though it took a while.

Dr. George Frank for getting me the hell out of there.

Ethel and Fred Schaefer for their generosity and caring.

Miss Mildred Windecker, my mentor.

Morris Jacobs for opening the door.

Jean Bernstein. My last social worker. And a real person.

Charlotte and Morey Bunin, my '60s surrogate family.

Martin Scorsese, for taking some of his "crazy time" for me. But above all, for being my friend.

Dr. Alan M. Levy for his compassion, generosity, and insight.

Bil Baird for hiring me and believing I could do strings.

Jack M. Perlman, Esq. for riding the bus just to hear my stories, providing I never told the same story twice, which I couldn't do if I tried.

Donald T. Gillin for his sage advice, encouragement, and friendship.

Willard Van Dyke, Laurence Kardish, Adrienne Mancia, and Ron Magliozzi, for their acknowledgment of my work.

Judith Crist for loving movies and encouraging a filmmaker.

Gail and William A. Henry III for encouraging me to "just tell a good yarn."

Harold Berkowitz, Esq. for being tough as nails, and as gentle as they came.

Royal E. Blakeman, Esq. for his generosity, loyalty, and lessons taught.

Dr. Wesley and Carolyn Halpert for their friendship and encouragement.

Elizabeth Cholakis for reading the damn thing. Constantly.

James R. Regan, PhD. For piercing the bureaucracy with dispatch.

Roland DeSilva for being from Brooklyn, going to New Utrecht, and keeping faith with both.

Philip Marella, Esq. for being as good on my side as when he sat opposite.

Timothy Seldes, my agent, a gentleman icon.

Walter Bode, my editor, who took a raw manuscript and enabled a book.

Philip Turner, editor-in-chief at Carroll & Graf, for seeing the value and giving me every consideration.

Linda Kosarin, a creative director par excellence.

Albert Maysles for his compassionate camera and for being my friend.

Laura Jacoby for finally meeting me, even though I'm not kosher.

Mr. Max Gluck, whom I never knew, but who I now know would have done more if he could have.

And finally, for Mr. Fisher. For taking us off the street.

And if I missed you, I haven't meant to (unless I did it on purpose).

Index